The Audible Life Stream

Ancient Secret of Dying While Living

The Audible
Life Stream

Ancient Secret of Dying
While Living

Alistair Conwell

BOOKS

Winchester, UK
Washington, USA

First published by O-Books, 2010
O Books is an imprint of John Hunt Publishing Ltd., The Bothy, Deershot Lodge, Park Lane, Ropley,
Hants, SO24 0BE, UK
office1@o-books.net
www.o-books.com

Distribution in:

UK and Europe
Orca Book Services Ltd
Home trade orders
tradeorders@orcabookservices.co.uk
Tel: 01235 465521
Fax: 01235 465555

Export orders
exportorders@orcabookservices.co.uk
Tel: 01235 465516 or 01235 465517
Fax: 01235 465555

USA and Canada
NBN
custserv@nbnbooks.com
Tel: 1 800 462 6420 Fax: 1 800 338 4550

Australia and New Zealand
Brumby Books
sales@brumbybooks.com.au
Tel: 61 3 9761 5535 Fax: 61 3 9761 7095

Far East (offices in Singapore, Thailand,
Hong Kong, Taiwan)
Pansing Distribution Pte Ltd
kemal@pansing.com
Tel: 65 6319 9939 Fax: 65 6462 5761

South Africa
Stephan Phillips (pty) Ltd
Email: orders@stephanphillips.com
Tel: 27 21 4489839 Telefax: 27 21 4479879

Text copyright Alistair Conwell 2009

ISBN: 978 1 84694 329 4

Design: Stuart Davies

Printed by Digital Book Print

O Books operates a distinctive and ethical publishing philosophy in
all areas of its business, from its global network of authors to
production and worldwide distribution.

CONTENTS

Music and sound have always been recognized as important components in spirituality, but seldom is sound mentioned as a catalyst and gateway into the preparation for dying. Through interesting analysis and real life examples this book skillfully opens those possibilities and inspires the reader to explore the Audible Life Stream as a pathway for more abundant living and conscious dying. In writing this book Alistair Conwell has made an important contribution to near-death literature.

Betty Bland, President of the Theosophical Society in America and a near-death survivor.

Your words have such lyricism and the great ring of truth about them...I wish you every success with this beautiful work...

Maggie Hamilton, Publisher Mind, Body, Spirit, Allen & Unwin Book Publishers (Sydney, Australia).

The Audible Life Stream: Ancient Secret of Dying While Living is an excellent, well-written work.

Nicholas Tharcher, Former Vice-President New Falcon Publications (USA).

I receive many submissions of work in what might loosely be termed new age, or dealing with spiritual material, but I have seen few...in the area of NDE or spirituality as lucidly and convincingly written as yours, in part because you have handled so well the scientific aspects of your theory.

Rosemary Creswell, The Cameron Creswell Literary Agency (Sydney, Australia).

To
the author of all that we know and of all that
we are ignorant — the Audible Life Stream

The teaching of the wise is a fountain of life, that one may avoid the snares of death.
The Book of Proverbs 13:14

Those who really apply themselves in the right way to philosophy are directly and of their own accord preparing themselves for death and dying...
Socrates (c.470–c.399 BC)

The art of living well and the art of dying well are one.
Epicurus (341–270 BC)

A wise man's life is all one preparation for death.
Cicero (106–43 BC)

As long as you do not die while living,
How will you obtain the true benefit?
Therefore die, and come out of your body.
O man, you have died many times,
But still you remain behind the veil,
For the method of true dying
You did not learn.
Jalaluddin Rumi (1207–1273)

...The world is dying, but knows none how to Die:
But, whosoever knows how to Die, dies not again.
Kabir (c.1398–c.1518)

Acknowledgments

Sincere gratitude is extended to the following publishers and individuals for granting permission for the reprinting of copyright material:

From *The Essene Gospel of Peace (Book 1)* © 1981, *From Enoch to the Dead Sea Scrolls* © 1981, & *The Essene Gospel of Peace: Book Four* © 1981 by E. B. Szekely. Reprinted with permission from Mrs Norma Szekely, **International Biogenic Society** (PO Box 849, Nelson, BC, Canada V1L 6A5).

From *Philosophy of the Masters (Abridged)* © 1973 by Sawan Singh, *Quest for Light* by Charan Singh © 1993, *Spiritual Gems* © 1996 by Sawan Singh, *Die to Live* © 1995 by Charan Singh, *The Science of the Soul* © 1994 by Sardar Bahadur Jagat Singh, *Sar Bachan* © 1991 by Soami Ji, *The Dawn of Light* © 1985 by Sawan Singh, *The Path of the Masters* © 1993 by Dr Julian Johnson, *Teachings of the Gurus* © 1987 by L.R. Puri. Reprinted with permission from Faith Singh & Shiv Singh, **Radha Soami Satsang Beas**.

From *The Light Beyond* © 1988 by Raymond Moody. Reprinted with permission of **Sobel Weber Associates Inc.**

From *The Infinite Harmony* © 1994 by Michael Hayes. Reprinted with permission of **The Orion Publishing Group Ltd.**

From *The Return from Silence* © 1989 & *Beyond Reality* © 1990 by D. Scott Rogo. Reprinted with permission of **Jack Rogo.**

From *The World is Sound: Nada Brahma* © 1983 by Joachim-Ernst Berendt. Reprinted with permission of **Suhrkamp Verlag.**

From *Music of the Mind* © 1994 by Darryl Reanney. Reprinted with permission of **Hill of Content Publishing Company.**

From *The Truth in the Light* © 1995 by P. & E. Fenwick. Reprinted with permission of **Headline Book Publishing.**

From *You Can See the Light* © 2001 by D. Morrissey. Reprinted with permission of **Citadel Press.**

Heartfelt thanks must also be extended to several individuals who have greatly assisted in the production of this book. Special mention must be made of the following:

My parents, who kindly supported me for more than three years while I wrote this book.

Nigel ('Nodi') Ipp for his encouragement and perceptive feedback on the manuscript.

Philip Gobetz for his scrutiny of every word and excellent suggestions about conveying what is essentially the ineffable through analogy.

Jennifer Moy and Dr M Bhaskaran for proofreading the early drafts.

Introduction

Physicians are aware that the sense of hearing is the last sense faculty to dissolve at the time of death. However, they, like the vast majority of people, are unaware of the fact that when this physical sense ceases to function our capacity to perceive spiritual sound naturally takes the ascendancy.

But why should we be concerned about death—after all we've all got lives to live? The answer is very simple; having complete knowledge of the spiritual significance of death will undoubtedly determine how we live our lives. For in the final analysis, it is through our knowledge and understanding of death that all the ultimate questions about the meaning and purpose of life can be fully answered. Yet, for most of us death remains the mystery of mysteries. Paradoxical though it may seem; mystics throughout history have said that it is possible to solve this mystery while being very much alive—to die while living. The secret is to consciously tune into and eventually merge with the phenomenon known in the West, at least, as the Audible Life Stream or Primordial Sound Current.

The Audible Life Stream is the central tenet of the most ancient spiritual teachings known. Mystics say it is the quintessential fabric of the entire universe—physical and spiritual. Without it nothing would exist. It is the essence of all things and, in fact, resounds continuously within each and every one of us. Put simply, this stream of conscious vibrating energy, which has the most enchanting musical quality, is our immortal spiritual essence.

Thus, this book is an attempt to provide convincing evidence of this timeless spiritual maxim and highlight its importance in the process of death—the one event of life that is the most heavily pregnant with spiritual potential—whenever it will eventually occur. Also given in the concluding chapters is advice about learning the science of dying while living to experience the Audible Life Stream for yourself.

As to the evidence; simply explained scientific principles in Chapters 2 and 3 will show that the Audible Life Stream phenomenon and the practice of dying while living are perfectly aligned with modern-day quantum physics theories, including the much talked about idea of a Theory of Everything based on the concept of superstrings. Believing these one-dimensional vibrating superstrings resonate in a musical pattern, some physicists agree that the theory is one which successfully unifies all the primary forces of nature, giving us a picture of ultimate reality.

Chapter 4 presents scriptural excerpts from the major religious traditions that make mention of mysterious sounds and music, foreshadowing the death of the physical body and birth of the spirit.

Yet arguably, Chapters 5, 6, 7 and 8 are the most compelling because they include testimonies from researchers, and ordinary people of diverse backgrounds, whose spiritual awareness has been profoundly deepened after their lives were unexpectedly touched by what could only have been the Audible Life Stream. For example, although seemingly unaware of the phenomenon, it was apparently through the vibrations of the Audible Life Stream that out-of-body experience (OBE) research pioneer, Robert Monroe, was able to astral travel at will. And when he heard its other-worldly musical tones he was left to ask himself if it was indeed God.[1] Also, internationally renowned music therapist and author, Don Campbell, was profoundly moved after being miraculously healed of a life-threatening condition by this potent force, which he refers to as an 'inner sound' not perceived by the physical ears.[2]

However, holding special importance in the weight of evidence are the numerous near-death experience (NDE) testimonials that include references to hearing wondrous sounds and enchanting music, notably far superior to even the finest music of this world. Like Monroe and Campbell, these people seemingly had no inkling of the Audible Life Stream phenomenon before their life-changing experiences.

In his best-selling book, *Life After Life*, celebrated NDE investigator, Dr Raymond Moody, admits:

> In many cases, various unusual auditory sensations are reported to occur at or near death.[3]

In such cases, however, death occurs unexpectedly and usually as a result of an accident or unforeseen complications during a medical procedure. The person has little or no idea what actually takes place and is totally ill-prepared.

Equally ill-prepared for death, are the vast majority of us. Despite its inevitability, medical professionals know that most people secretly deny death. American physician, Sherwin Nuland, observes:

> None of us seems psychologically able to cope with the thought of our own state of death... As with every other looming terror and looming temptation, we seek always to deny the power of death and the icy hold in which it grips human thought.[4]

So in setting the scene for the book, Chapter 1 will identify the true nature of our death denial and fear. Although we may not realize it, our death phobia impacts greatly upon how we live our lives. Yet, this fear can be overcome if we gain an experiential understanding of death through preparation. Preparation, in this sense, is not in terms of the drawing up of wills and testaments or making funeral arrangements. While these things are certainly necessary, it is the spiritual preparations that are far more important because death is a doorway into the realm of spirit, from where we have all originally come. We can enter through this doorway temporarily while still living in this world by consciously immersing ourselves into the current of the Audible Life Stream. By doing this, with proper guidance, a conscious experience of death can be knowingly induced—safely and without any threat to the physical body. Breathing and heart-rate continue very subtly, but for all intents and purposes one is dead to the physical world while very much alive to the realm of spirit.

This then is an invitation to, firstly, acknowledge the true nature of the spiritual doorway that death presents for us and, secondly, to learn what preparatory steps can be taken to open and actually enter through the door while still alive. Having done this, you will perhaps view life, which ultimately has no beginning and no end, in the widest of contexts with literally infinite possibilities.

Alistair Conwell
13 March 2009

1

Trembling on the Edge of Eternity

Death is psychologically as important as birth. Shrinking away from it is something unhealthy and abnormal which robs the second half of life of its purpose.

Carl G. Jung (1875–1961)

Some years ago in the west country of England, a man was found wandering the streets in a highly disturbed state. Determining that the man required medical attention, he was sent by a benevolent organization, called the Bed Bureau, to the local general hospital. The man was of no fixed address and doctors were unable to contact any friends or relatives. He was so afraid that no information about him, or what had happened to make him so unsettled, could be obtained. Totally unwilling to answer any questions, he instead kept shouting that he was going to die and was begging for help.

The then admitting physician of the hospital, Dr J C Barker, explains what transpired:

> He defied all our attempts to sedate or resuscitate him and continued to cry out that he was going to die. Then to our horror and amazement he suddenly stopped crying, fell back into the bed and quickly expired. He had been in hospital for about half an hour. A post-mortem examination showed him to be in perfect health and there was nothing to account for his demise, except perhaps fear... I was quite convinced that it was possible for a perfectly healthy man to be frightened to death.[1]

Such extreme cases as these (and this was not an isolated case that Dr Barker was involved with first-hand) highlight how strongly the fear of death can manifest in us. Psychologists have found that the vast majority of us harbor an intense fear of death. The medical profession has even coined the word thanatophobia, which is derived from the Greek word, *thanatos*, meaning death, for this fear.

Dr Barker believes emphatically that no one is exempt from the fear of death. In his book, *Scared to Death*, he describes thanatophobia as a very distinct, unique and sometimes all-consuming fear. The fear is so great and so deep that many of us deny the fear itself as a means to repress it.

A Paradoxical Obsession

But this repression is most insidious because we all know that literature, music and art have long had an obsession with death. Like the theme of romance, audiences in the main thoroughly enjoy witnessing death enacted on stage or the screen. Many operas include a death scene because, as the ultimate of tragedies, death is the perfect climax to drama. Puccini's deeply moving *Madama Butterfly* is perhaps one of the best known examples. After finally realizing that her unfaithful American husband has betrayed her and their son for another woman, a distraught and disillusioned Butterfly takes her own life. In this case, whether it's a question of honor or foolishness is debatable, but in the final analysis it is also immaterial because the power of Butterfly's actions overwhelms a cold, purely rational mind searching for reason.

Our strangely paradoxical fascination with death also goes beyond the realm of art. For instance, we've all witnessed the gawking crowds that quickly gather at the scene of fatal car accidents, or the angry mob that gathers at the prison gates in some countries on execution day. But this apparent display of fearlessness is deceiving. Psychologists term this disturbing reaction in the face of death 'disinterested emotion' or a glorious 'I'm all right, Jack' attitude. American psychologist Dr Gregory Zilboorg believes this to be a denial of the danger of death combined with the false assertion that one will somehow never be touched by it.[2]

Death is a Mystery

So, despite our paradoxical obsession, the sobering reality is that we are terribly afraid of death even though it's something we must all one day face—and face alone. But, it's true to say that many of us are afraid of several things precisely because we know they are inevitable—a visit to the dentist, an exam, a job interview, a driving test are only a few examples of countless things that instill stress and fear in us. Death, on the other hand, is different, if for no other reason than because the vast majority of us have absolutely no idea what to expect at the time. And this is the second important aspect of death—it is a mystery. It is a mystery that has haunted humanity since time immemorial.

The mystery associated with death is sometimes seen as the real cause of our thanatophobia, rather than a fear of death itself. Others, rather than say that they fear death, will instead explain that they fear the pain that may be associated with death if, for example, they were involved in an accident. Others may say that they fear losing family and friends; or leaving personal commitments and goals unrealized. Thanatologists have also observed that dying people dread having to face death alone, feeling they will be abandoned and vulnerable at the final moment. But surely all these reasons that purport to display a lack of fear of death itself are, in reality, symptomatic of that deeper darker fear of actually dying.

Psychologist Ernest Becker believes that '...the idea of death, the fear of it, haunts the human animal like nothing else; it is a mainspring of human activity—activity designed largely to avoid the fatality of death, to overcome it by denying in some way that it is the final destiny of man.'[3]

So although we can try to deny it, regardless of our social status, our influence or worldly knowledge, none of us can resist the clutches of the Lord of Death. And when that most compelling and wickedly seductive Grim Reaper beckons, none among us will have the capacity to even feign deafness. We might go kicking and screaming, and perhaps begging, but one day, go we will, for the choice will not be ours to make.

Fear is Based on Ignorance

Whether we are psychologically capable to acknowledge our thanatophobia or not, arriving at some understanding of this fear is important because all fear, without exception, is based on ignorance. There are numerous examples of ignorance instilling fear in entire societies and cultures throughout history. For instance, it was only some 500 years ago that a commonly held belief was that the Earth was flat and that anyone who sailed too far from the shore would fall over the edge! Given our modern-day scientific knowledge, we may well chuckle at this ludicrous idea but as progress continues and we acquire more knowledge, in 500 years time (or indeed earlier) our generation could well be the ones who will be the laughing-stock for our beliefs on a whole range of issues. Thankfully, men like Columbus were sufficiently courageous to challenge this flat-Earth belief and as a conse-quence the New World was discovered.

Like Columbus and those of his inspiring ilk, we must stand and face death—not as an enemy but as a friend. For no one succeeds in understanding an enemy simply because enmity prevails. But a friend is a friend because of an understanding, a knowing, a level of intimacy exists, whereby the two share so much that a great part of each is lost in the union. Potentially, death can be our greatest friend, but only if we learn to under-stand it and eventually master it. But while we harbor any shred of fear then it will remain our greatest foe, and, no doubt, our conqueror. As a consequence, we will be nothing more than the living dead. For our attitude to death ultimately determines our attitude to life. If we are afraid of death we will be afraid of life and, therefore, we will never truly live. Summarizing this attitude, Russian Orthodox Church bishop Metropolitan Anthony of Sourozh once wrote:

> If we are afraid of death we will never be prepared to take ultimate risks; we will spend our life in a cowardly, careful and timid manner. It is only if we can face death, make sense of it, determine its place and our place in regard to it that we will be able to live in a fearless way and to the fullness of our ability.[4]

So let's begin trying to understand our thanatophobia by looking at what some of the experts have learnt about it over the years.

Scales of Death

The behavioral sciences and mental health disciplines virtually ignored the anxiety associated with death until only the second half of the last century. Since 1955 various fear of death scales, based on responses to a rigid set of questions, have been developed. For example, the *Collett-Lester Fear of Death Scale* produces separate scores—one for the fear of one's own death and the other for the fear of the death of others. All these various scales produce similar findings, but the limitation of such instruments is that they can only assess the fear that one is willing to acknowledge. And therein lies the problem because few of us actually do acknowledge it.

Five Stages of Dying

Sufficiently sensitive medical professionals—people who witness death and dying on a daily basis and who are receptive to the psychological ebb and flow of patients—are really the only ones who are privy to our true feelings towards death. In America, and indeed around the world, Dr Elizabeth Kubler-Ross (1926-2004) worked with dying patients for many years. She wrote several books about her touching experiences that reveal much about our thanatophobia. While she didn't devise a formal scale that measures levels of anxiety associated with death, she observed that there are potentially five stages that a terminally ill patient will go through. The stages are detailed in her book, *On Death and Dying*. A summary of these stages follows.

Denial

The first stage is one of complete denial that death is immanent. The denial is so intense that the patient will often avoid speaking to anyone, probably because they don't want to listen to anyone reminding them, either directly or indirectly, that their remaining time is limited.

Anger

The second stage is one of anger, and it's categorized by rhetoric like: 'Why me? Why not someone else?'

Bargaining

The third stage a patient will experience is one of bargaining. They will bargain with their doctor for a reprieve as if the doctor was ultimately able to decide whether they die or live. Dr Kubler-Ross noted that very often patients would say things like, 'If I do as I'm told you will make me better won't you?'

Depression

Next comes a stage of depression. Denial, anger and all meaningless negotiations having failed, patients are often overcome with a feeling of total despondency.

Acceptance

Finally, usually on the actual verge of death, a state of calm acceptance is reached and it's not uncommon for patients to report hearing voices and seeing visions of dead relatives or friends. Such comforting visions are an integral part of their acceptance of death because it gives patients what they certainly believe to be a glimpse of what has been, up to this time, the great unknown. These types of episodes will be looked at in more detail when death-bed visions are explored in Chapter 6.

While the five stages of dying, as identified by Dr Kubler-Ross, delineate a fear of death in terminally ill people, it is not only those who are facing an immanent death who harbor this fear. After all, from the moment of our birth we are all in a sense dying. Each moment that passes brings us closer to the time of our death. American teacher, psychologist and former priest, Robert Kavanaugh writes that people '...we designate as 'dying' differ only in that they know the nearness [of death], while all know the inevitability... The basic mask all humans put on is to call ourselves 'the living', when we are equally 'the dying'.'[5]

The masking of our thanatophobia is so beguiling that many people avoid using the words 'death' or 'dying' altogether. In fact, Kenneth Krammer, an expert on comparative religion, identifies 66 euphemisms in the modern American vernacular to avoid using these two words. He cites many examples that we are all familiar with, like: 'kicked the bucket', 'passed away', 'checked out', to name a few.[6]

Religiosity and the Fear of Death

Some believe that our invisible fear of death is not as great in religious people because a religious person's belief in an after-life penetrates the veil of ignorance that normally surrounds death. However, some medical professionals believe that the fear of death is the same and often more intense in religious people as it is in the non-religious. It's a point made by Dr Barker who writes:

> The religious man has additional burdens possibly pertaining to his feelings of guilt, such as 'Will I go to heaven or to hell?' 'What about the expiation for my sins?' etc. In spite of a firm belief in heaven and a life hereafter, some religious persons still possess an intense personal fear of death.[7]

Accepting this, then two obvious implications follow:

1. A system of faith based on the belief in life after death must be failing if it cannot convince its adherents of this and remove the fear.
2. Our thanatophobia must be far deeper rooted than we imagine.

The first implication begs the question of whether successive guardians of the major religious traditions are truly aware of the fundamental teachings of the so-called founders of their respective faiths who all preached of an existence beyond the death of the physical body. In the case of the Christianity, it seems that for hundreds of years (perhaps even closer to two thousand) those who have administered this once all-powerful institution were not aware of Jesus' true teachings, and if they were they chose, for reasons best known to themselves, to make omissions and changes.

Modern scholarly research has found that a major proportion of the gospels were not written by those who actually knew Jesus, begging the question of whether he and his teachings are accurately depicted in them.

Scientist, author and long-time student of mysticism, John Davidson, writes:

They [the gospels] were almost certainly written between forty and seventy years after the death of Jesus, a lapse of two or more generations, presenting plenty of opportunity for things to have become distorted. It has also become evident that the gospel compilers, although incorporating the teachings of Jesus, had their own individual points of view and in some instances can actually be observed adjusting or presenting Jesus' sayings and teachings to fit these beliefs. The gospels then passed through a period of copying and general editorial tampering that lasted three or four centuries and it is only these edited and often differing versions which have survived to modern times.[8]

Regrettably, but not surprisingly, these edited versions are divergent from the very simple message that Jesus and indeed all mystics deliver, no matter at what period of history they appear, or for that matter, where.

Many, particularly those with a Christian background, may take exception to placing Jesus' teachings in a mystical context. This being so, we should consider that English author and lecturer on mysticism, Evelyn Underhill (1875–941), defined mysticism as '...the science of union with the Absolute, and nothing else...,'[9] adding that a mystic is, therefore, one who has attained this union through personal experience. The path of mysticism then, we can say, is not merely based on opinion. And it certainly has nothing to do with the pursuit of occult knowledge. Instead, Underhill writes that mysticism '...is the name of that organic process which involves the perfect consummation of the Love of God: the achievement here and now of the immortal heritage of man.'[10]

So while in Judaism and Christianity the Absolute is referred to as God, while Brahma, the Buddha Nature, the Tao, Allah and so on, are terms used in other religious systems, one can regard all the so-called founders of the great religions as being mystics of the highest order because their union with the Absolute can be easily inferred.

This potential union is the same for all, but unfortunately problems often arise when the mystic departs the scene and unenlightened humans seek to place their teacher's wisdom into an institutionalized package. History shows that this nearly always results in the mystic's original quintessential teachings, about how to prepare for death while living, being lost or grossly misunderstood. The prevalence of thanatophobia in the religious and non-religious alike is sufficient proof of this.

The Death-denying Culture

So, if both the religious and non-religious person fears death, the question then must be asked: Where does this ubiquitous fear of death come from? Some scholars contend that it is something that we are taught as children. Such a view was presented in an essay entitled *Education in Thanatology* that was co-authored by Gary J. Grad from Columbia University and Sir Stephen V. Gullo who both believe that no one is born with a fear of death but that instead we learn it from the superstitions and fear transmitted by our families and society as a whole.

This view is shared by parapsychologist D. Scott Rogo (1950–1990). Elaborating on the death-denying culture that prevails in many Western societies, Rogo observed:

Most people in Western societies fear death with a phobic terror. This lamentable situation isn't strange since we live in a death-denying culture where death is constantly divorced from the everyday realities of life. Popular illustrations of this widespread denial don't seem difficult to find. Death is a subject most people refuse to discuss in polite conversation, while the dying are usually shunted off to hospitals or rest homes, conveniently out of sight and out of mind from the standpoint of their relatives. We even try to shield our

14

children from the simple reality of death on the misguided premise that we're doing them a favor.[11]

But even if we accept that our modern societies are constantly perpetuating this widespread fear of death, and moreover, its denial, the question still remains: Where does this fear and subsequent denial of death stem from?

The late Australian academic and author, Darryl Reanney, had an interesting theory about this. Reanney believed our fear of death is so endemic that it is the root cause of many psychological ills like guilt and anxiety that today grip most, if not all, modern Western societies. Notably, this is in sharp contrast to Sigmund Freud's view that our psychological problems were caused by sexual repression. In his fascinating book, *The Death of Forever*, Reanney, who was an internationally acclaimed authority on the origin of life, penetrates deep into history and the human psyche in an absorbing investigation of our thanatophobia.

Nine-phase Cycle of Death and Time

Reanney believed our fear of death changes with age and is also dependant upon the period of history. He suggested that our attitude to death has changed dramatically over the centuries because of our increasing life spans, obviously largely due to advances in medical science. So, for example, an ancient Roman, who would have expected to live for an average of 20 years would have had quite a different perspective of death (and no doubt of life) than someone today, who can have an average life expectancy of between 70 and 80 years.

On the subject of modern man, Reanney suggested that our attitude to death depends on the age of the person and one's attitude to time. He illustrates this point with a nine-phase life cycle he devised based on his personal experience, anecdotal evidence and sociological studies. A summary of the nine phases follows.

Phase 1: The Genesis Dreaming (0–9 months)
The period in the womb, during which time we dream and have no subjective perspective of time and therefore no concept of death.

Phase 2: Growing Without Time (9 months–3 years)
Reanney described this phase of human development as the 'prehuman phase of consciousness'. While the child's language skills are fast developed, a sense of being an individual is still years away and there is still no subjective perspective of time. The child continues to have no concept of death.

Phase 3: An Infinity of Time (3–12 years)
The child's concept of time is one of infinity, so death is viewed not as a finality. For children in this age bracket, everything must have a purpose, just like a children's story. Therefore, they see themselves as being immortal, so they often cope with death much better than adults.

Phase 4: Footprints in Time (12–25 years)
In this phase the focus is on sexual activity, and although not always for procreation it often gives the person a psychological commitment to the future that succeeds in negating any fear of death. One is usually socializing and 'enjoying' life too much to even consider one's own mortality. Wisely, Reanney did qualify his comments about this somewhat psychologically problematic age bracket because he recognized that the psyche is at a particularly vulnerable stage of development, and also that much depends on personal experience.

Phase 5: Marching in Time (25–40 years)
In this phase, people are in the prime of life and usually too occupied with careers and/or family obligations to consider their own mortality. And a healthy body provides few indications of the ageing process to come.

Phase 6: The Denial of Time and the Shadow of Approaching Night (40–50 years)
Crisis time for those in most Western societies. Reproductive capabilities are impaired therefore diminishing one's importance to the process of evolution. Women sometimes experience post menopausal depression and for some men a mid-life crisis may take place. The fear of death often becomes starkly obvious because at this stage there is a high probability of a kin death— most likely one's parents. Compounding this is the fact that individuals in this age group tend to work within habitual boundaries and are largely unaware of the majority of what actually goes on around them. Therefore, time appears to contract, seemingly running more quickly.

Phase 7: The Acceptance of Time (50–69 years)
At this point, ageing is obvious but one usually develops defense mechanisms to cope with the concept of one's mortality. So although the awareness of death remains high, the fear of dying seems to recede psychologically.

Phase 8: The Blurring of Time (69–75 years)
Bodily and mental functions are often significantly impaired during this phase so the fear of death may become tainted and unfocused. A period of what Reanney called 'the dreaming of old age' begins.

Phase 9: The End of Time (75–120 years)
Game Over! (And you're completely out of coins). Your time is up! You can no longer run from the Lord of Death because if he hasn't already done so, he will definitely confront you during this final stage.

The issue of subjective time that Reanney consistently mentions in his life-cycle is significant and therefore will be discussed in the following chapter. For the present chapter, the point to be made is that the life cycle shows that the fear of death in a young adult is obviously different from someone who is, for example, in the twilight of life. The main reason for this is the development of the sense of being an individual that begins during the pre-school years. And this important point is also implied by Dr Kubler-Ross.

The Immortal 'I'

In her book, *Death is of Vital Importance*, Dr Kubler-Ross observed that we all have two natural fears—a fear of heights and a fear of unexpected loud noises. Of course, both these fears relate to self-preservation and so it's easy to see that these are both borne from our fear of death. This strongly suggests that the basis of our thanatophobia is the fear of losing one's self, or our sense of 'I-ness'. For while some people may say they fear the pain that may be associated with death, or the indignity that may come from a terminal illness, or the final judgment, or losing one's friends and relatives, or being alone, or even the unknown of death; all these reasons imply a strong sense of ego-self.

In fact, many experts believe that the ego robs the mind of the capacity to conceive of its own mortality and, therefore, that it's this psychological conundrum that compels us to a repressed state of thanatophobia. It was Freud who once said that in mankind's '...unconscious, every one of us is convinced of his [sic] own immortality.'[12]

Others, like psychologist Gregory Zilboorg, point out that our unconscious sense of an immortal 'I' is necessary to maintain a sense of normalcy. Of course this seems perfectly reasonable, especially in light of our repressed thanatophobia. Past and present mystics, however, would contend that if the fear of death is overcome by removing the ignorance then not only is a sense of genuine normalcy attained but, more importantly, a sense of ultimate reality too. But more on this in a subsequent chapter.

Since this 'I' is central to the issue of thanatophobia, we need to look more closely at what this 'I' really is.

The Conniving Brain

Mystics equate this 'I' with the 'little self', making a clear distinction between it and the great Self that is regarded as a spark of immortal divinity inherent in us all. They tell us that this 'I' is really superficial and illusory, and ultimately a product of the brain. Needless to say, materialists, on the other hand, equate the brain with consciousness, believing that consciousness necessarily requires the brain. Those who regard the physical realm as being the entire universe maintain that once the brain dies then consciousness is totally extinguished.

Coming to the defense of the mystics' view; philosophers, like Rene Descartes (1596–1650), believed that the body and consciousness are of totally different natures. In his *Meditations on First Philosophy*, which was published in 1641, the Frenchman makes this distinction clear, and although the word 'mind' is used, he is certainly not using it as a synonym for the brain as it is used today. Descartes believed that '...the natures of mind [consciousness] and body are not only different, but in some way opposite ... these arguments are enough to show that the decay of the body does not imply the destruction of the mind, and are hence enough to give mortals the hope of an after-life...'[13]

Descartes' dualistic approach contrasts with the monistic approach of Western medicine that assumes an inseparability of consciousness and the brain because these are regarded as different aspects of the one entity. The divide between the dualist and monist approaches is shaped by one's belief of whether consciousness originates in the brain or not. The eminent mythologist, Joseph Campbell (1904–1987), resolved the argument for himself by concluding that the brain is really a conduit of consciousness as opposed to being the source of it. He wrote that the head is not where consciousness originates but that it is '...an organ that inflects consciousness in a certain direction, or to a certain set of purposes.'[14]

A Distorted View of Reality

It is a plausible proposition to regard the brain as a type of filter for consciousness to ground us firmly in physical reality. Yet the word 'filter' implies a process of purification, which in fact is contrary to what the brain actually does. For the truth is that the brain sullies the flow of pure consciousness to provide us with a physical, but inherently distorted, view of reality. And the reason is quite simple—the brain cannot deal with non-physical realities so it conveniently rejects these, while necessarily allowing the flow of consciousness to continue.

Scientist David Darling, PhD, gives an excellent example of this insidious process by using our much believed and trusted organ for seeing the world around us—the eye. Explains Darling:

...the eye takes in light rays and focuses them, forming an image on the retina. Then via the optic nerve, it conveys the information in this image to the brain. But the eye does not add to what is already there—it takes away. The eye interferes with the light rays that fall into it. First it bends them from their original paths, then it destroys them completely by absorbing them. So the eye does not help us to become more conscious of the universe. Rather it denies any possibility of knowing what reality is like by altering and blocking at the source everything it comes into contact with. We cannot be conscious of *anything* that enters the eye because all such aspects of the universe are irrevocably changed or terminated in the process of 'seeing'.[15]

Moreover, the same is true of all our five senses! An analogy of the functions of the brain and senses is as submarine or scuba diving equipment. In a submarine or wearing scuba diving gear under the ocean depths one is better able to perceive the underwater world through the submarine's glass screens and the diver's goggles, just as our eyes and other senses are best suited to the physical reality above the water. So, in the same way that our naked physical senses are of little use in the ocean, they are also of little use (indeed mystics say they are an impediment) for perceiving any non-physical reality.

Therefore, on the one hand, marvelous though the brain is, from a purely physiological perspective of perception, when we understand that it is actually deceiving us into believing that what it reveals to us is a true image of reality, we can be excused for becoming more than just a little suspicious. We may even become mildly curious to find out what it is that we are actually missing. Death gives us that opportunity because at the time of death, it is the brain that dies, shutting down the physical senses, enabling our true selves, or pure consciousness as some mystics describe it, to prevail.

Therefore, in life, while the little self, or ego, holds sway through its accomplice the conniving brain, it is believed to be the cause of the biggest problem for us in terms of our spiritual progress. This is because the ego succeeds in blanketing more subtle levels of consciousness in a thick, seemingly impenetrable curtain, blinding us to ultimate reality.

Attachments and Habits Creates Ego

So what is this thing we call ego? For our purposes the term is used in a broad philosophical context beyond the purely psychological structures proposed by Sigmund Freud, namely the id, the ego, and the superego. Because each of these three psychological structures are subject to conditioning by the physical world, the word ego, as used here, will encompass all of these structures.

So if we investigate closely the nature of the ego, we find that it is really no more than a collection of attachments to the experiences of life and our genes. For it is only through the individual brain, via the individual physical body (our five senses), that we can experience sensual life. Therefore, persistently experiencing life as an individual entity cements the perception of 'I-ness' and of being separate from everything else. While we learn to avoid unpleasant sensual experiences, the enjoyable ones create in us habits. And we are, without doubt, creatures of habit.

Just consider for a moment all that you have done so far today, or yesterday. Doubtless, you will find that many of the things that you either did, said, or even thought, were as a result of habit. Habits dictate what, when and how we do almost everything. So in effect the ego diminishes our choices and limits our freedom.

The Mind's Quest for Happiness

Habits are formed because of the mind's restive nature and its unending quest for self-gratifying sensual experiences. Because the mind can only cope with a physical reality it, therefore, seeks satisfaction in material objects—whether that be cars or homes or jewelry or even another person. We all know that the ego is satiated through the association with and acquisition of such objects in the sense that it identifies with these external objects. But, as Russian psychologist Mihaly Csikszentmihalyi explains in his book, *The Evolving Self*, the more the ego identifies with external objects the more vulnerable it becomes because any threat to these material objects is a threat to the core of one's being.[16]

In our materialistic societies, where consumerism is the new religion, our minds chase objects in an endless cycle of desire and self-gratification, continually looking for another fix of 'happiness' like drug addicts—always hopeful that the next fix will be better and longer lasting. However, in identifying the problematic nature of the ego, this is not to argue for the notion of nihilism, a philosophy based on the negation of one or more aspects of life. Eliminating the trappings of egoism is argued only to the extent of ridding the ego of all the *unnecessary* desires that effectively inhibit one's freedom of choice because these psychological drives result in unhealthy attachments. Further, striving to be a completely selfless person is unrealistic because it ignores the individual physiological processes that each of us is subject to.

Instead, the type of egoless selflessness that is attainable is one where the individual identifies not with external material objects but with a common good beyond even the concept of humanity into the realm of the notion of universal spirit. Csikszentmihalyi argues that the evolution of the ego beyond material objects is fundamental for our survival in the third millennium, saying that unless we evolve we will continue to be controlled by the building blocks of ego—genes and culture.[17]

Ponder for a moment on the world's major problems today, and we find that there is a resounding ring of truth in what Csikszentmihalyi proposes, which is really no different to what the Buddha, Jesus, and others like them, professed thousands of years ago. There can be little doubt that all our global problems can be traced back to unnatural and unhealthy egotism. Greed for money and lust for power are the most obvious examples of gross egotism that have frequently and painfully plunged the planet into economic, social, political and/or ecological disaster.

Egotism Deceives its Victims

In separating people, an over-inflated ego-self creates division and enmity in all facets of society—not only in commerce and politics but in the home and also in religion. The late Dr Julian Johnson, theologian and surgeon, who practiced mysticism in India for many years, wrote:

...[egotism] has a thousand claws by which to dig into the minds of its victims. Its deadly poison infiltrates the entire being. Beginning generally in infancy, it seldom ceases to operate until death... It completely deceives its own victims, making them self-satisfied, when they ought to be seeking their own improvement. It will prevent people seeking new things [broader horizons]. It is the main friend and supporter of ancient superstitions. It establishes creeds, appoints a priesthood, and builds up organizations to propagate its own dogmas.[18]

The message of humility, which is the antithesis of egotism, is one that all genuine mystics attempt to deliver. They know that without sincere child-like humility, that has therefore negated the destructive sense of 'I-ness', one will be impeded from evolving into a greater being. We may recall the words of Jesus, who in the Gospel According to Matthew, is quoted as saying:

Whoever humbles himself like this child, he is the greatest in the kingdom of heaven.[19]

The significance of the child in this example is that a child, up to the age of around 12 years, has yet to develop a strong sense of ego-self—this was shown by Reanney in his nine-phase life cycle.

Only the 'I' Dies

A more recent example of the great importance mystics have attached to humility can be found in the *Adi Granth* (*Adi* meaning original and *Granth* meaning scripture). The *Adi Granth*, also known as the *Shri Guru Granth Sahib,* is the holy book of the Sikhs. It was compiled around 1604 by a mystic called Guru Arjan, the fifth successor to Guru Nanak (1469–1539), who is regarded as the founder of Sikhism. Arguably, it is the most complete scripture available today. It mentions, most emphatically, the importance of negating the sense of 'I-ness' for spiritual fulfillment and ultimately to overcome our fear of death:

Where there is 'I-amness', there, Thou art not; yea, when Thou

art within me, then 'I' am not.
Know this Unutterable Mystery, O ye Wise of God...
And one loses one's self, and Fear and Doubt, and is rid of the
fear of birth-and-death...[20]

Our thanatophobia, like all fears, is based on ignorance and symptomatic of the egocentric concept we have of ourselves. Ultimately, the thought of losing this 'I' underlies all the different manifestations of fear that surround death. Why this is so becomes clear when we understand that in death it is only the 'I' that dies and it's this vulnerability that frightens us the most. But the paradox is that death can only exist while the sense of 'I-ness' prevails. The *Adi Granth* states this unambiguously:

It is through Ego that one Dies; it is the sense of 'mineness' that Destroys...[21]

We know that our sense of 'I-ness' is created by our habits and attachments, which, in turn, are created and gratified through sensory input. As a result, consciousness constantly runs out to the receptacles of our senses to appease the mind in its never-ending quest for self-satisfaction. But happiness grounded in a physical object, which is the only form of happiness that can be derived via the physical senses, will always be ephemeral because of the restless nature of the mind. Physicists know that all physical objects are in a constant state of flux and molecular disintegration, in other words wearing with time, or in the case of living organisms—dying.

Under the constant flow of time, everything is weathered. More often than not, worn, damaged objects fail to satisfy a restive mind, so interest in such objects understandably wanes. Therefore, the mind continually seeks new objects or experiences. If you had the choice, would you rather live in a new, secure, sturdy dwelling or one that is dilapidated and dirty due to the weathering of time? Economic considerations aside, the self-satisfying mind would certainly choose the new dwelling. Even in situations where a new object was unavailable then usually any novel object will suffice. Notwithstanding the fact that people sometimes remain sentimentally attached to certain objects no matter how old and weathered, the point is that the mind always wants—wants that are the fuel for the concept of 'I-ness', which it can also be said, is the foundation of that sentimentality too.

Now, we have touched again upon the concept of time that Reanney first raised in his nine-phase life cycle. The concept of time is closely linked to the concepts of 'I-ness' and death. Time is an interesting phenomenon, one that physicists have been investigating for decades. Mystics tell us that time is a universal law that functions only in the lower realms of reality. This relationship between consciousness, time and death is one that requires further investigation and so is deserving of a chapter on its own.

2

The Death of Time and Birth of Forever

Time present and time past
Are both perhaps present in time future,
And time future contained in time past.
If all time is eternally present
All time is unredeemable...
Time past and time future
Allow but a little consciousness.
To be conscious is not to be in time...
T. S. Eliot (1888–1965) from Burnt Norton

Lord Krishna, the flute-playing Indian mystic who is believed to have been an incarnation of the Hindu deity Vishnu, is quoted in the *Bhagavad-Gita* as saying to his disciple Arjuna:

> Time I am, the great destroyer of the worlds, and I have come here to destroy all people.[1]

Powerful words indeed. Obviously, any discussion about death cannot avoid scrutinizing the concept of time, because it is *in* time that we all grow old and die (if, of course, we haven't met our death earlier in life due to any number of reasons).

So what exactly is time? Most of us regard time as a linear, forward-flowing phenomenon that runs in 60 second cycles for 24 hours each day, 365 days a year (or 366 in a leap year). Such a perception clothes time in a universal straight-jacket that is defined by our calendars and time pieces. This view gives time three distinct characteristics: the unalterable past, the always-changing present and the uncertain future. At any given moment we look back at the past, reliving a myriad of experiences, often with deep emotional ramifications, as well as look ahead into the future, frequently in either intense expectation or dread.

The Marriage of Time and 'I'

This concept of time is closely tied up with our illusory sense of 'I-ness'. As we discussed in the previous chapter, our experiences that are constructed by our sense faculties manufacture and shape our concept of 'I'. Our sense perceptions, therefore, imprint experiences upon consciousness that are stored away in memory, or the past. Thus, our memories become a reference to which we attach our concept of 'I-ness'. David Hume, the eighteenth century Scottish philosopher and historian, reiterated this important point when he revealed how his concept of himself was inexorably associated with his past perceptions. 'When I enter most intimately into what I call *myself*,' he wrote, 'I always stumble on some particular perception or other, of heat or cold, light or shade, love or hatred, pain or pleasure. I can never catch *myself* at any time without a perception and never can observe anything but the perception.'[2]

Fond memories of an experience will, naturally, encourage us to repeat the experience. While, on the other hand, the pain or discomfort of a negative perception will influence us in avoiding the particular experience wherever possible. So, in the course of a lifetime, the sense of 'I' becomes more defined and 'real' due to the entrenching and accumulation of habit-forming behavior. Notwithstanding the fact that sometimes our memories fail us, memory is an important element of our problematic sense of 'I-ness'.

Yet memory alone is not sufficient for shaping the sense of 'I-ness'. Even if, for example, you had no memory, the mere fact that time is perceived as a linear concept is the underlying reason why the sense of 'I-ness' is born and prevails so strongly.

Imagine for a moment that you had no memory resulting in

every experience you had being lost in a mental oblivion. In fact, such a frightening scenario can confront those suffering damage to the brain's hippocampus and amygdaloid nuclei structures. In such pitiful cases rather than no 'I' prevailing, a *new* 'I' is born in each new moment because the linear concept of time is maintained, albeit absent of the sense of the past. There is an actual and quite amazing case that illustrates this point, but before presenting this a brief explanation of memory and how it functions is necessary.

Mindful of Memories

Two broad classifications of memory are short-term and long-term memory. Short-term memory holds only a few pieces of information for up to about 20 seconds. Long-standing research by psychologists indicates that no more than seven (plus or minus two) items can be stored in short-term memory at any one time.[3] Long-term memory, however, is regarded as a limitless and relatively permanent storehouse of information. For information to be stored it must be encoded. Encoding can be automatic or require conscious effort. Interestingly, the type of information that is automatically encoded by our brains relates to space, time or frequency. Knowing you have met someone for the third time in the one day is an example of automatic encoding, as is knowing (all things being equal) when and where you had dinner yesterday. Psychologists have discovered that this type of encoding is impossible to switch-off.[4] Effortful encoding, on the other hand, requires a conscious effort to encode the relevant information and lay down a memory. Now it should be pointed out that scientists don't believe there is a specific location in the brain where memories are stored (and if there is, it has yet to be discovered), although there is clear evidence implicating key neural structures, like the hippocampus and cerebellum, in the encoding and recall of information.

Research involving unique amnesiac patients has shown scientists that there are two types of long-term memory. One is the explicit or declarative memory, so-named because it is a memory of facts and figures that one can consciously know and declare. The second type is implicit memory, which one cannot consciously recall but, nevertheless, we manage to retain. Movement and some cognitive skills are the kinds of information held in implicit memory. For example, although we all have to learn to walk, run and ride a bike, it would be very rare for someone suffering a typical amnesiac episode to also forget how to perform these movement, or motor, functions. This is because most amnesiac patients experience a disruption to their explicit memory only.

Clive Wearing, a world renowned conductor and expert on Renaissance music, is one such case in point. Unfortunately, Wearing lost the functioning of his explicit memory due to viral encephalitis (brain tissue inflammation). Although having intact language and motor skills, as is evidenced not only by his ability to walk and talk being unaffected but also by the retention of his earlier learned ability to deftly play the piano, he cannot store new memories. What is significant about his case, however, is that it seems because of the brain's ability to encode certain information (that is time, space and frequency) automatically, Wearing's sense of time, as a forward-acting linear phenomenon, appears unaffected. His diary, which he apparently keeps with obsessive fervor, gives us an insight into his psychological dilemma, which makes it impossible for him to *define* his persistent sense of 'I', but nevertheless his sense of 'I' still prevails:

9.04a.m. Now I am AWAKE
10.00a.m. NOW I AM AWAKE
10.28a.m. ACTUALLY I AM NOW FIRST TIME AWAKE for years

10.54a.m. Now I am awake for the first time.[5]

The scrawled diary entries continue like this ad infinitum.

Therefore, even despite the absence of the capacity to remember, we can see that a linear sense of the flow of time and our sense of 'I-ness' are both impossible to divorce.

The Illusion of Time

Given the illusory nature of our concept of 'I-ness' and the fact that this is knotted together with our sense of time, it can't come as any real surprise to learn that our sense of time is illusory in nature too. 'No way,' you say emphatically. 'The past is what has come before the present, which is a necessary precursor for the future—nothing can be more obvious than that!'

Well, just consider that the physicist's concept of time is quite different to how most people regard it. To discuss how the physicist views time we need to venture briefly and really only superficially into the esoteric world of quantum physics. And it's important to note that, although traditionally science has been seen as a kind of enemy of the seeker of spiritual truth, in recent years many quantum physics theories and discoveries have buttressed what the great mystics say about ultimate reality. British-born physicist, Prof. Paul Davies, write that several '...modern writers are finding close parallels between the concepts used in the quantum theory and those of Oriental mysticism, such as Zen.'[6]

Close parallels there are indeed in all genuine mystical traditions—in fact, much closer than most physicists are perhaps actually aware of, as we shall see later. But first, let's consider what exactly is quantum theory.

The Midas Touch of Consciousness

Quantum theory was born in the 1920s and is a significant pillar in a scientific endeavor that has become known as the 'New

Physics'. It's a branch of physics that deals with the micro-world of atoms and sub-atomic particles where energy is found to exist only in discrete 'packets' or quanta. The discovery of these quanta made scientists, for the first time, focus their attention on the relationship between the observer and the external world. Put simply, quantum theory provides convincing scientific evidence proving that consciousness is the single most essential factor in the materialization of the physical world. Physicist Nick Herbert elaborates:

> One of the main quantum facts of life is that we radically change whatever we observe. Legendary King Midas never knew the feel of silk or a human hand after everything he touched turned to gold. Humans are stuck in a similar Midas-like predicament: we can't directly experience the true texture of reality because *everything we touch* [through the brain] *turns to matter.*[7]

We simply cannot ignore the fact that the great mystics have been saying the same thing—for thousands of years. These knowers of ultimate reality have labored hard and sometimes even sacrificed their lives in telling us that the desirous mind/brain acts as a veil preventing us from experiencing ultimate reality. The poetic words of Jalaluddin Rumi, aptly sum up this point:

> Man is a mighty volume; within him all things are written,
> but veils and darkness do not allow him
> to read that knowledge within himself.
> The veils and darkness are these various preoccupations
> and diverse worldly plans and desires of every kind.[8]

This shared conclusion between mysticism and quantum theory is really a revolution of immense proportions because it goes against the traditional premise of science that separates the observer from what is observed. To better understand this paradigm shift we can look at the humble electron, that in the absence of an observer exists as a wave, or in other words, not a solid particle of matter. But, on the other hand, if the electron is observed it becomes a particle of matter! Confused? Well, Prof. Davies explains that this paradoxical wave-particle duality is very much akin to the computer hardware/software dichotomy.[9] The particle face of the atom can be seen as hardware, or as Prof. Davies describes, 'little balls rattling about.'[10] Yet the wave face of the atom is aligned with software. But this wave is quite different to anything that physicists have ever encountered. It is not a wave of any substance with a physical basis, but rather a wave purely of knowledge or information. It tells physicists what can be known about the atom, but is not a wave of the atom itself.

Thus, the logical conclusion that one must necessarily arrive at is that consciousness more than just changes our physical world, it actually creates it.

The astounding implications of consciousness being a fundamental creator of the world we see is that the world we do see cannot be regarded as ultimate reality, simply because it is a world that we have, in the very process of observation through the brain, created ourselves.

Relative Time and Space

Since Albert Einstein (1879–1955) was one of the major contributors to physics any discussion about time cannot overlook his theory of relativity because it is a hypothesis of motion, space and also of time. Einstein's revolutionary ideas proposed that *the* past, *the* present and *the* future are relative to the speed, or motion, of an entity. In effect, this meant that time could no longer be deemed to be an absolute phenomenon, flowing ever forward like a river towards the sea, but rather something more aligned with the water itself—dynamic and fluid, or as some physicists describe, elastic. Writes Prof. Davies:

> Einstein demonstrated that time is, in fact, elastic and can be stretched and shrunk by motion. Each observer carries around his own personal scale of time, and it does not generally agree with anybody else's. In our own frame, time never appears distorted, but relative to another observer who is moving differently, our time can be wrenched out of step with their time.[11]

Einstein himself described time as a '...tool invented by man to measure the movement of things,' and remarked that '...past, present and future are an illusion—although a persistent one.'[12]

In proving Einstein's theory, scientists have shown that rapid motion has the effect of slowing down time, and theoretically speaking, at the speed of light (186,000 miles per second) time would stop.

An example of the relativity of time involving two hypothetical twins is known appropriately in quantum theory circles as the 'twins effect'. Imagine a set of twins where one is an astronaut who blasts off in a rocket on a ten-year near light speed journey to a nearby star. The other twin remains at home and waits for their sibling to return. When the rocket does return, the Earth-bound twin would find that their astronaut sibling had aged only one year to their own ten. This is because the near light speed rocket would have enabled the astronaut twin to experience only one year of time, while on Earth ten years would have elapsed![13]

A Timeless State

Furthermore, modern-day physicists have put forward a theory of parallel universes whereby, in effect, the past, present and future exist in any one given moment. In substantiating this, physicist Dr Fred Alan Wolf confirms that this is also a belief in many spiritual traditions. He writes:

> The past, present and future exist side by side. If we were totally able to 'marry' corresponding times each and every moment of our time-bound existences, there would indeed be no sense of time and we would all realize the timeless state, which is taken to be our true or base state of reality by many spiritual practices.[14]

Aside from time, the other important aspect of Einstein's theory of relativity is space. And we discover that space, like time, is really elastic too. Einstein showed that when time is stretched (as in the example of the astronaut twin's time) space shrinks. To illustrate this point we can refer to an easy to understand example given by Prof. Davies. If you were to be a passenger on a rushing train as it passed through a station, the station clock would run slightly slower from your perspective than that of a station worker on the platform. Also in comparison with the railway worker, the station platform would be marginally shorter to you. Naturally, we don't notice such distortions of space and time because at the speeds we travel such distortions are exceedingly small, but sensitive scientific instruments do detect such distortions.[15]

Physicists regard these space and time dilations as a conversion of space (which shrinks) into time (which stretches). Therefore, rather than thinking of space and time as two separate phenomena, physicists regard them as one which is conveniently called 'spacetime', consisting of three dimensions of space (length, breadth and height) and the fourth dimension of time.

Cosmic Time Machines
Einstein also went on to include gravity into his theory of relativity by showing how it, like speed, can dilate time and this became known as his general theory of relativity. For example,

time does indeed run faster in space where the Earth's gravitational force is obviously weaker. Also, under converse circumstances, where there is a very strong gravitational pull present, time will slow, or stretch.

In recent years astronomers have discovered a unique type of star where the force of gravity is so rampant that not only is time there slowed but even light cannot escape from its pull. Because this type of star literally consumes all particles and even photons of light that venture too close, the star appears like a black void. Hence, these vortexes of unimaginable gravitational pull have become known as black holes.

Black holes are dead stars that have an enormous mass crammed into a tiny space. Having exhausted their nuclear fuel, these corpse stars continue to collapse in on themselves under the influence of their own gravity. Because they consume light they cannot actually be seen, but rather can only be inferred by intense X-ray emissions. Some scientists believe that most large galaxies have a black hole near their centers. A few years ago, University of Arizona astronomers discovered what they believe to be a black hole at the center of our Milky Way galaxy.

In line with Einstein's theory, the immense gravitational field that a black hole creates stretches time, making these enigmatic entities cosmic time machines.

Thus, a black hole can be regarded as a fast-track to eternity. Using the hypothetical twins as an example, the astronaut twin travelling into a black hole would not only reach the future before their sibling, but they would also venture beyond the end of time in an instant. This is because upon entering the black hole, time for this twin would literally stop, while outside the black hole an eternity would effectively pass. Physicists describes this highway to eternity as a journey to 'nowhere' and 'nowhen' — a 'nonplace' where the physical universe no longer exists. Surely such a 'nonplace' beyond the physical universe implies a doorway to the realm of spirit. Well this is certainly how some scientists regard black holes, believing them to be gateways to an infinite array of dimensions, or parallel universes, via a 'tunnel' or 'umbilical cord' that would eventually be severed.

In fact, scientist Clifford Pickover, PhD, believes there is no better way to die than to submit to the alluring magic and mystery of a black hole and to plunge straight into one. He admits candidly, '...if I had to choose the place and manner of my death I would certainly elect to plunge into a black hole. Black holes are essentially places that are gone from our universe. And within their hidden boundaries, time and space become magically intertwined.'[16]

But there's no reason for concern. While not implying that Dr Pickover has any criminal intentions, mastering the ancient art of dying while living does not entail hijacking a NASA space shuttle and flying directly into the first black hole you can find. Nevertheless, the intense gravitational field of a black hole resulting in unimaginable spacetime distortion makes the conceptual metaphor of the phenomenon remarkably poignant in terms of the art of dying while living, so we shall revisit it in the final chapter. For now, it's important to realize that time is not an absolutely linear phenomenon but can indeed be 'stretched' and 'shrunk' according to speed and also gravity.

However, the notion of speed should not be seen only in the context of rapid motion but also as a threshold of consciousness which delineates the realm of particles (that is the solid material world) from the quantum realm of vibratory waves. Indeed, Darryl Reanney made this significant point when he wrote:

...the speed of light should be thought of less as a movement than as a threshold; it represents the dividing line between the world of particles and the world of waves. All real entities have a quantum wave structure: below light speed they can express themselves as particles whereas at or above light speed they must remain as waves.[17]

Put another way, while our level of consciousness remains below the vibratory threshold of light speed, 'reality' will be perceived as particle-based matter. At the light speed threshold, however, reality takes on its inherent wave-form characteristic that cannot be subject to the linear concept of time because we know that at light speed time stops. As Reanney succinctly explained, wave-form reality exists in a timeless realm, beyond space and time, and he recognized that consciousness (knowing) is inherently a wave-form phenomenon:

> ...*when reality exists in wave form it is not stringently subject to the 'here and now' space and time limitations that constrain ordinary particle-based-matter.* And knowing by its very nature, exists in wave form![18]

The quantum world, therefore, is not bound by the linear flow of time. Physicists have demonstrated that quantum waves can function in a past-to-future sense as well as a future-to-past sense. Then, you may well ask, why it is that we harbor a sense of an absolute linear flow of time that creates a particle-based physical reality?

The Brain is Found Guilty Again

According to Reanney, our sense of time is structured by the sequential mode of brain function, of which memory is a crucial part. Reanney asserted that, '...our sense of time must depend critically upon the brain processes that underpin mechanisms of short-term memory.'[19]

In searching for a reason for this, Reanney suggested that the sequential flow of brain function is attributable to the origin of language. On the surface, maybe there seems a rather spurious relationship between the sequential functioning of the brain and the sense of the linear flow of time, but he explains quite convincingly that the serial ordering of speech is the basis for our illusion of time:

> To understand the meaning of any sentence it is essential that any given word in the set is successively removed from the focus of our attention so that the next word can be grasped and processed in a way that preserves the flow of experience. This serial ordering—bringing into focus (from the future state), holding (present state) and eliminating (past state)—is the very basis of the continuity of speech. [Thus]...it is also the basis of the continuity of time because the sequential this-after-that structuring which makes speech possible is a major source of the this-after-that structuring that creates our human sense of the passage of time.[20]

The penetrating use of silence, when of course no language is used, by the great mystics is perhaps testimony to Reanney's reasoning. In the light of this, the ancient words of the Chinese mystic, Lao Tzu, plumb new depths of understanding:

> Those who know do not say; those who say do not know.[21]

Decay with Time

Related closely with the concept of time is another scientific concept known as the second law of thermodynamics. Physicists regard this law as universal. It states that the level of molecular disorder in any given system will increase with time. Reanney outlined the principles of this law by using the example of a droplet of ink in a glass of water.[22] As well as being the antithesis of the black hole metaphor, we shall see that it's an example so perfect in describing the normal flow of consciousness. Consequently, like the black hole metaphor, we shall return to it in the final chapter also.

Over time, the droplet of ink will naturally diffuse and after perhaps an hour or two the ink would have evenly discolored the water. The reason why the droplet of ink disperses rather than remains a droplet is based solely on probability. That is to say, there is only one direction that the ink molecules can move to retain the droplet's perfect round shape, and that is towards the center of the droplet. However, there are many directions that the molecules can move in (that is in any number of outward directions) for the ink droplet to disperse. So therefore, over time there will always be greater molecular dispersion simply because there are more chances for the ink droplet to expand outwards than there are for it to contract back towards its center. Consequently, the ink diffuses in the water.

The second law of thermodynamics is fatalistic in that it determines that all physical processes, without any compensating input of energy, will move towards increasing entropy, or decay, with time. There are countless examples of this in our everyday lives. Over time buildings weather, coastlines erode, and all machines develop faults. But a more poignant example is the human body, which we all know grows old with time, making both physical and mental abilities impaired. The compensating input of energy in the form of food is the reason why we continue to function amidst this increasing disorder because the energy input allows new cells to generate. Thus, everything in the physical universe (that is everything that has been created) will eventually decay, and in the case of us humans, die.

The Universe is Dying

Therefore, the art of dying while living simply cannot be based on any physical concept since all physical entities must decay and eventually die. This is an inviolable law not just for all physical objects but for the entire physical universe too.

The second law of thermodynamics is one of the major factors that have enabled scientists to conclude that the physical universe was created by a profoundly dramatic event that has become known as the big bang.

Compelling evidence supporting the big bang theory came when in the 1920s American astronomer, Edwin Hubble, discovered that galaxies are actually pushing apart from each other—the second law of thermodynamics on a universal scale.

While some scientists believe that the universe is moving irreversibly towards further disorder, others believe that the disorder will one day cease and the universe will begin contracting in on itself. Data supporting this theory shows that the rate of the universal expansion is actually falling. Scientists, therefore, believe that if the expansion does halt then, due to the force of gravity, the universe will begin contracting at an increasing rate. In painting a dramatic picture of this scenario, Prof. Davies explains that initially '...the contraction will be slow, but over many billions of years the pace will accelerate. Galaxies that are now receding from one another will start to approach instead, gathering speed all the time. The stage is set for a monstrous cataclysm.'[23]

Scientists have called this monstrous cataclysm the big crunch. The physical universe will literally shrivel up and spacetime will disintegrate. This is basically a black hole scenario on a universal scale—the big bang in reverse. But this isn't necessarily considered by all to be the ultimate death of the physical universe. For some believe that at some fantastic density the universe will be reborn with another big bang, and another expanding universe will emerge.

The Birth of Space and Time

If the reversal of the big bang foreshadows the death of the physical universe (that is spacetime), then several billion (that's 1 followed by 9 zeros) years ago, the big bang itself must have been the conception of space and time. Without attempting to be overly dramatic, this seemingly bizarre scientific conclusion must be one of the most profound ever made. And from the point of view of mysticism, it is one of the most esoteric tenets.

Before physical creation, the universe was, therefore, a holistic and perfectly unified whole, not bound by time or space. In Western parlance, mystics translate this unity as God (or something culturally equivalent) while the typically prosaic term 'singularity' is used by the scientist. But both are mere labels and shouldn't distract us from the fact that time before the creation of the physical universe did not exist.

Of course it's impossible to imagine a universe without time because we know that our minds function in a necessary temporal mode. Yet the limitations of a conditioned human mind cannot alter the scientific theory of a non-physical universe, outside of time and space, existing prior to the big bang.

Since perfect unity can only exist, in its purest form, outside of time and space, then it seems reasonable to conclude that the creation of the universe—the beginning of disunity, time and space—was also the creation of our illusory sense of 'I-ness'. This is because the inherent nature of the ego, which is intrinsically linked with the concept of the flow of time, is to separate the 'I' from all else. And separateness, we all know, is the antithesis of unity.

NOW is the Time

Thus, we can begin to see the great wisdom in the teachings of the great mystics who encourage their students to be concerned only with the ever-present NOW. For in an eternal NOW, the past and the future cannot exist, stripping the illusion of 'I-ness' of all its destructive power.

The Japanese tradition of Zen is quite famous for rigorously attaching immense importance on the all-embracing and ever-present NOW. Ancient Zen scriptures contain sometimes terse phrases conveying the importance of being in the present totally—the NOW. By being completely focused on the NOW, the illusory 'I' is starved of past experiences and of the desires that it hopes will be fulfilled in the future. And a starved 'I' is a dead 'I'.

Remember that once we die to the illusory ego then we become enlivened to the immortal spirit.

On a visit to Japan, the late musicologist and author Joachim-Ernst Berendt was escorted through a Zen temple where it became all too apparent to him of the importance still attached even today to the concept of an eternal NOW. The evidence was found in a characteristic Zen temple garden. Observed Berendt:

> In the garden of the famous Kokedera moss temple in Kyoto (but also in other Zen gardens all over Japan), small creeks are regulated by bamboo lever pumps that periodically fill with water, tip over, and run out. Each time they tip, they generate a hollow, wooden bamboo sound to be heard all over the Zen garden and the entire temple area; this tone has been sounding for centuries, varied only by the creek's changing water-level. 'Do you know what the bamboo says when it goes 'click'?' asked the monk who was guiding us through the garden. Then he answered his own question: 'Now! Now! Now!'[24]

The well-known Japanese trait of taking countless photographs of their brief annual holidays is another means by which they remind themselves (consciously and unconsciously) of the importance of the eternal NOW. Berendt originally thought that the reason for the Japanese tourists' zealous photographic nature was due solely to mass advertising by the photographic industries. On the face of it this would appear to be the case. However, one of Berendt's Japanese friends explained that the photography is really a way of preserving the moment—the NOW.[25]

Yet, there is a disturbing aspect to the Japanese desire to be in the eternal NOW. Occasionally, Japanese newspapers report stories of two lovers who take their own lives when it appears that their love has brought them to a stage of unsurpassed happiness. Observed Berendt:

These lovers will gaze at a landscape all night long—a waterfall, a rock in the sea, or the full moon—but not for the sake of saying: Now I could die! That would suit Western romanticism, but the attitude of the Japanese is quite the opposite. They do not talk about it. They just do it. They die. As one way to preserve the 'now'.[26]

Obviously spiritual naiveté and misguided romanticism is a dangerous combination. While death is in one sense the embracing of the NOW, because it does intensely focus the attention in the present moment, taking life prematurely does nothing to shatter the illusion of time. In fact, it only entrenches it; for one of the most fundamental laws of the universe is the law of causation, which is inherently linked to the illusory flow of time.

Time for Karma

The law of causation is what the great mystics refer to as the law of karma. Karma is a Sanskrit word meaning action, so this is the law of action and the corresponding reaction. The law of karma operates in exactly the same way as the scientific concept of the law of causation, but from the stand-point of mysticism it is more far-reaching because it extends beyond just the physical realm.

Explaining how the law of karma operates spiritually, as well as identifying its scientific and social masks, Dr Julian Johnson wrote that karma

...requires that *every doer shall receive the exact result, or reward, of his actions*. In its last analysis, it is nothing more nor less than the well-known law of cause and effect. It is known in physics as the law of compensation or balance or equilibrium. In jurisprudence it is the law of justice. All the courts of the civilized world give official recognition to the law of karma every time they mete out rewards and punishments. In ethics, as in civil and in criminal law, it is the basis of rewards and punishments, the decisive principle of right and wrong conduct.[27]

Right actions will, of course, create good karma while wrong actions will have the appropriate opposite results. So, even if you are a saintly person who benevolently helps others all your life, all these good actions would effectively be adding to your karmic load.

As Sawan Singh (1858–1948), who many believe was a mystic, explained clearly, the Lord of Death, known in India as *Kal,* oversees the operation of the law of karma, which only functions in the lower levels of creation in which the ego, to varying degrees, prevails (and interestingly, *Kal* is a Sanskrit word that means both time and death):

> Karma is administered by *Kal,* the Lord of Death, who administers the three worlds, that is the material, astral and causal regions. *Kal* was created by the Supreme Lord; he administers the three lower regions under His orders. He dispenses justice (karma) impartially. In compliance with the orders of the Lord, *Kal* asks all living beings after their death to render an account of their good and bad deeds and he then deals with them accordingly.[28]

There are three types of karma, which the Indian mystics classify as *Pralabdh, Kriyaman* and *Sinchit. Pralabdh* karma is that which is allotted to the current life and so can be seen to be the underlying principle of fate or destiny. *Kriyaman* karma is the new karma that we create in the present life. The effects of new karma can be experienced at any time, either in the current life or else they will be 'stored' away as *Sinchit* karma that maps out future lives.

At the time of death, if there is any *Sinchit* karma—be it good or bad—one will be forced by *Kal* (a function of the linear

45

perception of time) to take another rebirth in one or more of the lower levels within his domain. And since we are engaging in new actions all the time, our karmic load is always increasing every new lifetime, consequently binding us in seemingly never-ending cycle of birth and death.

To get a better grasp of this ever-deepening karmic situation, think of it in terms of an unpaid mortgage to which more principle debt is constantly accruing while your repayments remain unchanged. The result is that the mortgage becomes impossible to repay. But unlike everyday life, where in such a situation the bank would simply foreclose the loan; in the case of karma we remain increasingly burdened by mounting debt.

Sawan Singh identified the two important powers at *Kal's* disposal, which resonate beautifully with the theories of the new physics:

> *Kal* has two powers, namely, Time and Space. These provide the warp and the woof of the creation. Space helps in spreading the creation, and time is ever bringing about changes.[29]

The realms of creation mentioned equate to levels of consciousness. These will be discussed in Chapter 10, but the point that needs to be made at this juncture is that karma is inexorably enmeshed with the concepts of time, ego and death. Outside of time (that is at the higher levels of consciousness beyond the causal realm), karma, and therefore death, simply cannot exist because action and the corresponding reaction are necessarily temporal events.

Christianity and Karma

It will come as a surprise to many Christians to know that the early followers of the faith were well aware of the law of karma. In explaining that the effect of whatever we do will return in like manner, St. Paul wrote:

...for whatever a man sows, that he will also reap.[30]

In effect, St. Paul was only echoing the message of Jesus who derided the barbaric 'eye for an eye and a tooth for a tooth' mentality in the context of the law of karma, by imploring the people of Palestine to break the karmic cycle with the example of offering the left cheek if slapped on the right one.[31] It's saddening that this particular Biblical passage is completely distorted and used by some religious folk whenever the issue of capital punishment is raised in certain societies, falsely implying that Jesus approved of the death penalty. Nothing could be further from the truth; for all genuine mystics regard all life, human and non-human, as sacred and know full well that the law of karma is completely infallible.

In understanding the relationship between karma and time, St. Paul also declared the need to see beyond the material world and its time-bound transitory things to the eternal spiritual things that are excluded from the clutches of the temporal and transitory:

...because we look not to the things that are seen but to the things that are unseen; for the things that are seen are transient, but the things that are unseen are eternal.[32]

He was perhaps alluding to what science has discovered only in the last century: that the generally held concepts of time and space are an illusion. Being an illusion, it is therefore solely dependant upon the level of consciousness. Recalling Reanney's speed of light threshold of consciousness (not involving any physical motion but instead vibratory frequency), together with the principles of Einstein's theory of relativity (approaching the speed of light threshold, time and space significantly distort) means that the vibratory level of consciousness determines the perception of space and time.

Words and Actions Spring from Thoughts

However, at the physical level—the lowest level of creation/consciousness—the absolute law of karma that requires a sequential flow of time has an important bearing on what we do and also everything we say and think. Mystics believe our thoughts are extremely important because they are precursors (albeit, sometimes unknowingly) to our words and actions. Sawan Singh explained that before one performs an action '...there is a desire, an intention or an urge in your mind. The desire is first formed within the mind, and then it is executed outside.'[33]

So while many of us think that we have a totally free will, the reality is that, in fact, we don't, because all that we say, do and think is not only subject to, but also determined to a large degree, by the law of karma. Only a will that is totally karma-less can be considered to be truly a free will, because such a will can have no previous causes limiting the 'free' choices available to it at any given moment. Once any karma is created then total freedom is lost and the will, while still free, is conditioned and limited by all the previous choices made.

This shouldn't, however, suggest that the conditioning of our wills makes it unnecessary for us to put in proper effort in all that we do, as an extreme cynic may believe, arguing that everything is destined anyway so why not sit back and enjoy (or endure) the ride. In answering this issue and elucidating further, Charan Singh (1916–1990), who many believe was also a mystic, wrote:

Everything in our life is predestined according to the karmas of our past life, but this does not preclude all effort on our part. The effort that we make is also part of our destiny. We, in fact have no free will as we call it... Our will is very limited and what we call free will is all circumscribed by our birth, the family we are born into, the country, the education and so forth, over which we had no control. All these circumstances have molded our thoughts and we act and think accordingly.[34]

Thus, the mystics see no contention between the concepts of free will and fate because although there was total freedom originally, before the birth of the illusion of time and the sense of 'I-ness', the very first action started the enormously complex cyclical process of action and further reaction that effectively limits our freedom. So while in one sense we are free to choose our destiny—and we certainly do—all our choices are subject to the decisions we have made previously, because no choice can be made in complete isolation of the previous choices. This would be against the law of causation.

On this issue, the mystics' view has some notable support; Einstein was adamant that there was no such thing as a free will, in the extreme sense of the phrase:

> Honestly I cannot understand what people mean when they talk about the freedom of the human will. I have a feeling, for instance, that I will something or other; but what relation this has with freedom I cannot understand at all. I feel that I will to light my pipe and I do it; but how can I connect this up with the idea of freedom? What is behind the act of *willing* to light the pipe? Another act of willing?... when you mention people who speak of such a thing as free will in nature it is difficult for me to find a suitable reply. The idea is of course preposterous.[35]

Like Einstein, the great mystics have asked what is behind the act of willing and discovered a divine will that functions through the temporal law of karma that effectively shatters the illusion of our capacity for totally independent action. In his characteristic poetic style, Rumi beautifully writes:

We are like bowls floating on the surface of water. How the bowls go is not determined by the bowls but by the water... There is no doubt that all bowls are floating on the water of divine might and will...[36]

Breaking Out of the Karmic Prison

So, since we are all subject to the law of karma there appears to be no solution to the ever-increasingly load of karmic burden that we have to bear. After each life we will obviously have more karma than before we were born—no matter how good or bad we were, meaning that we will be forced to take another rebirth again. The result is that we remain trapped in the karmic prison—life after life after life, and so on indefinitely.

But there is hope. Mystics contend there is an ancient and perfectly legitimate way to break-out of the karmic prison so that one will not have to take any further rebirths in *Kal's* domain. The ancient method is one through which we transcend the illusions of time, karma, and, therefore, 'I-ness', making it a confrontation with the Lord of Death. And importantly, this is done while still living; for it would be most unwise to wait until the physical body finally dies to try to break the Lord of Death's magical spell. If we confront the Lord of Death unprepared, victory will be assuredly his and we shall remain his victim.

To defeat death, the ancient message has been to awaken from the dream of illusion, or as T. S. Eliot advised to '...Allow but a little consciousness,' thereby breaking through the illusory reaches of time, space and 'I-ness'. It's surely for this reason that Buddha Shakyamuni was known as the 'Awakened One' because he was truly awake, or conscious, to the ultimate nature of reality and liberated of the deceptive sense of 'I' and time; for it's only the superficial 'I' that exits within time and consequently dies before taking yet another rebirth at some *future time*. The timeless, karma-less and I-less immortal core of our being, however, is logically beyond birth and death. If we can shatter this destructive illusion of 'I' then the spiritual immortal aspect of our being can be fully realized. The Lord of Death will be deprived of its victim and the basis for our mostly invisible thanatophobia will be usurped.

The Sound and Light of Freedom

The great mystics have long since told us that realizing our immortal selves is achievable within a single lifetime by practicing the art of dying while living. This ancient art is based upon the concept of a universal soundless sound. In the West, this spiritual vibration is known as the Primordial Sound Current, or, more aptly, as the Audible Life Stream because it is the essence of all life, and although inaudible to the physical ears (hence it's often referred to as soundless) it resounds ceaselessly. Resounding within each and every one of us, the Audible Life Stream is quite simply the Universal Principle, God-power, Allah, Brahma, call it whatever you like.

Inevitably, however, using mere words to describe what is ineffable will always prove inadequate. To only see this universal principle as a one-way flowing stream or river is misleading because, as Dr Julian Johnson explains, there is a two-way current in each wave of the Audible Life Stream, one moving out from the creative source of the universe and the other that returns:

> This wave has two aspects, a centrifugal flow and a centripetal flow. It moves outward from the central dynamo of all creation, and it flows back toward that dynamo. Moving upon that Current, all power and all life...flow outward to the outermost bounds of creation, and again upon it all life [returns] toward its source.[37]

Mystics contend that dying while remaining very much alive is the beginning of this return journey.

While all major religious traditions—both East and West—are founded on the concept of a supreme God or God-like concept, the spiritual vibratory principle of this universal force is largely unknown because over the centuries, for various reasons, this quintessential spiritual tenet has been grossly misunderstood. Consequently, the original message of the ancient mystics has been in the main lost, and so today most people are completely unaware of the Audible Life Stream and its spiritual significance, believing that at the time of death one needs only to go to the light. This belief is understandable given the emphasis on the light in spiritual literature. But nevertheless, mystics say this is a tragic mistake. For the light, in fact, emanates from the Audible Life Stream. Being vibratory in nature, the Audible Life Stream, thus, encompasses both light and sound, since both are vibratory in nature too. Explained Sawan Singh:

> Both Light and Sound are within us. The Sound and Light are related to the two faculties of the soul namely Surat (hearing) and Nirat (seeing).[38]

Once these two soul powers of hearing and seeing are fully developed, the soul can rise up to the highest spiritual regions beyond the illusion of death.

Certainly, the light is necessary for illuminating the spiritual path but, say the mystics, the sound is equally necessary to pull the soul in the correct 'upward' direction. They believe that without the magnetic force of the sound we cannot ascend through the higher spiritual levels.

The Book of Genesis tells us that '...God *said*, 'Let there be light'...'[39] (the italics are added) meaning that the voice of God—the sound of God—preceded the light. This is why mystics place emphasis on the Audible aspect of the God-power—the spiritual

Life Stream of consciousness.

Believed to be the most fundamental way that the God-power manifests itself to human consciousness, the Audible Life Stream is considered by mystics to be like a spiritual highway along which all souls will have to travel in order to reach the source of this power. But a far more poetic analogy, used by Sawan Singh to sum up the importance of the Audible Life Stream, is to view the universe as an ocean of spirituality:

> The Sound Current is a wave of the ocean of spirituality of which the soul is a drop. The ocean, wave, and the drop are alike in nature. All three are one. If the soul catches the Current and follows it, it can reach its destination, the ocean—and, by merging itself in the ocean, can itself become the ocean.[40]

So the Audible Life Stream is believed to be a universal and inherently non-material vibratory force manifesting as countless sounds and even music, that is said to be infinitely more enchanting than the very best music composed here in the physical world. The type of sound perceived, whether music or not, depends upon the level of vibrational frequency of one's consciousness.

In a very real sense the Audible Life Stream is a cosmic symphony to which all things, seen and unseen, unknowingly dance. Underpinning all physical and spiritual levels of creation; this symphony is endlessly being performed at the very essence of our being, since we are a microcosm of the entire universe. Yet, so few of us are aware of this. Even fewer understand that this sweetest of music can be perceived if we are prepared to truly *listen* for it. Being beyond the mental constructs of space and time, this harmony, therefore, cannot be apprehended through any physical means because, as has been shown, the brain neces-sarily filters and sequences our sensory input to create an illusory material perception only. Accordingly then, such a concept is understandably difficult to comprehend because our ears are the very organs designated by nature to perceive sound. Therefore, it's prudent to next discuss the nature of worldly sound, which most of us are familiar with, because the vibratory principles are the same as those pertaining to the sonorous and spiritual Audible Life Stream.

Hear! Hear! The Universe is Sound

The hidden harmony
is mightier
than what is revealed.
Heraclitus (c.540–475 BC)

Sound is constantly reverberating all around us although we can only hear those sounds within a certain frequency range. Put simply, sound is created by pressure waves (or spheres as some researchers like engineer and scientist John Stuart Reid believe) transmitted from a vibrating source. Since sound is a form of energy, sound waves are the means by which this auditory energy is transferred from one location where it is produced, to another where it is received. With time, this energy dissipates because the sound waves have a greater distance to travel.

The density of the environment through which sound waves travel will determine how fast the vibrations pass through it. The more dense the environment—or in other words, the more tightly packed the atoms—the quicker the sound waves will travel. We know that a sound wave will travel 340 meters per second in air, but this jumps to 1500 meters per second in water because there are more atoms in water than in air. So it doesn't matter what the source of the sound is—whether it be a tiny buzzing mosquito or a Concorde aircraft—the sound waves created will travel at exactly the same speed through the air.

Of course, anyone with a normal sense of hearing will know that there are two very noticeable differences between the sound of a mosquito and that of a Concorde aircraft. The first would be in volume. The loudness of a sound is determined by the energy within the sound wave itself. Graphically, this is depicted as the height of the sound wave (that is the amplitude). Decibels are the measuring unit for the loudness of sound. Zero decibels is below that which can be detected by the human ear, while at about 125 decibels the sound would cause discernible pain.

The second obvious difference between the sound of a mosquito and a roaring Concorde would be in the pitch. The pitch, or frequency, refers to the number of waves that are produced each second. The more waves that are produced in any given second, the higher the pitch of vibration. Sound wave frequency is measured in hertz. So, if a sound registers 300 hertz, it means that 300 sound waves are produced each second. An adult human with normal hearing can detect sound between 16 and 20,000 hertz.

Light is also produced by vibration. It is a form of electromagnetic radiation vibrating at an extremely high frequency. The rate of vibration is so high that it's measured in gigahertz, or billions of cycles per second. Therefore, sound and light, are both created by vibrating energy but of differing frequencies. Following the Hermetic edict, 'as above, so below', this vibratory relationship between sound and light is believed to be mirrored in the spiritual realm, as will be discussed later. But for now we'll remain firmly in the physical world.

Sound for Life

The ability to detect sound or vibration is important to all life on the planet. Several species of animals have extremely sensitive hearing mechanisms which are vital for communication and ultimately their survival; marine creatures like dolphins, porpoises and whales make sonic clicks to communicate, detect other marine life and for echolocation; whales are well known for their alluring 'singing' to each other, sometimes across entire oceans; bats also have an acute sense of hearing for receiving the echo of high pitched sounds that they emit. Echolocation is a characteristic of the micro species of bat and enables the creatures to navigate and capture their insect prey.

The Musical Life of Plants

Plants are organisms that are also highly tuned to sound, despite the fact that they have no recognizable hearing mechanism. The flute-playing Lord Krishna was believed to have had the ability to encourage enthralling plant growth. And Mian Tan Sen, a sage in the court of the Moghul emperor, Akbar, is said to have performed many miracles like starting rain, lighting oil lamps, as well as inducing plants to blossom, simply by intoning ragas— the traditional Indian spiritual music characterized by improvised tones, rhythms and melody.

Stories such as these may well be regarded as scientifically baseless folklore having little relevance to the facts. Yet, deities and monarchs aside, scientific experiments on this issue of whether sound can affect the life of plants have been done with some remarkable findings.

Prompted not by Indian folklore but by earlier unsuccessful experiments by Charles Darwin and German plant physiologist Wilhelm Pfeffer, Prof. Julian Huxley (brother of novelist Aldous Huxley) experimented further during a visit to India in 1950. When Prof. Huxley visited Dr T. C. Singh, then the head of the department of botany at a Madras university, he was studying the live streaming protoplasm under the microscope in the cells of *Hydrilla verticillata*, an Asian aquatic plant with long transparent leaves. This gave Prof. Huxley the idea to see if the magnification would be sufficient to see any observable changes in the streaming process if the plant was exposed to sound.

Dr Singh was accommodating to Prof. Huxley's idea, and since he knew that the streaming of protoplasm naturally sped up after sunrise, he conducted the experiment before 6am by placing an electrically operated tuning fork six feet from the *Hydrilla*. Observing the protoplasm under the microscope, Dr

Singh discovered it sped up to a rate more consistent with what would be expected later in the day after the plant had been exposed to the tuning fork's vibration for 30 minutes. When Dr Singh later asked his young assistant, an accomplished violinist, to play her instrument near the *Hydrilla* the protoplasm stream was accelerated again.

Encouraged by the findings, Dr Singh decided to conduct larger, more controlled, experiments incorporating Indian raga music that had purportedly been used to such good effect during the reign of Emperor Akbar. Consequently, Dr Singh arranged for his assistant to play a south Indian raga to mimosas. In their book, *The Secret Life of Plants,* authors Tompkins and Bird wrote about the marvelous results. 'After a fortnight,' they explain, 'to Singh's intense excitement, he discovered that the number of stomata per unit area in the experimental plants was 66 per cent higher, the epidermal walls were thicker, the palisade cells were longer and broader than in control plants, sometimes by as much as 50 per cent.'[1]

Further experiments with a number of other plant species like petunias, white spider lilies and food plants including: sweet potatoes, sesame, radishes, onions and tapioca all produced similar results. So convinced was Dr Singh of the efficacy of the raga music on plants that in an Indian agricultural college magazine published at the time he emphatically stated that he had proven beyond all doubt that harmonic sound waves affect not only plant growth, but also flowering, fruiting and seed-yield.[2]

The obvious next step that Dr Singh realized was to see if music could increase the yield of crops. The importance of such a question in a highly populated country like India is all too apparent, and it's one that has become increasingly important to other countries in the last couple of decades. Between 1960 and 1963 Dr Singh piped raga music via a loud-speaker to six varieties of paddy rice growing in seven villages in the State of

Madras and in Pondicherry on the Bay of Bengal. The harvests were consistently 25 per cent to 60 per cent higher than the regional average.

Similar findings using other types of crops in North America and exposing them to European classical music have also been reported. A Canadian man named Eugene Canby broadcast Johann Sebastian Bach's violin sonatas to a test plot of wheat which had the effect of producing a crop 66 per cent greater than the average and with larger and heavier seeds. Remarkably, the test plot of wheat was planted in an area where the soil was poor yet it did just as well as those growing in richer earth. Canby, therefore, concluded that the music was as good, if not better, than soil nutrients.

Cultured Plants

Furthermore, astounding results were achieved in the experiments of an American mature-age music student in the late 1960s that created unexpected intense public interest. Using European classical music under strict laboratory conditions, Dorothy Retallack discovered that plants respond very positively. While, on the contrary, those that were exposed to rock music tended to use more water and had deteriorated root systems. In one experiment some plants that were bombarded with raucous rock music died after only two weeks!

Wondering what effect more sophisticated music of both Eastern and Western cultures would have on plants, Retallack set-up an experiment using music, including Johann Sebastian Bach's choral preludes and Ravi Shankar's sitar music. Tompkins and Bird write:

> The plants gave positive evidence of liking Bach since they leaned an unprecedented 35 degrees *toward* the preludes. But even this affirmation was far exceeded by their reaction to Shankar: in their straining to reach the source of the classical

Indian music they bent more than halfway to the horizontal, at angles in excess of 60 degrees, the nearest one almost embracing the speaker.[3]

When Retallack introduced jazz to the experiment she was most surprised. Being exposed to Duke Ellington's *Soul Call* and recordings by Louis Armstrong, 55 per cent of the plants leaned 15 to 20 degrees towards the source of the music, and compared with the plants in the silent control chamber, growth was more abundant.

The Harmony of the Spheres

Like plants, humans can also either benefit or suffer from the sounds that we are exposed to—and this includes all sounds not just those that are audible. The fact that the human hearing mechanism has a limited range means that there are a great deal of sounds that we cannot perceive. Advances in technology have enabled scientists to detect a myriad of sounds that the human ear is deaf to. Although Pythagoras, Plato and the seventeenth century astronomer, Johannes Kepler, all believed in the 'music of the spheres', for decades mainstream modern science maintained that the cosmos was utterly silent. With the invention of the radio telescope in 1937 by Grote Reber, scientists became aware of the enormous array of sounds, in the form of cosmic radiation, constantly raining down upon us. Radiation is a vibration, but one so high in frequency that it is outside the range of our ears. Yet radio astronomy has shown that the planets, together with suns, pulsars, quasars, supernovas and a host of other heavenly bodies all contribute to a cosmic symphony of sound, rhythm and harmony. As Joachim-Ernst Berendt explained:

> Some pulsars sound like bongo drums, others like castanets, still others like the scratching needle of a record player. Most of them are simply ticking and tocking away as they have

done for millions of years, some in a strangely rhythmical manner. These 'living sounds' often change from one day to the other, even from one hour to the next, growing or diminishing, expanding or contracting as if they were being emitted by a living creature.[4]

Of particular interest are the sounds created by the orbits of the plants. Being elliptical, they have been shown to produce even more beautiful sounds. But remarkably, of all the possible elliptical orbits that the planets can move in, they have 'chosen' those that oscillate and sound in proportions of whole numbers—in other words harmonically. The mathematical proportions that are the basis of our earthly music are, therefore, the same that structure the music of the planets!

So aeons before our beautiful worldly musical harmonies were composed there has existed a universal harmony that still resounds today through the 'dancing' and 'singing' of the planets and stars.

Some years ago, Willie Ruff and John Rogers of Yale University input the angular velocities of the planets, based on their elliptical orbits, into a synthesizer. Based on Kepler's astronomical calculations, they assigned keys from the standard piano keyboard to each planet's movements. The results, while being fascinating, were also somewhat predictable as Berendt pointed out:

> To nobody's surprise, the sounds of the planets (as realized by Ruff and Rodgers) correspond with the conceptions traditionally attributed to the different celestial bodies. Mercury, the fast and restless 'messenger of the gods,' symbol of intelligence and businesslike agility, does indeed have a quick, busy, chirping, 'quicksilver' sound. Aggressively and 'ruthlessly,' Mars slides up and down across several notes. Jupiter has a majestic tone reminiscent of a church organ, and

Saturn produces a low, mysterious droning. The sound spectrum of the six visible planets including Earth covers eight octaves, almost identical with the human hearing range.[5]

Therefore, although most regarded the concept of the 'music of the spheres' as being nothing more than a poetic indulgence, the fact is that we now know that Pythagoras, Plato and Kepler were absolutely correct. Yet, there is evidence that Pythagoras and Plato, at least, may well have used the phrase in a mystical context as well because it's possible that they could have been aware of the Audible Life Stream phenomenon. But more on the spiritual music in later chapters.

The Musical Cosmic Vibratory Continuum

Further evidence of the harmonic vibratory principle of the universe is found in the experiments conducted by Swiss scientist Hans Jenny in the 1960s. Using electronic sound oscillators and highly sensitive photographic equipment, Jenny documented the beautifully elegant and geometrically perfect sound mandalas created by various substances spread on a metal plate when he directed different frequencies, tones and music through it.

Jill Purce, who researches the relationship between sound healing and the transformation of consciousness, witnessed Jenny's work and recalls:

He [Jenny] vibrated all kinds of materials with sounds in a variety of ways. He used liquids and pastes and fine powders and subjected them to different kinds of sounds. As I watched, I saw heaps of matter which had no form take on the precise and exquisite patterns that I had seen in nature. The longer the sound was maintained the more differentiated these patterns became. If the materials or the sound changed, so did the patterns.[6]

This relatively new field of research, which Jenny called cymatics, showed that the vibratory principle underlying all matter has a symmetry that eludes to harmony. More recent work in the field of cymatics has been conducted by John Stuart Reid, who invented the 'CymaScope', which is the world's first commercially available machine that makes sound visible.

Support for the notion of a harmonious universe comes in the form of the so-called Theory of Everything, put forward by physicists. A Theory of Everything is the physicists' 'holy grail' because it is an attempt to unify the four elementary forces of nature, namely: electromagnetism (the force that produces light, electricity and magnetism); the weak nuclear force (the force that results in radioactive decay); the strong nuclear force (which is responsible for keeping sub-atomic particles together); and gravity. Einstein's theory of general relativity essentially describes how the law of gravity works in relation to big objects like stars and black holes, while quantum physics deals with the laws governing the three remaining elementary forces operating in the sub-atomic world. The problem is that the theory of general relativity (the laws governing the world of big objects we see and know) is incompatible with the laws governing the world of the very small (the quantum world). In other words, the principles of Einstein's theory of general relativity breakdown in the quantum world. Superstring theory is regarded by some as the best candidate for a grand Theory of Everything because it seems to resolve the incompatibility between the laws governing the world of big objects and those governing the world of the very small. It is based on the notion that the universe is made of extremely tiny vibrating strings not unlike rubber bands.

Superstring theory was first proposed in the late 1960s but it wasn't until the early 1980s that the theory began to gain widespread acceptance. Put simply and very briefly, physicists predict the sort of energy required for the four forces of nature to unify is astronomical (specifically 4.9 gigajoules), known as the

Planck energy because it was physicist Max Planck who arrived at the calculation.[7] Superstrings allow for this kind of incredible energy because they are so small that they are beyond our concept of space and time, which means that their energy is infinite since energy dissipates only *in* time. As physicist Steven Weinberg explains in his description of superstrings:

> These strings can be visualized as tiny one-dimensional rips in the smooth fabric of space. Strings can be open, with two free ends, or closed, like a rubber band. As they fly around space, the strings vibrate. Each string can be found in any one of an infinite number of possible states (or modes) of vibration, much like the various overtones produced by a vibrating tuning fork or violin string. The vibrations of ordinary violin strings die down with time... In contrast, the strings that concern us here are truly fundamental and keep vibrating forever; they are not composed of atoms or anything else, and there is no place for their energy of vibration to go.[8]

Thus, physicists theorize that at the very essence of ultimate reality is an infinitely powerful vibratory phenomenon that could follow a musical pattern. This is wholly consistent with the concept of the Audible Life Stream. As Charan Singh once wrote in a letter to one of his students:

> Music, no doubt, is beautiful to listen to; but the music of this world only impresses the mind and is not permanent. The real Music that is resounding within you affects the soul, gives genuine peace and happiness...[9]

It seems then that the key is to somehow contact this real music, for to do so would mean that one has apprehended the all-pervasive, all-powerful, eternal energy of the universe—ultimate reality, a vibratory phenomenon of which both the mystics and at least some physicists both essentially agree.

Another point of agreement between physicists and mystics is that to apprehend this level of vibratory energy requires concentrating energy. Physicists can do this at the sub-atomic level, which is what hugely expensive particle accelerators do. However, they concede that no accelerator yet conceived could ever reach the required Planck energy level, not even the multi-billion dollar Super Collider that has been proposed in America. The problem is not so much with the energy level but more with the ability to concentrate the energy.[10] Physicists Paul Davies and John Gribbin accept that this sort of concentrated energy is only possible during an event like the big bang. They write that '...to probe distances one billion times smaller than a nucleus requires energy one billion times greater than nuclear energies. The only place where such energy was concentrated was in the big bang.'[11]

The death of a star, you will recall, or indeed the universe, is the reverse of the big bang—being a black hole or the big crunch respectively. Therefore, the same enormous levels of concentrated energy would be expected to be present at these events as physicists know were present very shortly after the big bang. Being unable to concentrate energy to this level is an obvious problem facing physicists, and with no apparent solution. We will necessarily have to return to this significant impasse in the final chapter, but for the present let's continue to unearth more material evidence of the underlying spiritual musical phenomenon that is the Audible Life Stream.

The Harmonic Foundation of Religion and Science

Since some physicists theorize that the very fabric of the universe is a non-material vibrating energy, it comes as little surprise to learn that musical structures are believed to be the basis of science and even religion. This is precisely what Michael Hayes posits in his insightful book, *The Infinite Harmony*. His persuasively argued theory is one which he applies to specific domains and also to the arrangement of some ancient religious scriptures, as well as to the genetic code of all life—DNA (deoxyribonucleic acids). DNA and RNA (ribonucleic acids) are the fundamental substances of all living things, carrying genetic information that determines the shape, form and function of future generations.

Hayes contends that all physical and metaphysical phenomena are created because of the harmonious interaction of two fundamental laws of nature. This, of course, complements the physicists' superstring theory from which all phenomena, including the laws of nature, would be derived. Hayes calls the first law the 'law of triple-creation' consisting of three forces: attraction, repulsion and time.[12] He points out that these forces are found in all natural phenomena as a passive or negative force (attraction), an active or positive force (repulsion) and a neutral force (time). Of course, these terms are merely labels to depict the relationship between the forces. The reality is that all three forces are effectively active.

The 'law of seven-part formation and sequence' is the second fundamental law that Hayes identifies and is otherwise known as the law of octaves.[13] And as we know, the law of octaves is a principle of music. Summing up the significance of interpreting the first and second fundamental laws of nature together, Hayes writes:

According to the second law of nature, each of the three creative forces are themselves subdivisible into seven distinct but interacting orders of energy and form. Taking the first of these forces as being positive, or active, we may say that it is composed of seven fundamental aspects or tones. Upon achieving a condition of optimum resonance these seven tones then combine together to generate, simultaneously, an *eighth, transcendental* tone. Having thus succeeded the scale of its origin this transcendental signal then becomes the *first* tone of the next scale—the second, negative or passive force. This negative or passive manifestation will also be composed of seven fundamental tones. Upon achieving a condition of optimum resonance this second set of seven tones will also combine together to generate, again simultaneously, a second eighth or transcendental tone, which then becomes the first tone of the next and final scale—the third, neutralizing or mediating force. The completed optimum development of this final set of seven tones results in the simultaneous generation of the third and last transcendental eighth note of the whole series.[14]

Viewed in this way, all phenomena, including ourselves, can be described in musical terms as being created by three octaves of resonating energy. The number twenty-two precisely represents three octaves sounding together because although there are three sets of eight notes in each octave, the last note of each set is simply a repetition, on a higher scale, of the first. So, eight notes plus seven notes plus seven notes equals twenty-two notes. Twenty-two is a significant number—one that the Pythagoreans believed was sacred because of its musical link, and it's, thus, a cornerstone of Hayes' theory.

Transcendental Symmetry
Those mathematically minded may recognize that the relationship between the twenty-two tones of a given triple-octave and the seven tones that are generated in each successive octave constitutes a famous mathematical relationship. That relationship stated as 22 divided by 7 is, of course, *pi* (π) that denotes the ratio of a given circle's circumference to its diameter. It's generally accepted that it was Pythagoras who discovered this relationship; however, Hayes holds the view that it must have been known by the ancient Egyptians for them to have been able to construct the geometrical/mathematical symmetry that

characterizes the Great Pyramid of Cheops.

Mathematicians regard the number *pi* as a transcendental number because it cannot occur as the root of a polynomial (that is algebraic) equation with rational number coefficients. In simple terms, it means that the number, when displayed as a decimal, continues indefinitely without a repeating pattern. So in one sense the circle can be seen as a transcendental symbol and one cannot avoid seeing the circular symmetry of a black hole and the holistic unity of the perfectly round droplet of ink (discussed in Chapter 2) in precisely the same way.

According to Jung, the circle (or more specifically the mandala, which encompasses all circular symmetrical images) is the most fundamental of religious symbols.[15] Certainly there is a beauty and elegance in a perfect circle or sphere that is imbued with a sense of eternity—no beginning, no end. Deathless.

The Eye-dominated Culture

Thus, we should be able to see a perfectly logical scientific basis for the Audible Life Stream phenomenon. Mystics have long since said this musical quality of the Audible Life Stream is the key to achieving a state of pure symmetrically balanced consciousness that is beyond the reach of death. As one would expect, the Life Stream, being primarily an 'audible' aspect of pure consciousness, translates into the material world in such a way that makes our physical sense of hearing superior to all our other senses. This, of course, doesn't overlook the fact that all our physical senses prop up the destructive ego. However, our spiritual capacity to hear means that our physical hearing ability has a special significance that the other senses don't. Yet, it's apparent that our hearing sense faculty is one that is usually sorely neglected. Such a view is supported by anthropologist and musicologist Marius Schneider who wrote, 'One of the most remarkable manifestations of the degeneration of modern man is an increasing weakening of his acoustic sense.'[16]

The main reason for this acoustic neglect is possibly a result of the eye's dominance over the other senses—a phenomenon psychologists refer to as visual capture. One example of visual capture is when watching a film taken from a roller-coaster carriage and which is displayed on a larger than usual wrap-around movie theater screen. People in the audience will automatically brace themselves as if they are actually taking the roller-coaster ride, despite their other senses (and prior knowledge) telling them that they, in fact, are stationary.[17]

Whether it be because of visual capture or not, as a society we attach far greater importance to our eyes and seeing. For instance, Joachim-Ernest Berendt believed that our modern culture is basically eye-dominated and that the eye has become a dictator to our other senses, including, of all things, our sense of taste. In his book, *The Third Ear*, he wrote that we as a society, '...live in a predominately visual civilization, so we tend to 'visualize' our senses. We even try and influence our taste nerves optically. That is why food is artistically 'embellished' in shop windows and restaurants.'[18]

Berendt regards the shift in emphasis from radio to television to be a step backwards in human development because, according to him, it takes us back to a nomadic existence in a figurative sense. His reasoning is that our eyes are constantly on the move as if searching for prey like a nomadic hunter. Conversely, the ears are more often associated with stillness. Certainly, whenever we want to listen intently the first thing we usually do is to stop whatever we're doing, even if that means stopping moving completely. Our sense of vision, on the other hand, has a predatory nature that implies power and aggression. Wrote Berendt:

A person can have 'piercing eyes' but certainly not 'piercing ears' or any other attribute which could give the ears a puncturing quality. The epitome of visual acuity are the eyes of an eagle: from up high the eagle spies its prey and in that instant anticipates seizing it in its claws and piercing it with its beak. It is a single act: spotting and seizing. Not only for the eagle but for the eyes. For human eyes too.[19]

This is a view that Aristotle ascribed to having found differences between the behavioral patterns of those who are blind (and who therefore rely more heavily of their sense of hearing) and those who are deaf (and are consequently heavily reliant on their eyes). He wrote that '...the blind are more understanding than the deaf because hearing exerts a direct influence on the formation of moral character, which is not immediately true of what is seen.'[20]

The wisdom of Aristotle's words are relevant to the whole of society because it's not only those who are deaf who fail to listen. We all know that people with near-perfect hearing do not always have the capacity to truly listen.

Hearing is Different to Listening

The late French ENT (ear, nose and throat) specialist, Dr Alfred Tomatis (1920–2001), was the first to make a clear distinction between hearing and listening. His research into sound and the ear is so highly respected that some of his colleagues regard him as the 'Einstein of sound' and the 'Sherlock Holmes of sonic detection'.

Born in Nice, Dr Tomatis' findings showed that hearing is really a physiological process because it relates to the ability of the auditory system to receive sound. Listening, on the other hand, is primarily a mental process requiring concentration to selectively focus on, remember and respond to sound.

Dr Tomatis, whose major discovery was that the voice can only reproduce sounds that the ear can detect (which has become known as the Tomatis Effect) also firmly believed that the ear is a superior organ to the eye. Substantiation of his claim can be found in the fact that the ear has greater influence on the brain because there are three times as many nerve connections between the brain and the ear as there are between the eyes and the brain.[21]

The Eye Says 'I'

Given the mental and physical superiority of the ear to the eye, and the influence that these senses have over our behavioral patterns, the eye-dominated culture that we presently live in seems somewhat seriously unbalanced. Perhaps, if this situation was reversed, a more compassionate and tolerant society with less crime could be shaped. Such a claim might at first appear too idealistic to be taken seriously despite the sense of power and aggression that a vision-dominated society has been shown to create. But consider that our eye-culture, in successfully separating us from our 'prey' and the rest of the world, further fattens our destructive ego-self.

Certainly, all our five senses feed the ego-self, but the eye does so to a far greater extent. With the eye we project ourselves outwards, perpetuating a metaphoric aggressive masculinity (frequently symbolized by an arrow) which is in contrast to the ear (often symbolized by a sea-shell) that is passive and metaphorically feminine.

Our aggressive eyes say 'I', asserting the sense of self on the world that can often appear to be spiritually short-sighted and destructive. Thus, it cannot be merely an accident that the words 'eye' and 'I' sound exactly alike and can only be distinguished by the context in which they are used. This same quirk of language is true also in the primal tongues of South American Indians and Australian aborigines.[22]

While the dominating eye and our other senses bolster the ego, creating a division between ourselves and everything else, the spiritual implications of hearing give listening to the world great importance. When we listen we don't put as much emphasis on ourselves and, therefore, the ego. Instead, we bring the world into us rather than project ourselves out into the world. Listening is a passive process of relationship integration rather than relationship delineation. Listening, therefore, attempts to establish unity as opposed to division. And unity is the paramount goal of the mystical path.

Listening—Gateway to other Dimensions

Not only does the eye separate us from other entities in this physical realm as we observe everything else to be outside of ourselves, but it also deprives us of being aware of the other realities too. As we know the eye bends, distorts and filters the incoming light onto the retina before passing it onto the brain via the optic nerve, thereby only showing us what it wants us to see and not what is actually there to be perceived. In fairness to the eye, however, it should be said that there is a very good reason for this censorship. The eye can only comprehend three dimensions at most—length, breath and height. And this highlights an extremely important difference between the ear and the eye, because the ear can perceive any number of dimensions.

It was only early in the last century that a Russian scientist named Elsie von Cyon made this ground-breaking finding public knowledge. Cyon wrote:

The spatial and temporal qualities of the sense of hearing are of much greater importance—thanks to the inner ear's sensitivity to location—than their counterparts in the spheres of touch and vision. We owe...the concept of the infinitude of space to those perceptions. Direction is in its very nature indivisible and unlimited. It is to perceptions of sound or resonance, supplying us with knowledge about numbers, that we owe our concept of the infinity of time since numbers can essentially be developed infinitely.[23]

This unique quality of the physical hearing mechanism is a

reflection of our spiritual capacity to perceive spiritual sound of varying energy levels or dimensions. What other dimensions one may well ask? Superstring theory enables physicists to hypothesize about a multi-dimensional reality, some taking six as their starting point! In 1995, a team led by Prof. Edward Witten of Princeton's Institute for Advanced Study, successfully united different superstring theories into a single theory that has become known, somewhat cryptically, as 'M-theory', and in doing so predicts a universe with 11 dimensions.

Ears of the Soul

Interestingly, mystics speak of a multiple dimensional reality also, and regard listening as the means to tune into these other dimensions. However, they speak of listening in terms of our spiritual sense faculty, being quite independent of the physical ears. Listening, remember, is solely a mental function. It is primarily dependant upon consciousness rather than a physiological mechanism. The significance of this spiritual aspect of listening is that it undermines our sense of 'I-ness' that we've previously established is the only victim of death.

Mystics contend that beyond our vibrating physical world are other higher vibrating worlds and beings that inhabit them. Most of us may not readily perceive these realms primarily because we are normally too engrossed in the physical realm as a result of the continuous stimulation of our physical senses. The situation will certainly be different when our senses shut down for the last time. When this happens we will get an inkling of the spiritual nature of reality and may well experience the vast dimensions beyond the material world. Normally this would happen completely beyond our control. But not so, say the mystics, for those who know how to contact the infinitely powerful vibrating current of the Audible Life Stream here and now.

For, mystics believe, as all-pervasive as air is to the atmospheric bubble around Earth so is the Audible Life Stream to all dimensions in the universe. Mystics point out that by contacting, listening to and ultimately merging with the Audible Life Stream of vibrating energy we break down the illusion of 'I-ness' and, therefore, death. However, this necessarily requires the spiritual knowledge of vibration/sound because, say the mystics, it is the only means by which to achieve perfect unity—immortality, eternity, deathlessness. Wrote the late Sufi teacher, Inayat Khan (1882–1927), who many believed was a mystic:

> By the knowledge of sound man obtains the knowledge of creation, and the mastery of that knowledge helps man to rise to the formless. This knowledge acts as wings for a man; it helps him to rise from earth to heaven, and he can penetrate through the life seen and unseen.[24]

Mystics have long since advised spiritual seekers to obtain this precious knowledge—to hear the Audible Life Stream so that the soul can begin to live. Intimations of such precious knowledge have been handed down to us in the form of volumes of scriptures from all over the world. In the following chapter we shall look more closely at some of these texts to see that the message of dying while living has been the same from many of the great mystics of the past regardless of when or where they appeared to teach.

4

In the Beginning Was the Sound

God has no religion.

Mahatma Gandhi (1869–1948)

Death and the after-life are common themes in all religious traditions—both East and West. Yet, religious speculation about what
happens after death is based solely on respective scriptural texts,
and rarely on any personal experience of the guardians of
modern-day religion. It seems apparent, however, that the great
mystics of the past around whose mystical message the religious
scriptures are based, knew, through their own transcendental
experiences, exactly what happens when the physical body dies.
They, like any genuine mystic, must also have known that
whatever name by which to call the innate spiritual nature
within us all, either God, or Allah, the Buddha Nature, Jehovah,
and so on, it cannot be boxed into one particular religious
doctrine to the exclusion of the rest. Mystics not only believe that
there is one God-principle but that this principle applies to all—
Christian, Muslim, Buddhist, Jewish and so on, even atheist.
Since all humans, regardless of religion, race, culture and gender,
have the same innate spiritual quality, it seems perfectly logical
that the way to realizing this spiritual quality must be the same
for all.

Religions, it should be noted, are not created by mystics but
usually by uninformed followers, possibly with sincere intentions, after the mystics depart. Hence, today there is a heavy
reliance on outward ritual and ceremony in nearly all religious
traditions without a deeper understanding of the original
mystic's message. True mystics realize that all outward forms of

ritual stand as obstacles on the path to genuine spiritual realization. For this reason, scriptures and other elements of external worship play no significant part in a mystic's universal message.

So, although religious scriptures are important historical documents often with passionate, inspirational and devotional content, and thus should be treasured, relying solely on these texts for spiritual development can be most unwise. We need to be extremely cautious about the true spiritual significance of scriptures that are hundreds, and in some instances thousands of years old, that have been translated numerous times, and even on occasions been subject to unscrupulous teams of editors and censors.

However, having historical and emotional significance requires that we should never totally disregard such documents because despite being subjected to the flaws in human nature and to its darker side, all scriptures are, to varying degrees, imbued with the ageless truth about life and death. Identifying this truth is no easy task and so can only be properly done by those who have actually experienced this ultimate truth just as have great mystics of the past. The few genuine modern-day mystics, who have in all likelihood soared to the same spiritual heights as their predecessors are the only ones capable of incisively and accurately discerning what elements of the scriptures are kernels of truth and what (for whatever reason) amounts to only the chaff of ignorance. Significantly, these kernels of truth can be found in almost all the major and most influential of scriptures. To prove this we can begin with the oldest religious literature in the world, the Vedas.

The Flame-tongued Gods of the Vedas

The Indian Vedas date back at least 3,500 years to the period when the Aryans invaded north-west India. *Nada brahma* is a Sanskrit mantra that dates back to the Vedas. *Nada* means sound and a related term, *nadi*, means river or stream of consciousness. Brahma refers to the all-pervasive cosmic principle, which in Christian terms is the equivalent of God. Therefore, according to Joachim-Ernst Berendt, the mantra, *nada brahma*, can mean that God is sound, indeed that everything is sound.[1] Perhaps, the ancient Vedic mantra, *nada brahma*, means, in fact, that God is a sounding stream of consciousness. Importantly, the Vedas also make a distinction between audible sound, known as *ahata*, and the spiritual cosmic sound, referred to as *anahata*, which is said to be inaudible to the physical ears.

Of the four Vedic texts, the Rig Veda is the oldest, and there is considerable importance to be attached to the fact that these writings makes mention of the spiritual sound and light. Scholars believe that the authors of the Rig Veda were actually recording knowledge that was already in their own distant past. So the Audible Life Stream phenomenon should not be seen to be solely as an Indian concept, or for that matter an Aryan belief, because mystics believe that spiritual truth is the foundation upon which all humanity, and indeed the entire creation (spiritual and physical) is based. In the Vedic context, however, the ancient Indian sages documented that spiritual sound and light are at the fundamental core of ultimate reality. They described the gods as being 'flame-tongued', which is a beautifully compact metaphor for the transcendental light (the flame) and sound (the tongue from which vibratory energy in the form of words emanates). Even scholars who are seemingly uninformed of the Audible Life Stream phenomenon acknowledge that the Vedic sages must have taught a subtle science of Sound.

The concept of vibrating spiritual energy is referred to as *Vac* in the Vedas. *Vac* translated means word. The *Vac* was regarded as being of equal importance to the spiritual light, which is sometimes called *agni*. For the Vedic rishis, the creative power of *Vac* emanated from the 'highest heaven' and held all the other worlds together. According to Vedic scholar Jeanine Miller, '...*Vac*, the verbum, and Agni, the flame, are two sides of the one power...Agni pervades all the worlds and he is born in the waters. *Vac* extends over all and her home is in the waters...*Vac* is the formative sound hidden behind or within all manifested lives...'[2]

So for the rishis, the spiritual light came from the sound, both of which were regarded as fundamental aspects of the creative power of the universe.

The Tree of Life

Central to Vedic eschatology is the concept of a Tree of Life that is perhaps the oldest and most widespread metaphor for the Audible Life Stream. Trees and plants, after all, are the primary source of sustenance for life on the planet. They are the lungs of the Earth, absorbing carbon dioxide and providing the necessary oxygen that we require to live. Food is another necessity that trees and plants provide not just for humans but for all physical life, either directly or indirectly. Their timber is also extensively used in the manufacture of our buildings and homes. Furthermore, all trees have an all important creative function as evidenced by the fact that all species are seed-bearing. Thus, trees are the pivotal element on which all life on the planet rests. Without them we simply couldn't survive physically, making the Tree of Life metaphor so perfect for denoting the Audible Life Stream, the life-blood of the entire cosmos.

In one verse of the Rig Veda, the Tree of Life is described as having its roots in the spiritual regions, meaning it is inherently spiritual in nature, and with its branches within us, intimating of its bridging capacity between the physical and spiritual realms:

Varuna [the lord of righteousness]...sustaineth erect the tree's stem in the base-less region [spiritual realm]
Its rays [branches], whose root is high above, stream downward.

Deep may they sink within us and be hidden.[3]

So, we have an image of an inverted tree sprouted from a spiritual seed, with its branches spreading out to all creation. We, then, can be seen as the fruit of that one seed that will one day ripen, in death, and return to the soil of spirit.

The same tree metaphor is also used in the *Bhagavad-Gita*, which interestingly means *The Song of the Lord*—clearly a reference to the musical qualities of the Audible Life Stream. Considered by many Hindus to be the most significant part of the Upanishads, the *Bhagavad-Gita* records a long discourse between Lord Krishna and his foremost disciple, Arjuna, on the eve of a momentous battle (which some regard to be merely metaphorical). Incidentally, those who have ever wondered why Krishna is nearly always pictorially depicted with a 'transcendental flute' in hand (as opposed to a mundane flute) may now be able to appreciate that this is a symbolic way of showing that this great mystic was a master of the transcendental sound. But anyway, during Krishna's profound exchange with Arjuna, which covers all aspects of spirituality and mysticism, Krishna, at one point, describes himself as a banyan tree.[4] In all likelihood, he does so because genuine mystics are believed to be one with the Audible Life Stream since they have attained union with ultimate reality—but more on this in Chapter 9. The banyan tree is one of the tallest and most beautiful trees grown in India, characterized by its plethora of aerial roots that descend from branches into the ground, perhaps explaining why Krishna would use it to symbolize the Audible Life Stream.

Buddha Shakyamuni talked of a bodhi tree under which he sat to attain enlightenment and destroy the illusion of death. Bodhi is a Sanskrit word that means wisdom. The words buddha and bodhi are derived from the root word *budh* that means 'to know'. Thus, a Buddha, one who is all-wise, becomes so by taking shelter under a Tree of Wisdom. It is likely not a literal tree, as millions of Buddhists around the world believe it to be, even to the extent of sanctifying a tree in northern India that is said to be a descendent of the original.

The prophet Mohammed, around whose revelations Islam is based, is another mystic who it seems symbolically referred to the Audible Life Steam as a tree. In the Koran, like the Vedas, the term 'Word' is also likely to be a reference to the Audible Life Stream, and in the following sura (chapter of the Koran) both the Word and Tree metaphors are used. Through the vibratory energy of the Word, which is likened to a tree from heaven, Muslims are told that they can be enlivened spiritually:

Dost thou not see how Allah [God] sets forth the case
of a good Word, which is like a good tree whose root is
firm and every one of whose branches reaches into heaven?
...Allah strengthens the believers with the Word that is
firmly established, both in the hither life and the Hereafter...[5]

Centuries before Mohammed, the Essene Brotherhood—to which Jesus has been linked—also taught of a Tree of Life as a spiritual bridge linking humans to the spiritual world. The Essenes were a mystical Jewish community located at Qumran near the Dead Sea. For them, the Tree of Life was a figurative way of speaking about the Law of God. It was regarded as the way to acquire spiritual life and the means through which one could fully understand the Law of God. The Essenes believed that through the Tree of Life one could journey from the physical world to the spiritual realms—in other words, to die while living.

The late Dr Edmond Bordeaux Szekely (1905-1979), a biblical scholar and philologist in Sanskrit, Aramaic, Greek and Latin, found the Tree of Life symbol in the written teachings of almost all religions, strongly suggesting that the concept of dying while living was originally a core religious concept. He believed that the mystical Tree of Life symbol '...has been imbedded in almost all religions... In outer legend and inner wisdom man's deepest intuitions have focused about it.'[6]

In the Thanks-giving Psalms of the Dead Sea Scrolls, the Tree of Life is said to be watered by an eternal stream—almost certainly a reference to the eternal Audible Life Stream:

> I thank Thee, Heavenly Father,
> because Thou hast put me
> at a source of running streams,
> at a living spring in a land of drought,
> watering an eternal garden of wonders,
> the Tree of Life, mystery of mysteries,
> growing everlasting branches for eternal planting
> to sink their roots into the stream of life
> from an eternal source.[7]

Additional evidence linking the belief in the Audible Life Stream with the Essene Brotherhood can be found in the following excerpt from the *Essene Gospel of Peace*, discovered by Dr Szekely. It was translated from texts he unearthed in the secret Vatican archives and what was formerly the Royal Archives of the Austrian Habsburg family. In the document, the Audible Life Stream is referred to as the Holy Stream of Life, the Holy Stream of Sound and the Holy Stream of Light, highlighting its three important aspects. The following extract counsels readers about the fact that since we will all one day die, we should contact the eternal Holy Streams:

> One day your body will return to the Earthly Mother; even also your ears and your eyes. But the Holy Stream of Life, the Holy Stream of Sound, and the Holy Stream of Light, these were never born, and can never die. Enter the Holy Streams, even that Life, that Sound, and that Light which gave you birth; that you may reach the kingdom of the Heavenly Father

and become one with him, even as the river empties into the far-distant sea.[8]

Like the teachings of the Essene Brotherhood, at the heart of Judaism and Christianity is the mystical concept of a Tree of Life as well as one of knowledge of good and evil. It is the Tree of Life that leads to conscious awareness of our spiritual immortality, while the tree of knowledge of good and evil leads only to death, as the Old Testament proclaims:

> And out of the ground the Lord God made to grow every tree that is pleasant to the sight and good for food, the tree of life also in the midst of the garden, and the tree of knowledge of good and evil... And the Lord God commanded the man saying, 'You may eat freely of every tree of the garden; but of the tree of the knowledge of good and evil you shall not eat, for in the day that you eat of it you shall die'.[9]

Today we know that God wasn't making an empty threat. Eating of the tree of good and evil led to Adam and Eve being expelled from the Garden of Eden. This story is, of course, steeped in mystical symbolism so it would be unwise to interpret it literally. In all probability, the Garden of Eden is an abundant sanctuary of spiritual unity because there duality (good and evil) doesn't exist. Duality can only prevail when there is a sense of 'I-ness' because it's the ego that creates the illusion of separateness and division. Thus, it seems likely that Eden is a metaphor for a perfect state of consciousness unsullied by a desirous ego that perpetuates the illusion of 'I' and death.

Once Adam and Eve desired the fruit of the tree, a sense of 'I' and a concept of linear time was immediately borne. Perfect unity was, thus, destroyed and a veil of death was drawn across the reality of deathlessness. Then, having eaten of the tree, both of them were filled with fear for themselves (perhaps making theirs the first

recorded cases of thanatophobia) when they next *heard* the sound
of God. They became aware, for the first time, that they were naked
and their spiritually atrophying self-consciousness is apparent:

> And they heard the sound of the Lord God walking in the
> Garden...and the man and his wife hid themselves... But the
> Lord God called to the man, and said to him, 'Where are you?'
> And he said, 'I heard the sound of thee in the garden, and I
> was afraid, because I was naked; and I hid myself'.[10]

Like Adam and Eve, we have all desired the fruit of ego and
eaten of the tree of duality. Mystics advise that we now need to
climb back up to the Garden of Eden via the branches of the Tree
of Life because they reason that the fruit of this tree is the
revelation of perfect unity and immortality. The great Indian
mystic, Kabir, poetically wrote that rare is the person who eats of
this fruit to die while living:

> Tall is that tree [of life],
> Its fruit is in the skies within;
> Rare is the bird who tastes it.
> He alone will eat that fruit, O Kabir,
> Who dies while living.[11]

The Water of Life

Jesus used another natural element—water—to convey to the
desert-dwelling peoples of Palestine the spiritually quenching
and life-giving qualities of the Audible Life Stream. This is
shown by the well-known story of a thirsty Jesus meeting the
Samaritan woman at a well. After surprising the woman with a
request for some water, Jesus unambiguously makes a
distinction between the water in the well that the woman can
offer him and the living water that he can offer her, which he
mentions can reveal the secret of death. Jesus says to the woman:

Everyone who drinks of this water [in the well] will thirst
again, but whoever drinks of the water that I shall give him
shall never thirst; the water that I shall give him will become
in him a spring of water welling up to eternal life.[12]

In the same gospel Jesus also draws an analogy between bread —
still a staple food in the Middle East as it was during his time —
and the Audible Life Stream. In the gospel, he is quoted as saying
of this spiritual nourishment:

This is the bread which comes down from heaven, that a man
may eat of it and not die...if any one eats of this bread, he will
live for ever...[13]

Saying that the bread comes down from heaven indicates that
Jesus was speaking metaphorically and not referring to ordinary
bread. By using a simple and easy to understand metaphor to
denote an abstract mystical concept, Jesus successfully conveyed
these ancient spiritual teachings, highlighting his immense
wisdom and profound intellect.

The Word of God

Jesus also makes the same point in the Gospel of Matthew where
it's written that he spoke of humans being unable to live by bread
alone, again alluding to the fact that true life comes from a
spiritual source. In the same excerpt, he also speaks of the
Audible Life Stream as being a 'word' emanating from the mouth
of God, as was the case in the Vedas and the Koran, saying:

Man shall not live by bread, but by every word that proceeds
from the mouth of God.[14]

The Audible Life Stream is also described as the 'Word' of God in
the Gospel of John. This particular text begins:

In the beginning was the Word, and the Word was with God, and the Word was God.[15]

Since this Word is said to be with God and indeed is God, it cannot be any mundane word of human language. Instead, say the mystics, this Word floats on the breath and life of the God-power, or universal principle. The beginning of the Gospel of John must be one of the clearest scriptural passages indicating that the God-power is a vibratory energy that can be heard. But, maintain the mystics, to hear this Word of God, to ascend this Tree of Life and drink of this spiritually quenching Water, our physical ears are of no use because we know they can only perceive the sounds of this material world, and even then within only a limited frequency range. Mystics tell us that material sounds are really only echoes of the Word, or voice, of God.

Death can only beget death, while life begets life. Mystics advise that until we are put in touch with the Audible Life Stream we are alive only to the ephemeral physical world but dead to our eternal spiritual nature. If true, then we are, in other words, the living dead, remaining the Lord of Death's victims. However, mystics say that through the divine Sound Stream one can really begin to live because for the first time one will be conscious and alive to the life-giving spirit. As Jesus remarked emphatically:

> Truly, truly, I say to you, the hour is coming...when the [spiritually] dead will hear the voice [of the Audible Life Stream]...and those who hear will live.[16]

Further, evidence indicating that the original Christians had intimate knowledge of the process of how to die while living, and therefore by implication, had knowledge of the Audible Life Stream, is found in St. Paul's bold declaration, '...I die every day!'[17] And when Jesus speaks, seemingly in riddles, about finding life when losing it and losing life when finding it, he is in all likelihood telling us to learn how to die while living:

> He who finds his life will lose it, and he who loses his life...will find it.[18]

Buddha's Drum of the Deathless

As has already been discussed, comparing the Audible Life Stream to music is not simply a poetic metaphor because, say mystics, at the higher levels of consciousness it is possible to hear melodious spiritual music. Interestingly, the Buddha spoke about this music in the form of a drum immediately after his enlightenment, apparently linking the music of the Audible Life Stream with states of consciousness beyond death's door. Theravadin Buddhist scriptures quote the Buddha as saying:

> I alone am a Fully Enlightened One
> Whose fires [of desire] are quenched and extinguished.
> I go now to the city of Kasi [Varanasi]
> To set in motion the Wheel of Dhamma.
> In a world that has gone blind
> I go to beat the drum of the Deathless.[19]

Thus, the state of deathlessness and complete enlightenment are essentially one and the same. To be deathless is to have realized that the spirit does not die when the physical body perishes. This realization can only come when one's level of consciousness is sufficiently raised; in other words, the vibratory frequency of consciousness approaches light speed. This is the true meaning of enlightenment. The Audible Life Stream, say the mystics, is the most effective means through which to achieve this because they say that not only is it resounding within us at all times but it's also the fundamental manifestation of pure consciousness. To use a Buddhist phrase, it's our Buddha Nature.

Elsewhere in the same Buddhist text, the Buddha again seemingly alludes to the audible means for achieving realization of deathlessness, when he is quoted as saying:

Open for them are the doors to the Deathless,
Let those with ears now show their faith.[20]

The *Surangama Sutra* is another Buddhist scripture, but of the Mahayana tradition, that appears to refer to the Audible Life Stream as being the most effective way to achieve enlightenment and thus penetrate the illusion of death. Moreover, the sutra records that all of the Buddhas of the past used spiritual sound to escape from the wheel of birth and death. This is said to be achieved only when material sounds are sublimated and the spiritual sound is heard. Explains Manjushri, who is believed to have been a Buddha in his own right and noted for his immense wisdom:

I now submit to the World Honored One [Buddha Shakyamuni]
That all Buddhas from this world escaped
By following the teaching, here most suitable,
Which consists in sublimating sound...
Realized by means of [spiritual] hearing.[21]

Later in the same sutra, Manjushri is quoted as saying that when the sounds of the physical world are sublimated, the sound of the drum emanating from the higher deathless dimensions of reality can be perceived:

...When one dwells in quietude,
Rolls of drums from ten directions
Simultaneously are heard...[22]

It should be noted, however, that the Audible Life Stream can be perceived as several different types of musical sounds and not just that of a drum, particularly in the early stages of practicing dying while living. Some of the other sounds that are heard include that of a flute, cymbals, harp, trumpet, bag-pipes and tinkling bells, to name a few.

Ancient Books of the Dead

References to a variety of spiritual sounds and music are stated in ancient books of the dead like the popular *Tibetan Book of the Dead*, *The Egyptian Book of the Dead* and the *Aztec Song of the Dead*. The Aztec text mentions that the spirit, upon leaving the dead physical body, would hear the sound of flutes as it travelled through a city of light and over hills of many colors.[23] In the ancient Egyptian document there is mention of the spirit hearing various voices before what's referred to as a long boat trip through a dark tunnel and finally merging into a bright light. Chapter 178 of the Egyptian text, among other things, is devoted to the idea of spiritual seeing and hearing, being described as the chapter '...of making the eyes to see, [and] making the ears to hear...'[24]

As for the Tibetan equivalent, it's interesting to note that the title of this text is not an accurate translation of the original Tibetan title, which is *Bardo Todrol Chenmo*, meaning the great liberation (from birth and death) through *hearing* in the *bardo* (the after-death realm). Naturally, the only sounds that can be perceived when the physical body dies are those of a spiritual nature since our physical senses are no longer operable. Notwithstanding this fact, today devout Tibetans traditionally read the book out aloud to the deceased for up to seven weeks after their death, believing that it is the message of the text that the spirit needs to hear for liberation. Not so, say the mystics, because even if the dead person could still hear, the words or sounds of this world have no significant spiritual bearing.

The *Tibetan Book of the Dead* itself seems to refer to the spiritual Audible Life Stream calling it the 'natural sound of Reality'. It states that in the *bardo*:

> ...the natural sound of Reality, reverberating like a thousand thunders simultaneously sounding, will come. That is the natural sound of thine own real self.[25]

Elsewhere in the text, mention is made of the spirit hearing trumpets, drums and other '...kinds of musical instruments, filling the whole world-systems and causing them to vibrate, to quake and tremble with sounds so mighty as to daze one's brain [consciousness]...'[26]

The term 'daze' is possibly used to refer to the Life Stream's capacity to draw the mind away from the physical senses—but more on this in the final chapter.

In the first half of the twentieth century, adventurer Alexandra David-Neel wrote of an amazing encounter she had with a Tibetan lama during her remarkable journey across the Himalayas. The wise old man who was known as the 'master of the tone' was playing an ancient Tibetan cymbal when David-Neel and her companions met him in a temple within a monastery's confines. David-Neel describes an unearthly sound that shook the temple walls and penetrated her brain. Her fellow travelers all heard the sound too. Later the lama confided to the travelers:

> I am the master of the tone. With the tone I can kill living things and revive dead things... Each being, each thing produces a special, characteristic tone which, however, changes as the states of the being or thing by which it is produced change... In the beginning was the wind. With its whirl, it created the *gjatams*, the primordial forms and the prime base of the world. This wind sounded; thus it was the

sound which formed matter. The sounding of these first *gjatams* brought forth further forms which, by virtue of their sounds, in turn created new shapes. That is by no means a tale from days long passed, it is still that way. The sound brings forth all forms and all beings. The sound is that through which we live.[27]

The Trumpet of Allah

The Audible Life Stream is also referred to, numerous times, as mystical trumpet sounds in the Koran, usually in connection with a so-called day of judgment that clearly implies a time of death. In one sura, not only is the Audible Life Stream referred to as a mystical trumpet blast but also as the creative Word of Allah:

...the day He says concerning that which He wills: Be; it will be. His word shall be fulfilled. His will be the kingdom on the day when the trumpet will be blown.[28]

Yet Mohammed's mystical message of the Audible Life Stream is perhaps more easily discernible in the Islamic Sufi tradition. The reason that music, song and dance is an integral part of modern-day Sufi worship is because the original Sufi's were apparently in touch with the sound and music of the Audible Life Stream. The original Sufis called it *saawt-e-sarmad*, meaning the divine song; *kalma,* meaning word; *kalam-e-qadim,* the ancient sound; or *nida-e-asman* that means the sound emanating from heaven.

Listening to the divine sound, the Sufi's believed that the soul could be freed of the limitations of the material world. One of the most respected ancient Sufis, Jalaluddin Rumi, wrote reams of devotional poetry, much of it replete with references to transcendental music. His writings also unambiguously confirm that the original Sufis practiced the art of dying while living:

As long as you do not die while living,
How will you obtain the true benefit?
Therefore die, and come out of your body.
O man, you have died many times,
But still you remain behind the veil,
For the method of true dying
You did not learn.[29]

Rumi also told us that to hear the transcendental music one must consciously ascend to the spiritual realms; in other words, raise one's level of consciousness beyond just the physical realm:

Bring the sky beneath your feet
and listen to celestial music everywhere.[30]

The Old Testament also records that the voice of God was like the sound of a trumpet, as well as like thunder. In describing the Israelites exodus from Egypt, it's written:

Then Moses brought the people out of the camp to meet God... And as the sound of the trumpet grew louder and louder, Moses spoke and God answered him in thunder...[31]

A Revelation of Sound

The New Testament book of Revelation, attributed to the disciple John, is a record of what can only be an experience of death while still alive. The text explains that John was in the spiritual realm when he heard a voice like a trumpet instructing him to later write down what he was to see. The voice is also said to sound 'like the sound of many waters,'[32] comforting John by saying:

Fear not, I am the first and the last, and the living one; I died, and behold I am alive for ever more, and I have the keys to Death and Hades.[33]

This key to death, as is indicated in numerous other biblical passages, is strongly suggestive of the Audible Life Stream. Several times in the revelation account the voice tells an astounded John:

> He who has an ear, let him hear what the Spirit says... To him who conquers [death] I will grant to eat of the tree of life, which is in the paradise of God.[34]

The Subtle Music

The musical qualities of the Audible Life Stream, as well as its significance to the ancient practice of dying while living, are abundantly stated in the *Adi Granth*. In the following excerpt, the divine stream of sound is described as being the soul's subtle music, leading beyond birth and death:

> Nectar-sweet is the Lord's Gospel of Equipoise:
> But, rare is the one who has witnessed it with his
> (Mind's) Eyes.
> There rings the Subtle Music of the Soul to which the men of
> Spirit Attune...
> There is neither birth there nor death...[35]

Further east, we discover that the ancient Chinese sage Lao Tzu, who is believed to have authored the poetic *Tao Te Ching* described the Tao, or Way, as the Great Tone and at other times as 'unimpeded harmony', again an apparent allusion to the sound/music of the Audible Life Stream:

> The Way is unimpeded harmony;
> its potential may never be fully exploited.
> It is as deep as the source of all things:
> it blunts the edges,
> resolves the complications,

harmonizes the light,
assimilates to the world.[36]

Chuang Tzu, who lived some 300 years after Lao Tzu, also confirmed that the Way is an audible phenomenon when he advised:

...hear with the mind instead of the ears; hear with the energy instead of the mind. Hearing stops at the ears, the mind stops at contact, but energy is that which is empty and responsive to others. The Way gathers in emptiness; emptiness is mental fasting...have your ears and eyes penetrate inwardly...[37]

All these selected excerpts from the various scriptures seem to unambiguously suggest that the so-called founders of the world's major religious traditions most likely perfected the art of dying while living because of their apparent knowledge of the Audible Life Stream. In all likelihood, it was this knowledge that was their quintessential message, but which sadly has been forgotten or grossly misunderstood over the centuries.

Although theirs is an ancient message, it is one that is just as relevant today. Death is still the great mystery it has always been, and the search for meaning and purpose of life in its foreboding shadow has continued unabated ever since humans first embarked on this eternal quest.

Yet, despite these scriptural references there will be those who will remain unconvinced about the Audible Life Stream phenomenon, attaching little importance to religious texts of sometimes dubious origin. Such skepticism isn't altogether unwise. But what other evidence is there? In fact, there is modern-day evidence of the Audible Life Stream available. The contemporary status of such evidence and its nature makes it starkly more compelling. There can be no question of translation errors, misinterpretation, authorship or even political censorship because such evidence is not the property of religion. Instead several open-minded and esteemed researchers have collected voluminous data from average people from different parts of the world who have described their extraordinary experiences in simple language, having no reason to veil their testimonies in mystical metaphor. Their unique experiences have become known as the near-death experience (NDE).

History of the near-death phenomenon is rich and detailed, but nevertheless it has not enjoyed a consensus of opinion among all commentators. Therefore, a qualification of the true nature of the near-death phenomenon and discussion of its profoundly transformational effects is necessary before presenting the testimonials themselves. So this will be the subject of the following chapter.

Sounds Like Death—But is it?

Do not, I beg you, look for anything behind phenomena. They are themselves their own lesson.

Johann Wolfgang von Goethe (1749–1832)

A 1982 Gallop poll concluded that up to eight million Americans, approximately 1 in 20, believe they have lived through an NDE.[1] On 2003 US Census Bureau adult population estimates, that translates to over 10 million people![2] A much smaller Australian survey conducted in 1989 by Allan Kellehear and Patrick Heaven of 173 people found that 10 per cent reported experiencing at least one element of the NDE.[3] This equates to over 1 million people using 2001 Australian Bureau of Statistics adult population figures.[4]

So what is an NDE that so many millions of people are reporting?

David Lorimer, former Chairman of the International Association for Near-Death Studies in the UK, defines an NDE as '...the continuation of conscious experience while the person is clinically dead—no heart-beat, breathing or skin resistance response and, in some cases, no detectable EEG [electroencephalogram] activity.'[5]

A closely related phenomenon that has become known as an out-of-body experience (OBE) is often a common and important element of the NDE. However, it's clear that by definition the NDE does not include those OBEs that occur in situations where there is no obvious threat to the physical body. These OBEs are nevertheless an important link in the chain of evidence of the Audible Life Stream; therefore, they will be discussed separately in Chapter 7.

Although David Lorimer's lucid definition states that an NDE is an experience of death, there are many who disagree with this assessment. There are numerous alternative explanations that have been put forward discounting the NDE as something other than a profound spiritual experience of death. These alternative explanations can be broadly classified as either psychological, whereby the prospect of impending death is believed to affect the person's psychological state; and physiological, whereby the physiologic processes associated with death are believed to alter a person's perceptions.[6] But before we examine some of these alternative theories something of the phenomenon itself needs to be said.

Evidence of Life after Life

The term 'near-death experience' was first used by Dr Raymond Moody in his book, *Life After Life*, that became a best-seller around the world, having been translated into many different languages. The seed for the book was planted in an atmosphere of scholarly sobriety when Dr Moody was a 20 year-old student of philosophy. It was at this time that one of his professors told him about a strange experience that a psychiatrist named Dr George Ritchie had. Essentially, after being pronounced dead of double pneumonia, Dr Ritchie was somehow successfully resuscitated. After the drama, he reported a remarkable experience of travelling through some kind of tunnel and seeing beings of light. All this purportedly happened when he was dead! Yet, despite the remarkable story, at that time Dr Moody's interest wasn't sufficiently aroused for him to investigate further.

Having finished his doctorate in 1969 and taken up an alma mater teaching position, Dr Moody was told a similar story by one of his students, who had been in a car accident the previous year. Later, when Dr Moody told both stories to his students, they offered noticeably similar accounts involving either their relatives or friends who had also experienced what appeared to be a temporary death.

In 1972, Dr Moody entered medical school and while there was able to collect more such cases. It soon became plainly obvious to him that the phenomenon was much more common than he had originally thought. *Life After Life* eventually contained over 100 cases of people who had had a brush with death and returned to tell their remarkable stories.

Since the publication of *Life After Life*, a number of other researchers have published their findings about the phenomenon, with obvious similarities between them all. People like Dr Cherie Sutherland, in Australia; Dr Margot Grey and Drs Peter and Elizabeth Fenwick in the UK; and Dr Kenneth Ring, Dr Michael Sabom, Dr Melvin Morse and others in America.

NDE Transformations

Interestingly, researchers have found that in the overwhelming majority of cases, the NDE has a profound transformational effect on those who believe they have glimpsed the other side of life. In a report published in 1998 in the *Journal of Humanistic Psychology*, researchers found that individuals who have an NDE are more likely to undergo major attitudinal changes compared to those who have similar life-threatening experiences but without having an NDE.[7] In other words, it is the NDE that initiates the transformational effect within individuals, not exposure to a life-threatening situation.

In the cited 1998 psychological study, 52 individuals (average age of 48) who reported having had an NDE were compared with 27 others (average age of 47) who had been in life-threatening situations but, in contrast, did not report an NDE. Ratings about changes in the individuals in both groups were also obtained from 45 significant others (close family relatives)—26 rated a relative in the NDE group while 19 rated a relative in the non-NDE group. The results of the study were consistent with results of similar previous studies. The researchers found that the changes in people in the NDE group included becoming more generally concerned about others, a stronger belief in an after-life, a lessening of anxiety about death, an increased awareness of spiritual phenomena, a greater appreciation of the natural environment, increased feelings of self-worth and a reduction in materialism.

Importantly, the documented changes in people were found to be significantly greater in individuals who reported having an NDE compared to those in the other group who did not report an NDE despite being exposed to a life-threatening situation. Furthermore, there was a significant positive correlation between the depth of the NDE and the extent of psychological transfor-mation. Put simply, the deeper the NDE, the greater the psycho-logical transformation.

Based on an Australian study conducted by Dr Cherie Sutherland that involved over 400 people, changes that NDE percipients reported include a shifting in their attitude to religion (whether it was favorable or not) by subsequently grasping an acute sense of spirituality. This is in contrast, however, to simply becoming interested in mainstream religions and, for example, going to church. One Australian NDE subject named 'Edwina' reported:

> I now have a strong view that church and religion are totally divorced from spirituality. It doesn't matter what sort of religion you get involved with. It just doesn't help each individual along the path to understanding or spirituality. The only way people do it is by looking in themselves, and looking in and in and further and further, and most religions I feel take people away from that.[8]

Reflecting this willingness to go within as opposed to expressing their spirituality in an outwardly religious way, in Dr Sutherland's Australian study a massive 60 per cent of NDE percipients began to meditate regularly after their experience. This compares to a mere 12 per cent of those surveyed who did some form of meditation on a regular basis before their NDE.[9]

Consistent with the American 1998 study, the Australian study found that NDE percipients also tend to develop a more holistic compassionate attitude to life and no longer set or crave materialistic goals. A desire to work in an area where others can be helped is often a conscious choice that many make. Such a noble decision is frequently shaped with a greater sense of purpose, even if it means leaving a current, and often higher paid, job. As an example, another Australian subject called 'Harriet' described her willingness to assist homeless boys after her experience, something she believes she most likely wouldn't have contemplated before her NDE:

> I found that as my children grew up, it doesn't seem as if we've ever had an empty house... My mother always said other people collect stray dogs but I collected stray boys. We always seemed to have a boy living here—one on probation, one who'd run away from home, a Chinese-Malaysian student who thought I ran a boarding house because he'd heard about these boys that kept coming in. I picked one up off the street one day, and he looked so wet and bedraggled... Whereas perhaps before I would have driven past, or I would have said no to some of those.[10]

Frequently, NDE percipients also become acutely conscious of their lifestyle. An increase in their perception of their self-worth and self-understanding, and a generally more positive attitude to life resulted in many reducing, or sometimes totally avoiding consuming animal flesh, alcohol, tobacco and other harmful substances.[11]

Overcoming the Fear of Death

However, clearly the most widely observed change reported by people who undergo an NDE relates to the fear of death. Researchers in America and Australia have compiled similar results on this particular aspect. Dr Kenneth Ring, who supervised a study involving 102 respondents in the Connecticut area of US, identified five stages of the NDE which he termed the 'core experience'. In his scholarly book, *Life at Death*, Dr Ring writes that the data he collected '...clearly demonstrates that core experiencers, as a group, tend to show a sharp decline in fear [of death] where no such pattern is evident for nonexperiencers.'[12]

In an Australian study, 33 per cent of subjects had a fear of death before their NDE, however, only 2 per cent (one person) harbored a fear of death after their experience.[13] As one female respondent to the study said confidently '...I have no fear of death! Now I know that I'm not the body therefore it's possible to take another body. When you die it's not the whole of you that dies.'[14]

In documenting these major shifts in attitude, researchers have identified slightly different elements of the NDE that are most commonly reported. These elements can be best summed up by the Gallup poll findings:

A feeling of peace	(32 per cent)
A life review	(32 per cent)
Visiting another world	(32 per cent)
OBE	(26 per cent)
Accurate visual perception	(23 per cent)
Encountering other beings	(23 per cent)
Perceiving sounds or voices	(17 per cent)
Perceiving light	(14 per cent)
Travelling through a tunnel	(9 per cent)
Subsequent incidences of precognition	(6 per cent)

Being actually close to death seems to be a defining character-istic of the NDE phenomenon. A 1990 study published in *The Lancet* found that most (62 per cent) who were actually close to death based on their medical records also reported enhanced cognitive functioning using criteria like speed, clarity and logic of thought, vividness of colors, and auditory and visual perception.[15] In contrast, the study found that 81 per cent of those who were not actually physically close to death during their perceived NDE reported no cognitive enhancement.

An Ancient Phenomenon

However, it would be incorrect to conclude that the NDE is only a modern-day phenomenon. Sir William Barrett, who was one of the founders of the British Society of Psychical Research in 1882, reported NDEs in his book called *Death-Bed Visions*, which was originally published in 1926. The book included near-death accounts that he and his gynecologist wife collected while at the bedside of dying hospital patients.

Furthermore, scholars like Carol Zaleski, a well-known Harvard theologian, believes NDEs can be found in Roman, Greek, Egyptian and near-Eastern myths and legends.[16] Through the translation of ancient hieroglyphics, Egyptologists have learnt that this great civilization had an intimate knowledge of what we now call the NDE. Such knowledge would have given rulers a sense of all-knowing and immortality because for them it proved that life continued after the death of the physical body. Perhaps it was this spiritual understanding of death that enabled them to shape such a remarkably advanced society that is regarded as one of the greatest in history, having prevailed for more than 2000 years.

Unfortunately, like the modern-day descendants of this ancient culture, modern-day researchers of the NDE phenomenon are apparently unaware of the spiritual nature of sound. Consequently, they have failed to see the importance of the auditory elements that a notable proportion (17 per cent) of NDE percipients report. To those who have knowledge of the Audible Life Stream, it seems clearly apparent that the sounds/music that are reported are the various manifestations of this spiritual phenomenon. The testimonials to be presented in Chapter 6 suggest that the source of the sounds was unlikely to be anything within the material world. Indeed, it will be shown that percipients sometimes even make a clear distinction between the sounds they perceived in the after-death state and those mundane sounds of the physical world.

What the Researchers Say

Only one parapsychologist, American D. Scott Rogo, has displayed a keen interest in this aspect of the NDE (due in no small part to his interest in music); he wrote:

> Whatever its core nature, this impressive music is a common feature of the NDE. But is it a real property of the other-worldly realms or merely a hallucinatory component of the NDE? My own feeling is that this music is an objective part of the experience since, on rare occasions, people visiting the dying have heard it too.[17]

Notwithstanding this apparent general lack of insight into this aspect of the NDE, which must be a major factor as to why specific research has not been done in this area, Dr Moody acknowledged that reports of various 'unusual auditory sensations' are made by many NDE percipients.[18] Further NDE research prompted him to be more specific about the type of sounds that his subjects described, writing that some '...hear a *whoosh* as they go into the tunnel. Or they hear an electric vibrating sensation or a humming.'[19]

Dr Ring's Connecticut study observations regarding the perception of audible sensations were a little more cautious and, indeed, he regarded such reports as insignificant. He writes that '...only fourteen people reported remembering any unusual voices or sounds and this feature was more commonly reported by core experiencers...'[20] However, he does add, with his own use of italics that, nevertheless, '...this is *not* to say that it *never* occurs'[21] and notes that some of his reports corresponded with those published by Dr Moody.

Dr Cherie Sutherland's research findings also buttress those of researchers in other parts of the world, particularly regarding the aspect of auditory perceptions. It's noteworthy to mention that she believes she had an NDE herself while giving birth to her youngest son in January 1971, and describes hearing a mysterious 'whooshing' sound during the incident. She recalls, '...I found that I was moving very quickly through a dark tunnel towards a magnificent bright light, hearing a 'whooshing' sound as I went.'[22]

Another researcher to have had an NDE is British humanistic psychologist, Dr Margot Grey. Her NDE episode occurred when she was travelling in India in 1976. Indeed, she believes she was on the brink of death for three weeks during her sub-continent sojourn after contracting a mysterious illness. On returning to England, she became determined to study the phenomenon, which she was aware had changed her life dramatically. In her British study conducted in the 1980s, of 41 near-death cases, Dr Grey observed that 11 per cent of subjects reported hearing music. Eleven per cent also reported hearing a 'rushing noise'.[23] It should be said that some of those who reported the rushing noise may be the same subjects who reported hearing the music; however, the given testimonials do not indicate whether this was or was not the case.

After a more recent British study, lead by Dr Peter Fenwick and his wife Elizabeth, they concluded that those who report '...mystical experiences sometimes describe hearing 'heavenly music', and about 20 per cent of people who wrote to us heard music during their near-death experiences. Here too the music is always described as 'beautiful' or 'heavenly'.[24]

The NDE Theories

As mentioned earlier, however, several other hypotheses have been proffered by skeptics in an attempt to dismiss the NDE as something other than an experience of death and resuscitation. And it's to this issue that the remainder of the chapter will focus.

As noted earlier, aside from the spiritual theory of the NDE, alternative explanations can be said to have a psychological or physiological basis. Some skeptics believe that the NDE is nothing more than a form of mental illness, or an hallucination triggered by drugs or anesthetic, or even the result of some neurological factor. Emily Kelly, PhD, of the University of Virginia notes that most scientists have focused only on the physiological implications of an NDE and in describing the after-effects of the experience, while ignoring the more profound question about the continuance of consciousness.[25] She explains that many researchers have begun questioning the mainstream scientific assertion that mental processes are fully dependent upon biological processes.[26] Furthermore, researchers like Drs Moody, Ring, Sabom and others have considered the main physi-ological and psychological explanations and all concur that none of these theories are valid.

Some have suggested that an NDE is a result of a mental disturbance falling into one of two categories:

1. a major psychoses like schizophrenia; or
2. an organic brain disorder like delirium or a condition known as temporal lobe epilepsy.

Dr Moody is steadfastly dismissive of the notion that an NDE is caused by a major psychosis like schizophrenia—and for good reason. Schizophrenia is a complex and extremely serious psychological condition of which there can be five types: the paranoid type is characterized by delusions and hallucinations; the disorganized type is characterized by unusual speech and behavior; the catatonic type is identified by excessive or a complete lack of movement; the undifferentiated type captures those who do not fit into any of the previous types; and the residual type is for those who have one or more schizophrenic episode but no longer display any of the major symptoms.[27] The condition is usually associated with severe cognitive and emotional dysfunction. In contrast, those who have reported an NDE have been characterized by enhanced cognitive functioning, as is evidenced by the 1990 study published in *The Lancet* cited previously.

On the question of whether the NDE is really just an organic mental disorder like delirium, which is a cognitive disorder characterized by impaired cognition and consciousness, Dr Moody notes that those suffering from this condition do not report the typical features of an NDE.[28] And again, impaired cognitive functioning is the opposite of what NDE percipients actually report.

Drs Moody, Ring and Sabom have also discounted temporal lobe epilepsy as a trigger for an NDE because they found that this hypothesis could not support all the different traits of the near-death phenomenon.[29]

Skeptics have also tried to explain an NDE in terms of an autoscopic hallucination since many NDE subjects report the OBE. An autoscopic hallucination is basically an experience where one believes one sees one's own image. It's believed to be quite a rare phenomenon that mainly affects people suffering from severe migraine headaches or epilepsy. Dr Moody rules this theory out in very simple, easy to understand, terms:

In the typical out-of-body experience, or OBE, the person reports that he has a point of view outside of his physical body. And he is viewing his physical body from a distance... The OBEer also reports a center of awareness that is outside his physical body. In an autoscopic hallucination, awareness is still from inside one's physical body, just like your experience now, in reading this book.[30]

Dr Moody has also eliminated the theory that the NDE is an hallucination triggered by stress or drugs. Although he does acknowledge that the EEG, which measures the brain's electrical activity, is not an infallible machine, he believes it provides the strongest case against this hypothesis. To explain, one needs to understand that brain electrical activity goes on as long as someone is alive, even during dream states. So therefore, whenever there is anything happening in the brain, an EEG reading will occur. Thus, during hallucinations the EEG will give a reading. He has found that in many cases where a flat EEG reading was made—that is when there is no electrical activity in the brain—the subject, when resuscitated, reported an NDE, thereby showing that the NDE cannot be classified as being hallucinatory in nature.

Dr Ring looked to the effects of anesthetics and drugs on subjects as a way to explain the elements of the NDE as some sort of drug-induced trip. He discovered, however, as have other researchers, that pharmacological substances were often not used in cases where NDEs were reported. In fact, he found that in most cases when drugs were involved they often interfered with the occurrence or recall of the NDE. He noted that '...the evidence suggests that drug usage tends to be negatively associated with the [NDE] experience.'[31]

The depersonalization theory, whereby a person faced with the imminent prospect of death initiates a defensive psychological reaction allowing the person to cope with the stress of the situation, has also been proposed. But as Dr Ring articulates '...to force the near-death experience into the procrustean bed of depersonalization, they [those offering the hypothesis] have to make numerous ad hoc assumptions for which there is little support.'[32]

Meeting Deceased Relatives

Secondly, Dr Ring observed that the depersonalization argument could not accommodate one important characteristic of the NDE, which is the meeting of a deceased relative that the dying person is unaware has died. These types of cases have been reported by Dr Elizabeth Kubler-Ross and others. She tells of an incident involving an American Indian woman that deeply touched her. A woman told Dr Kubler-Ross that when her sister was hit by a car and left to die hundreds of miles away from her reservation, another driver kindly stopped to render assistance. Moments before the woman died, she told the kind-hearted man to be absolutely sure to tell her mother that she would be all right because she was going to be with her father. The dying woman's father had, in fact, died on the reservation about an hour before her accident and there was no possibility of her knowing about this.[33]

This aspect of the NDE also prompted Dr Ring to rule out the wishful thinking theory because it is so similar to the depersonalization hypothesis. He further points out that such a theory simply cannot explain the consistent pattern found in NDEs reported. He explains that '...the *consistent patterning* of the core experience across different people is itself evidence against the hypothesis. Presumably, people *differ* in their wishes in regard to a hoped-for afterlife, yet the sequence of experiences they go through on coming close to death is remarkably alike.'[34]

Emily Kelly, PhD, investigated the survival hypothesis (that is that an NDE is evidence of consciousness surviving the demise of the physical body) and the alternative 'expectation' hypothesis that suggests that a person facing the prospect of death will wish or expect to be reunited with deceased loved ones and, therefore, will perceive them.[35] To test these competing hypotheses, Kelly examined 553 NDE cases from USA, Canada and Australia. Of these cases, 13 per cent (74 cases) involved the perception of a deceased loved one. However, it should be noted that for 37 out of the 74 cases there were no medical records available to verify the person's proximity to death. Yet some of the key findings of this study included that people who were truly close to death (based on the medical records) were more likely to perceive a deceased loved one compared to research participants who were not close to death. Another important finding was that many figures perceived by people were unidentified. This finding made Kelly question the expectation hypothesis because if valid then most figures perceived would be likely be someone recognized (even a religious figure) by the person because of the nature of expectations.

Also counter to the expectation hypothesis was the finding that there were so few cases (only two) involving the seeing of a deceased pet, to which people can often be strongly emotionally attached. One participant even expressed her disappointment at not seeing her deceased pets because of her emotional attachment to her animals.

When looking for other psychological factors to explain the NDE, Dr Ring, like Dr Moody and others, found that the experience tends to be independent of religious expectations, although he observes that an individual's interpretation of their experience is often colored by their religious beliefs. For example, someone with a Christian background is more likely to interpret a being of light to be Jesus, while someone with East Indian ancestry may well perceive a being of light as a Hindu deity. This, of course, seems hardly surprising.

Does Carbon Dioxide Play a Part?
But, one of the most seemingly plausible explanations for the NDE phenomenon is a condition known as cerebral anoxia that

results from insufficient oxygen reaching the brain. The same condition is induced if there is a build-up of carbon dioxide in the blood. Therefore, heart-attacks or a respiratory failure can both trigger this condition. One of the main reasons why this hypothesis has been proposed is because of findings of a now discontinued form of psychotherapy that was used in the 1950s that required patients to inhale carbon dioxide. Upon doing so, patients reported going through some kind of tunnel and seeing bright lights. However, NDE researchers have found that many NDEs were reported by people who had been breathing normally up to the time of their experience. Furthermore, Dr Moody noted that in a sample of his subjects who underwent a deeper 'core experience' NDE, a cut-off of blood supply to the brain that would, for example, occur after a heart-attack (thus reducing the level of oxygen getting to the brain) never took place.

Also, Dr Moody cites a case reported by Dr Sabom, in which he coincidentally measured the blood oxygen level of a patient, who at that particular time was later found to have experienced a profound NDE. Dr Sabom discovered that the patient's blood oxygen level was above normal.[36]

Children's NDEs

The fact that children of varying ages have also reported NDEs shows that social conditioning cannot be considered as the likely basis for the phenomenon occurring. Dr Melvin Morse headed a Seattle study which looked at the NDEs specifically reported by children. His interest was sparked after resuscitating a nine-year-old girl named Katie who reported an NDE after nearly drowning in a pool. Naturally, she didn't understand that she had had a spiritual experience, rather that just something quite unusual had happened. After she reluctantly reported seeing 'guardian angels' and travelling through a tunnel to 'heaven', Dr Morse understandably wanted to determine if Katie had been indoctrinated with religious beliefs that could well result in such a story being created.

When Dr Morse suggested this to Katie's mother she strongly denied this possibility. Although she accepted that as a Mormon, she had raised her daughter to believe in the after-life and took her to Sunday school regularly; she was, however, emphatic that no one in the family espoused a belief in spiritual guides or tunnels to heaven. Dr Morse was, therefore, left to conclude that there was very little similarity between Katie's experience and the religious teachings to which she had been exposed.[37]

Memories of Birth?

Perhaps knowing that many children report NDEs, and of the universality of the phenomenon, author and astronomer Dr Carl Sagan suggested an interesting hypothesis. He suggested that NDEs are merely memories of birth. He wrote:

> The only alternative, so far as I can see, is that every human being, without exception, has already shared an experience like that of those travelers who return from the land of death: the sensation of flight; the emergence from darkness into light; an experience in which, at least sometimes, a heroic figure can be dimly perceived, bathed in radiance and glory. There is only one common experience that matches this description. It is called birth.[38]

While Dr Sagan's theory does have an alluring element of logic to it, many NDE researchers have been dismissive of it. Studies into infant perception have shown that new-borns don't normally have the mental capability nor visual propensity to remember what happens during the birth process.[39] Dr Morse also makes the point that there is little comparison between travelling, at speed, through a tunnel and a baby being squeezed out of the mother's narrow birth canal. During birth, the baby's face is pressed hard up against the walls of the birth canal so the sense of freedom and space that NDE percipients report contrasts sharply with a new-born's entry into the world. The birth theory also doesn't explain the precognitive aspects of NDEs or the sometimes reported seeing of dead relatives.

Interestingly though, the Drs Fenwick study found one British woman who believes she experienced an NDE when she was born in 1947![40] However, far from buttressing Dr Sagan's birth theory, the important point of this most unique case is that the woman definitively described an OBE and tunnel experience that occurred moments *after* she was born, thereby ruling out the possibility that she was merely recalling the experience of her birth.

The woman reported that it was years later that she learnt that when the doctor arrived at the family home after her delivery he thought she was dead because she was blue-black all over. It was only after he dipped her body in cold water that she breathed for the first time. Therefore, her proximity to death as a newborn is clearly consistent with her recall of an NDE.

Sensory Cuing

Finally, there is one more hypothesis concerning the NDE that needs to be considered. Mention of auditory sensations experienced by people who are believed to be near-death must bring to the minds of some readers the phenomenon of synaesthesia. Synaesthesia is believed to be a rare phenomenon where input from one sensory channel, like for instance the ears, is transcribed and transformed into a secondary sensory mode. This is the condition which leaves some people 'seeing' music or 'hearing' colors. Coupling this with the fact the doctors have known for decades that the hearing faculty is the last sense to cease functioning when one dies, one can see the obvious implications for the NDE. For if one is 'unconscious' yet for an unknown period is still capable of auditory perception then visual images could be created synaethesially. And, of course, the other important question is whether the sounds reported by NDE percipients could be those coming from their immediate physical environment.

While a rigorous researcher would probably find a few cases where synaesthesia could be used as an explanation of a purported NDE, there is a vast volume of cases where the theory simply could not be applied even by the most hardened critic. For instance, precognitive NDEs where percipients get glimpses of future events and those where the percipient reports details that would not normally be known, unless the subject experienced an awareness outside of their unconscious physical body, are obvious examples.

As to whether the phenomenon of synaesthesia can be applied to the extracted NDE testimonials in the following chapter, two questions need be asked to assess the credibility of the reports:

1. Is there evidence to suggest that what was heard by the percipients emanated from the percipients' immediate physical vicinity?
2. Does the researcher identify the source of the sounds perceived thereby precluding the sounds being of a spiritual nature?

In all cases, the answer to both questions is no. In fact, in some reports, the NDE percipients state unambiguously that the sound they experienced was something unique and other-worldly, particularly those who perceived the Audible Life Stream as music. Moreover, when external mundane sounds were by chance heard, the subject clearly recognized them as being of a material nature.

Therefore, the findings of NDE researchers from around the world, who have methodically discounted all the most common psychological, pharmacological and neurological theories put forward by skeptics, leave little doubt about the NDE being a deeply profound spiritual experience that we will all have to face at the end of our earthly sojourn. Because rather than being an experience *near* death, it is perhaps reasonable to say that is a glimpse of death itself. The consistent pattern, the recurring elements, the profound personal changes that often take place and the unexplainable factors, like the seeing of dead relatives that the subject would normally be unaware had died, all indicate that the NDE is a unique experience that has enormous transformational potential.

All these conclusions can be best summed up by Dr Melvin Morse who wrote:

A near-death experience is in fact the dying experience. We will all have one when we die—rich or poor, murderer or saint. I used to think that when we die, we simply enter into darkness and end our lives. As a critical care physician I had seen many children and adults die and never had any reason to think otherwise. It was only after I took the time to ask those who survived clinical death what the experience was like did I learn that the process of dying is often joyous and spiritual.[41]

This being so, it seems that the NDE cases where subjects perceived the Audible Life Stream, albeit unknowingly, have occurred within a definite spiritual context. Although their experiences began, more often than not, with a fearful accident of some kind or some unforeseen complications during a medical procedure, the fact that they were able to return to the physical body to continue their earthly existence makes them extremely fortunate. They themselves would no doubt agree, given the many positive personal changes that the vast majority have undergone. No longer does death hold any fear for a major proportion of these people because they believe that the body is only a temporary dwelling for the immortal spirit. And having realized their own inherent spiritual nature many understand that all physical beings are inherently spiritual in nature too. What often follows then is that the importance of living a physical life within a spiritual context becomes a natural progression for them, clearly with immensely beneficial repercussions for others.

Therefore, dying while living, which is a way of essentially safely inducing an NDE but without any possibility of prematurely extinguishing life from the physical body, is as much about spiritual evolution as it is about leading a more fulfilled physical existence; for a physical existence is equally a part of our spiritual evolution as is a purely spiritual state. Death, we've established, is merely a dark illusory veil dividing, but not permanently separating, these two forms of existence. The mystics' essential teachings are simply about penetrating this illusory veil. This is precisely what many millions of NDE percipients have done unexpectedly, irrevocably transforming their lives for the better. So it's to some of their remarkable testimonies that we shall next turn our attention.

6

Embraced by the Sound

Twilight and evening bell,
And after that the dark!
And may there be no sadness of
farewell,
When I embark;
For though from out our bourne of
Time and Place
The flood may bear me far,
I hope to see my Pilot face to face
When I have crost the bar.

Alfred, Lord Tennyson (1809–1892) from *Crossing the Bar*

After experiencing death and returning to this side of life, Australian Prof. John Wren-Lewis, said in a TV interview that it was '...as if everything was there and everybody was there. The sense was of absolute, total fulfillment. And yet there was no sense that I was there. That's the most extraordinary thing—John vanished at that moment.'[1]

This feeling of 'I-lessness' highlights the fact that it is only the ego, which we know is inexorably tied to the illusory sequential sense of time, that is subject to death. This is not to say that the whole ego always dies completely at death, although this would seem surely possible, and indeed is the ultimate spiritual goal. But since any entrenched habits and attachments, which constitute the ego, are still empowered with conscious energy after the physical body dies, these, together with the law of karma, will ensure another rebirth. Consequently, these attachments and desires can be fulfilled through a physical body.

So ironically, death is the one critical process by which the immortal spiritual aspect of consciousness can be revealed, if one knows how. However, mystics tell us that without the knowledge of how to tune into the Audible Life Stream one risks remaining trapped in the illusion of a never-ending cycle of birth and death. They say that through the Audible Life Stream one can develop the necessary control in the death process so that the transition from this physical existence to the spiritual is done fully conscious. Being fully conscious, however, does not imply the continuance of an ego-based consciousness that the average person maintains while alive. Like Prof. Wren-Lewis, many NDE percipients report the automatic loosening of the sense of 'I-ness' and often articulate this as a state of reality where time, as we normally (and falsely) perceive it, distorts—implying a state at least approaching the eternal NOW. For example, one NDE percipient reflected on the experience by saying, '...I learned there was no time, and no word for time. Our terms, 'past,' 'present,' and 'future' blend together, coexisting on one plane at the same moment as a harmonious part of the whole.'[2]

In Chapter 10 we shall see that there are different degrees of ego-consciousness that must be surmounted even after the physical body dies before a state of pure timeless consciousness can prevail. But the fact that NDE percipients report a distortion of time is further proof that the illusions of ego, time and death are all interrelated.

Another important feature of the NDE accounts to follow is that it seems highly unlikely that at the time of the experience percipients had any knowledge of the Audible Life Stream phenomenon. Yet, many will tell how they were touched by something awesome; something that has the mind scrambling for words it always finds are inadequate; something unmistakably spiritual, and which we have already discovered has had profound repercussions in many cases.

Also significant is that none of the testimonials are from

people who were trying to induce a mystical experience. The value of this is that the skeptical reader has no reasonable grounds to dismiss such evidence as biased or unreliable. Although subjects were ignorant of the Audible Life Stream phenomenon when they died, some indicate that they did become aware of the spiritual nature of the sound they perceived. But this will be shown to be dependant on the type of sound perceived and sometimes on the duration of exposure.

Another important point to note is that the following extracts show that there are many sounds that are reported. The reason for this is simple. Because we are all at different levels of consciousness, one will only perceive what one is capable of at any given time. This possibly explains why some NDE percipients do not report any auditory perceptions at all, and similarly why some are more profoundly affected than others.

The Sound-of-Being

So, now to the testimonials: these first two cases were reported to Australian researcher, Dr Cherie Sutherland. The subjects perceived the sound as a vibration and a torrent and both were deeply affected by what they heard. The first case involves a woman who returned from death after being in a car accident in which her husband was killed. The case is also interesting because the woman describes the sound and light in similar terms, which one would expect since mystics say that these are two aspects of the one vibratory phenomenon:

> We died together, he and I, and as entities of energy, we moved together to a place outside of time and space... I became aware of the LIGHT. I struggle to find earth-words to describe it. It is the light-of-being, pulsating from each of us. And the sound! It is the sound-of-being, radiating from each of us to create a community of pure, sacred vibration![3]

The Sound of Silvery Moonbeams

In the second case, a law graduate recounted her NDE, which occurred when she was 15 years old. She describes the sound as a *'whshshshsh'*, which is almost exactly the same as how some of Dr Moody's subjects described it, as well as how Dr Sutherland described the sound after her own NDE during the birth of her child. The university graduate recalled:

> I was coming out of the operating theater—it happened in the recovery room—and I just remember going... I found I was looking down at myself, and then I was flashing to a place which was all light... It was like going through a tunnel, like shooting through something and seeing the light at the end. I heard a sort of whooshing sound, like fast wind or something like that—a sort of *whshshshsh*. It was like every wind and every sea combined in a torrent, but not deafening, not like a deafening roar. It was sort of like silvery moonbeams and the noise they'd make on water if they were going to make a noise... A sort of brushing sound.[4]

The next account is from a woman who suffered from a heart disease. She described seeing the light as well as hearing the sound as vibrations:

> The next thing I remember was being carried or projected very rapidly through what appeared to be a cylindrical void. I could see in the distance a light, very bright light. As I rapidly came closer to this light it grew brighter and wider. I heard sounds around me that appeared or felt almost like an echo, but they were not frightening; they were vibrations...more than anything else.[5]

A psychotherapist who suffered a major heart-attack felt comfortable when the Audible Life Stream began vibrating through his whole body. The experience left the man feeling uncomfortable about using the word death because, for him, like most, it implies a total extinguishing of life when, in fact, he realized that it's not. He explains what happened:

> I then felt my body begin to tingle followed by the sensation that every cell in my body was vibrating. As this increased my whole body glowed. It was very beautiful and incredibly comforting. It wasn't as if I was taken somewhere, but it was as if I allowed this to continue there would be no coming back. But it isn't death, that's not the right word.[6]

Some of American researcher Dr Kenneth Ring's respondents reported the Audible Life Stream as a kind of buzzing, or like the sound of a siren. Two very brief case extracts identify these other tones. For example, a woman who experienced death during a difficult childbirth said, 'I felt like I might have had a buzzing in my ears. It was just a 'zzzz'.'[7] There is no suggestion by the researcher or the percipient that the woman suffered from tinnitus, which certainly isn't something symptomatic of child-birth. The fact that the woman believed the buzzing to be in her ears is only because we are so accustomed to hearing worldly sound with our ears that when the Audible Life Stream is perceived some immediately think it's our ears that are picking up the sound. But as mentioned previously, the Audible Life Stream, being transcendental in nature, is registered not by the physical ears but by our innate spiritual faculty to perceive vibratory phenomenon.

The Wind in the Willows of Death

A man who was in a serious car accident reported his experience of death by saying, 'I think I went through a tunnel and it *seems* to me that I heard something like a siren. A siren and something that might have been like a high rustle of trees. High wind of trees.'[8]

This case has parallels to a passage in the New Testament where Jesus is quoted talking about the Holy Spirit (the Audible Life Stream) and describes it as the wind blowing:

> The wind blows where it wills, and you hear the sound of it, but you do not know whence it comes or whither it goes; so it is with everyone who is born of the Spirit.[9]

A case collected by British physicians, Elizabeth and Peter Fenwick, involves a female social worker who was involved in a serious car accident on a dark, wet day. The woman, whose name is given as Avon Pailthorpe, lost control of her vehicle after it aquaplaned and spun. Although she didn't crash into the car she was trying to avoid, she lost consciousness and had the following NDE in which she heard the Audible Life Stream as a loud roaring noise. The sound is accompanied by a feeling of shooting through the often mentioned tunnel, highlighting the pulling effect of the Audible Life Stream, although it is not too common for someone unfamiliar with the process of how to contact the Audible Life Stream to experience its magnetism. Dr Carl Sagan would have likely delighted in such a case because the woman equates her experience to what she imagines birth to be like, but clearly she knows that the two experiences are different. Yet the death of the physical body is, in a very real sense, actually a birth into the spiritual world and a new level of consciousness. So, drawing an analogy between the NDE and physical birth is perhaps most appropriate since both events foreshadow an entry into a new realm of existence. Ms. Pailthorpe explained:

> I was in a black tunnel, or funnel, shooting through it incredibly fast. I was spinning, too, yet it was a different movement from that of the car. I felt I was shooting through this tunnel, head first, spinning round the edges—like water going down a plug, or like a coil. There was a loud roaring—

it was very noisy, like the moment of birth. I had no time to feel afraid. I was very interested in what was happening, but I felt completely safe.[10]

Death is Alive with the Sound of Music

The following percipients had deeper NDEs because they reported hearing the Audible Life Stream as the most wonderful music they have ever heard. Mystics say that generally the Audible Life Stream, when apprehended correctly, is extremely enchanting. This is particularly so when it is heard as the melodious strains of music. Most of us would be well aware of how worldly music can be so engaging. A favorite song can sometimes stop us in our tracks. But as some of the NDE percipients themselves will say, no mundane music can compare to the universal symphony of the Audible Life Stream. And, declare the mystics, this is one reason why the Audible Life Stream is so important to our spiritual progress because it provides consciousness with something far more captivating and satisfying than the short-lived pleasures derived through the physical senses, which succeed only in bolstering the ego.

Mary Lowther's NDE occurred when she was eleven years old. She suffered acute peritonitis (an inflammation of the smooth membrane that lines the abdomen cavity) after her appendix burst. Like other NDE percipients, she saw the light, but as she explained, the most wonderful part of the experience was the sound of music that she heard. In recalling her experience she said:

I remember still, with total clarity, the feeling of utter overwhelming peace and tranquility. I was looking down on myself in the bed, my mother sitting beside it, and my father standing by the window. I knew he was crying. I seemed to 'float' along a corridor towards, then into, all-enveloping brightness and light, with indefinable shades of pastel-like colors. There were what I can only describe as billions of beautiful shimmering forms, no outlines, and they were all 'cloaked' in what looked like a garment of translucent light. The most wonderful thing was the music, which I can only describe as almost a tangible joy emanating from, yet part of and encompassing these forms, of which one appeared to be the source and somehow embraced all else.[11]

Definitely Not of This World

The late Dr Robert Crookall collected this next case in the 1960s from a 42 year old woman named Kathleen Snowden, who had her NDE while critically ill as a teenager. This case shows clearly how the percipient could easily distinguish between the Audible Life Stream, this time in the form of singing, emanating from the other-worldly regions, and those sounds from the physical realm, which in this case was the voice of her mother:

I was only sixteen years old, ill in bed. I told my mother I thought I was going to faint... I felt myself drifting away from her. Suddenly I realized a feeling of great excitement, wonder, and delight surpassing anything I had ever experienced as I felt my body weightless and floating upwards in a golden glow towards a wonderful light around hazy welcoming figures and the whole air was filled with beautiful singing. I floated joyfully towards the voices and the light and then I heard my mother's voice calling me... My whole being revolted against going back. Her voice grew nearer and to my great distress, I felt myself slipping away from the wonderful light and merging into a dull black cloud where my heaviness of body returned... My mother thought I had died; I had seemed to stop breathing...[12]

The following two testimonials were given by adults recalling an NDE that occurred when they were children. 'Ed' was only five years old when he experienced his NDE. Like the previous account he also heard singing, but in his case it was accompanied by music. The incident occurred after Ed released the hand-brake in the family car and he became trapped in the car door when it rolled down the steep driveway onto the road. He was pinned under the car's rear left tire and his father had to dig him out and give him mouth-to-mouth resuscitation. Ed described the scene, in which his parents rushed him to hospital in their car, as if he were witnessing the event from a point outside the car window. He observed the panic on his parents' faces, and his own bruised face. He then felt himself floating upwards with great speed in total darkness. Suddenly, he found himself standing on what he described as a loading dock where a bright light hung over his head from which thoughts were entering his mind. He goes on to say that he heard '...beautiful music and vocals like a choir that I couldn't quite understand.'[13]

As a six year-old, 'Jim' had a serious bout of scarlet fever. One night, gasping for breath, he felt himself receding into the clutches of death, and as he did he heard the music with a discernible rhythm:

> Suddenly, I found myself in a long dark tube, with some strange and different music. There was a continuous rhythm that reminds me of the sound you can hear when you place your ear against the mouth of a long pipe... I was convinced that I was dead and I really wanted to get to the end of the tunnel to see what the next life held. But I never reached it, and I don't know why.[14]

An Expansion of Consciousness

This next case shows how the Audible Life Stream can have a dramatic affect on a person's state of consciousness. It was reported by a woman who died temporarily while under-going surgery due to a cardiac arrest:

...I became conscious of seeing my body lying there on the operating table... While I was in that out-of-body state...I then felt myself moving off very fast, exceedingly fast, into what seemed like outer space... I could also hear beautiful music, wonderful music. I'm not sure if it was instrumental music, but somehow I think it was more massed voices giving that sound. But there were no words—it was more just a resonance of sound. And my consciousness seemed to increase dramatically, to the point where I felt all-knowing. I felt I was in touch with all knowledge—I just knew and understood so much more.[15]

Sounds of a New Order

A woman who related her experience to investigator Dr Kenneth Ring believed she died after two major operations. She later reported hearing harmonious music that she described as 'nameless', possibly because of its ineffable quality. She also makes the point about the distortion of time and space as she explains that '...pain disappeared, comfort seized me. Only my essence was felt. Time no longer mattered and space was filled with bliss. I was bathed in radiant light and immersed in the aura of the rainbow. All was fusion. Sounds were of a new order, harmonious, nameless (now I call it music).'[16]

Here is a case of an accident victim who implies that the spiritual music actually had a transporting effect:

During the night I started to feel as if I was falling down and down a well, which was going round and round. At the end of this deep well I could see a wonderful blue light which was coming up and enveloping me. It was alive, like a living light. I could hear beautiful music all around me. I felt as if I was going back somewhere I belonged. There were people all around who I sensed were loving friends.[17]

The Sound of Love

Next, a woman glimpsed death after her crinoline dress ignited while at a New Year's Eve fancy dress party. She suffered severe burns and doctors didn't expect her to live. It's difficult to comprehend the trauma of such a tragedy, and yet this is poignantly contrasted by the description of the scene that greeted her on the other side, with particular mention of the music that embraced her:

> At some point I suddenly found myself in this beautiful place. I was greeted by such warmth and happiness that it was utter bliss. I was in a beautiful landscape, the flowers, trees, the colors were indescribable, not at all like the colors you see here. The peace and joy were overpowering. I felt warm and glowing. There was a blinding light, but it was not harsh and did not hurt my eyes. The beauty of the landscape is beyond description. Somewhere I heard the most wonderful music and there was an organ playing as well. I felt embraced by such love, it's beyond description.[18]

The Valley of Death

While undergoing surgery for a chronic intestinal disorder, an American woman in her mid-thirties had her NDE. Apart from recalling a meeting with her dead grandfather, she also remembered hearing what must have been the Audible Life Stream. This is what she said when asked about her experience:

> ...I remember being first above my body and then I remember being in, like a valley. And this valley reminded me of what I think of as the valley of the shadow of death. I also remember it being a very *pretty* valley... And I felt very *calm* at this point. I met a person in this valley. And this person—I realized it later on—was my [deceased] grandfather, who I had never met. I remember my grandfather saying to me, 'Helen, don't

give up. You're still needed. I'm not ready for you yet.' It was that kind of thing. And then I remember *music*. (Can you describe it for me?) It was kind of like church music, in a sense. Spiritual music.[19]

In this next case, the comforting quality of the Audible Life Stream is again made apparent, even for someone suicidal and whose mind must have been steeped in utter confusion. The young man who, temporarily at least, succeeded in his attempt, reported hearing the music that made him relaxed and filled him with hope:

I also heard music—different music. (Tell me what it was like.) It was usually like classical music; I like classical music. It wasn't *exactly* the music I've heard, but it was along that line. (Do you recall how the music made you feel?) It made me *relaxed*. The fears went away when I listened to it.[20]

This next case stands out from the others for a couple of reasons. Firstly, the subject is blind, and has been since the age of three months due to excess oxygen being pumped into her incubator. And secondly, the woman, who is called 'Emily', reported three different types of sounds. She first describes what, to her, sounds like massive fans as she is sucked into the tunnel, then she hears hymns, and finally she reports hearing a 'rushing wind' immediately prior to returning to her physical body. Her NDE occurred when she was 22, after a car accident which left her in a coma for three days:

The first thing I clearly remember was being on the ceiling, looking down and seeing this body. I was really terrified by this ability to see. At first, I couldn't relate to that body, and then I realized it was me... Then I was pulled up through the roof and I had this glorious sense of freedom. I could move wherever I wanted to... Then that suddenly ended. I was sucked into a tunnel, and heard a sound like monstrous fans. It was not actually that, but it's the closest way I can describe it. It was a beautiful sound. The tunnel was dark, with regular open spaces in the side, through which I could see other people travelling in other tunnels... Then I saw the distant light, and I heard these hymns...[21]

No doubt due to her Christian background, Emily believes she saw Jesus at this stage, followed by deceased school friends, relatives and neighbors. She then said she experienced a very rapid but detailed life-review. She explains that she then '...started careering backwards. I heard this rushing wind, backwards. Then I felt this thud and I was back in my body with a lot of pain.'[22]

A Powerful Tornado

The following testimony comes from a woman who Dr Ring regards as having the deepest experience of all the people in his study. She had the NDE after a cardiac arrest in her home, after which she lay comatose and undiscovered for three days! Here the Audible Life Stream is first described as a powerful tornado that obviously pulls her spirit out of her physical body, then later, as comforting music unlike anything that she had ever experienced before. Detailing her experience, the woman told Dr Ring:

The first thing I remember was a tremendous rushing sound, a tremendous [searching for words]... It's very hard to find the right words to describe. The closest thing I could *possibly* associate it with is, possibly, the sound of a tornado—a tremendous, gushing wind, but almost pulling me. And I was being pulled into a narrow point from a wide area. (Sort of going into a funnel?) Yes! Yes. And it was [pause] nothing painful. There was nothing frightening about it. It was just something that I felt I gave myself into completely. And it felt *good*.[23]

The woman then reported seeing her deceased mother who informed her that she and her dead husband (the percipient's father) have been waiting for her. In explaining how she felt at this point of her experience, the woman recounted:

...all I felt was a tremendous kind of happiness, of pleasure, of comfort. And then somehow she took me by the hand and she took me somewhere [pause] and all I could see was marble all around me; it was marble. It *looked* like marble, but it was *very beautiful*. And I could hear beautiful music; I can't tell you what kind, because I never heard anything like it before... It sounds—I could describe it as a combination of vibrations, many vibrations. (How did that music make you feel?) Oooh, so good! The whole thing was just very *good*, very happy, very warm, very peaceful, very comforted, very—I've never known that feeling in my whole life.[24]

Embraced by the Sound of Light

At the time of her NDE, American Betty Eadie was 31 years old, a mother of seven children and otherwise in good health. Her death experience is possibly the most widely read and detailed account that has yet been documented. She wrote about her remarkable experience in her touching book, *Embraced by the Light*, which was published in 1992. Her NDE, however, actually occurred in November 1973 after she was admitted into hospital to undergo a partial hysterectomy. Although apparently unaware of the Audible Life Stream, she heard many of its different tones and as her experience deepened the more profoundly she was affected by the sound.

It was on the night after the successful operation, while she was resting in her hospital bed that Eadie's NDE occurred. Unbeknown to her and the nursing staff, who were changing shifts at the time, she had hemorrhaged.

Spirit Drawn Upwards

To begin with, as she lay in bed while becoming increasingly uneasy about her condition, Eadie heard the Audible Life Stream as a buzzing sound after trying unsuccessfully to signal a nurse to come to her assistance. Then the Audible Life Stream pulled her spirit out of her body, as she explains:

> I heard a soft buzzing sound in my head and continued to sink until I felt my body become still and lifeless. Then I felt a surge of energy. It was almost as if I felt a pop or release inside me, and my spirit was suddenly drawn out...and pulled upward, as if by a giant magnet.[25]

Having exited from her physical body, Eadie saw three old sagacious-looking men wearing monastic robes. She was told telepathically that they are her guardian angels and that she had died prematurely. She became anxious for her family and so went, as spirit, to her home to see if they were all right. When she returned to the hospital she found the three monks waiting for her. She again heard the Audible Life Stream, but this time as a rushing sound just prior to her spirit being transported elsewhere.

Awesome Sound and Power

Having returned to her physical body, Eadie again heard the Audible Life Stream, in a variety of tones, and this time she was very deeply moved. She mentions the tremendous power and hypnotic qualities that the sound possesses, and described feeling like being swallowed up by a tornado, which is precisely how a woman in Dr Ring's study described it earlier:

A deep rumbling, rushing sound began to fill the room. I sensed the power behind it, a movement that seemed unrelenting. But although the sound and power were awesome, I was filled again with a very pleasant feeling— almost hypnotic. I heard chimes, or distant bells, tinkling in the background—beautiful sound I'll never forget. Darkness began to surround my being... Common sense told me that I should have been terrified, that all of the fears of my youth should have risen up, but within this black mass I felt a profoundly pleasant sense of well being and calmness. I felt myself moving forward through it, and the whirling sound became fainter.[26]

The Living Waters

Eadie's death experience continued as she was taken into what she describes as a garden surrounded by mountains, valleys and distant rivers. After approaching a waterfall, she again perceived the Audible Life Stream, this time as beautiful classical type music, just as other NDE percipients have described it. Given Eadie's Christian background, it's perfectly understandable that her interpretation of certain elements of her experience is given from a Christian perspective. For example, she even mentions the 'living waters' (recall that this was a term coined by Jesus to denote the Audible Life Stream) when describing the waterfall, which she believed was the source of the music:

A melody of majestic beauty carried from the waterfall and filled the garden, eventually merging with other melodies that I was now only faintly aware of. The music came from the water itself, from its intelligence, and each drop produced its own tone and melody which mingled and interacted with every other sound and strain around it... We simply don't have the capacity to comprehend the vastness and strength of the music there, let alone begin to create it. As I got closer to the water the thought came to me that these could possibly be the 'living waters' mentioned in the scriptures, and I wanted to bathe in them.[27]

Eadie was then attracted to a rose that appeared to her to be creating the music just like all the other flowers in the garden. She described the music as being perfectly harmonized, creating in her a feeling of utter joy.

Spiritual Salve

As her experience continued, Eadie was taken to other worlds, but the Audible Life Stream never left her. In fact, she was increasingly awestruck by it. And unlike any of the previous NDE cases, she became aware of the healing propensities of it. With the aid of the Audible Life Stream and under the guidance of two beings of light, she journeyed on and described how the music was pleasant and comforting, making her feel intensely happy:

> It was a tone similar to a note of music but was universal and seemed to fill all the space around me. It was followed by another tone at a different pitch, and soon I noticed something of a melody—a vast cosmic song that soothed and comforted me. The tones produced soft vibrations, and as they touched me I knew they possessed the power to heal. I knew that anything touched by these tones would receive the effects of their healing; they were like spiritual salve, expressions of love that mended broken spirits.[28]

Eadie also learnt from her spirit guides that not all musical tones are healing, that some, in fact, can also do damage.

The way that Eadie describes the music she heard after deciding to return to her physical body can leave little doubt about the Audible Life Stream's divine source. As the angels rejoiced in her decision, she was touched like never before. When she heard the angels around her singing she was filled with an unsurpassed love. She remembered fondly:

> No music I had heard in my life, even the music in the garden, compared to this. It was grand, glorious, awesome, and meant especially for me. It was overwhelming... Their voices were pure and each note was clear and sweet... I wept only, soaking in their love and celestial music...[29]

Death-bed Visions

As remarkable as the Eadie case is, perhaps even more thought-provoking are cases in which others who are with the dying actually hear the Audible Life Stream. Since the NDE is, in fact, a death experience, such cases as these are more apt to be called *near*-death experiences since those reporting hearing spiritual sound are *near* someone who is dying and not actually experiencing death themselves. However, the late Sir William Barrett, who collected such cases referred to them as death-bed visions.

In one such case dating back to 1881, an elderly woman, a Mrs L, died in her home in the presence of a number of family and friends, including a doctor. Everyone present at the time of the woman's death heard the Audible Life Stream, except her son. Quite remarkably, even two ladies who had left the room heard the music as they went back upstairs.

In a letter sent to Edmund Gurney of the British Society of Psychical Research, one of the chief female witnesses recalled:

> Just after dear Mrs L's death between 2 and 3 am, I heard a most sweet and singular strain of singing outside the windows; it died away after passing the house. All in the room...[except Mrs L's son] heard it, and the medical attendant, who was still with us, went to the window, as I did, and looked out, but there was nobody. It was a bright and beautiful night. It was as if several voices were singing in

perfect unison a most sweet melody which died away in the distance. Two persons had gone from the room to fetch something and were coming upstairs *at the back of the house* and heard the singing and stopped, saying, 'What is that singing?' They could not, *naturally*, have heard any sound from outside the windows in the front of the house from where they were at the back.[30]

In a corroborating letter about the incident, the doctor in attendance wrote not about singing but about harp music. While it may seem anomalous that some heard singing, another heard music, and the woman's son heard nothing at all, this, in fact, shows how the perception of the Audible Life Stream is dependant upon one's level of consciousness. Furthermore, this aspect of the story proves that the Audible Life Stream did not emanate from the street, as the witnesses first thought, or from any physical source because if this was the case then all present would have surely reported hearing the same thing. Also, while the level of consciousness determines a subjective aspect of the experience, the fact that there was more than one witness highlights the objective nature of the actual phenomenon. The doctor noted:

I was sent for about midnight and remained with Mrs L until her death about 2:30am. Shortly after we heard a few bars of lovely music, not unlike that from an aeolian harp—and it filled the air for a few seconds. I went to the window and looked out, thinking there must be someone outside, but could see no one though it was quite light and clear. Strangely enough, those outside the room heard the same sounds, as they were coming upstairs quite at the other side of the door.[31]

And the Deaf Shall Hear

Another case of this type, which was first published by the

British Society of Psychical Research in the 1880s, arguably incites even more thought provocation than the previous one. It involves a man named John Britton who was dying of rheumatic fever. What is exceptional about this case is that the man was a deaf mute, and not only did those who were with him hear the music but so did he! This substantiates the mystics' claim that the Audible Life Stream is not perceived by the physical ears but by a spiritual perceptual faculty.

Britton's brother-in-law, Mr S Allen and his wife, who were summoned to the home vigil by the family doctor, were the first to hear the music. At the time they were staying in the room below Britton's. While they believed the music came from somewhere upstairs they could not find any appropriate source for it. Mr Allen later wrote:

> We found Jack [that is John] lying on his back with his eyes fixed on the ceiling and his face lighted up with the brightest of smiles. After a little while Jack awoke and used the words 'Heaven' and 'beautiful' as well as he could by means of his lips and facial expression... After Jack's partial recovery, when he was able to write or converse upon his fingers, he told us that he had been allowed to see into Heaven and to hear most beautiful music.[32]

According to psychic researcher D. Scott Rogo, an Italian researcher named Ernesto Bozzano published similar cases in his 1923 French published book entitled, *Phenomenes Psychiques au Moment de la Mort*, but this was never translated into English. In the late 1960s when Rogo tried to collect contemporary cases of this type to match those of Barrett and Bozzano he was largely unsuccessful. Some years later, he realized why. During Victorian times, people often died in the intimate company of their relatives and friends, which is in stark contrast to the hidden deaths of today that in the main take place in high-tech hospital rooms, being symptomatic of our death-denying culture. Perhaps if we overcame our fear of death and regained a sense of intimacy during a dying person's final moments the Audible Life Stream would touch and transform more people—not just the dying.

Certainly, John Britton, Betty Eadie and the many others who unexpectedly perceived the Audible Life Stream, were profoundly touched as a result of their experiences. Britton's experience foreshadowed his own death, but for the others, they were given the opportunity to fulfill their uncompleted missions on this side of life. Most have no doubt about the spiritual nature of their experience, although it seems none fully understood the spiritual significance of what they heard.

Yet the NDE is not the only phenomenon in which people have become unknowingly exposed to the Audible Life Stream. Not surprisingly, an OBE, which, for all intents and purposes, is exactly the same as the core element of the NDE except that, as mentioned previously, it occurs in a situation where there is no obvious threat to the physical body, also produces similar testimonials. Since the OBE phenomenon requires further explanation and there are numerous reports, the following chapter will have to deal with these.

7

Out of Body and into Sound

I know a man in Christ who fourteen years ago was caught up to the
third heaven—whether in the body or out of the body I do not know,
God knows. And I know that this man was caught up into Paradise—
whether in the body or out of the body I do not know, God knows—
and he heard things that cannot be told, which man may not utter.
2 Corinthians 12:2–4

Dianne Morrissey, PhD, was 28 years old when she died—
temporarily that is. At the time she was an office manager for a
large construction company and played the clarinet profes-
sionally for several local orchestras. Her electrocution, which
occurred at her home while she was preparing to host a party,
changed her life profoundly. Some time after her recovery she
quit her jobs and became a certified hypnotherapist. She also
began lecturing about her experience at universities and colleges,
eventually establishing a Friends of IANDS (International
Association for Near-Death Studies) group in California.

After her death experience in 1977, Dr Morrissey wanted to re-
connect with that sense of timelessness and absolute love that she
remembered so vividly while in the spiritual realm. She was so
changed by what had happened that she felt compelled to learn
as much as she could about the phenomenon. In order to do this,
she reasoned that she needed to be able to induce an OBE
consciously. She explains '...that every out-of-body journey,
whether near-death or not, can change the life of the percipient.
Both types of out-of-body experience can provide knowledge
otherwise unattainable... Both can awaken the deepest sense of
peace and well-being. Both can even, on occasion, bring healing

and recovery.'[1]

As a result, over the past several years Dr Morrissey claims she has taught over 25,000 people to have an OBE while asleep. She rightly sees the NDE as being closely linked spiritually to the OBE. However, not usually occurring in life-threatening situations, OBEs are generally not as deep an experience as an NDE.

Like NDE percipients, OBE percipients also often report a distortion of time and space, which not only shows that both phenomena are closely linked but also adds further support to the belief that, at the gross level, the illusory sense of 'I-ness' is dependent upon the physical senses. Researcher and author Celia Green noted that a majority of OBE subjects (53.9 per cent) frequently used expressions like: 'There was a sense of timelessness', 'Time seemed to stand still', or 'Time ceases to exist' when speaking about their OBEs.[2]

The Tomb of the Body

Since both the NDE and OBE are inherently spiritual in nature it is hardly surprising that both phenomena have been reported since ancient times. Some of the earliest philosophers who have greatly influenced Western thinking believed that the soul or spirit can take leave of the physical body while it is still alive. Socrates (c.470–c.399 BC) and his disciple, Plato (c.428–347 BC), accepted and promulgated the Pythagorean belief that the body is like a tomb or prison that temporarily houses a free and immortal spirit. According to American psychical researcher, Dr Janet Mitchell, there are written records of experiences by both Socrates and Plotinus (205–270), which closely resemble what we now call an OBE. And Plutarch's (c.46–120), *On the Delay of Divine Justice*, is said to present an OBE account experienced by Aridaeus of Asia Minor in AD 79.[3]

OBE Research

Modern research into OBEs began in both America and UK

decades ago. In trying to determine the rate of incidence of OBEs, American sociologist Prof. Hornell Hart surveyed 155 university students in the 1950s. His findings were that 27 per cent of the student sample claimed to have had at least one OBE.[4]

A UK survey in the 1960s arrived at similar results. Celia Green, who worked as the director of the Institute of Psychophysical Research in Oxford, surveyed undergraduates at two British universities. Students were asked if they ever had an experience where they felt they were out of their bodies. In the first sample of 115 students, 19 per cent answered yes. And of the 380 students who constituted the second sample, 34 per cent answered in the affirmative.[5]

Yet such statistical data stands for little in the minds of medical professionals who still regard the OBE phenomenon as having a psychological or neurological basis. Not surprisingly then, many of the same arguments that have been put forward in trying to discount the NDE have frequently been raised in connection with the OBE. Hypotheses like: depersonalization, dissociation, ego-splitting, autoscopy, dreams, fantasies, and mental imagery or archetypes, are the most common theories put forward to try to explain the phenomenon as something other than an objective spiritual experience. However, since the NDE and OBE phenomena are so closely related, the same points of rebuttal concerning depersonalization, dissociation and autoscopy that were stated in relation to NDEs still apply. Naturally, though, since the hypotheses of: ego-splitting, dreams, fantasies and mental imagery or archetypes have not yet been discussed, the reasons why these too can be ruled out as valid theories needs to be stated.

A Spiritual Experience is the Only Valid Theory

Firstly, the possibility of ego-splitting can be quickly dismissed. Ego-splitting is defined as the dissociative reaction to acute stress in which one is overcome by an unnatural calm feeling as though one is 'outside' of oneself. However, while there have been a few OBEs reported during times of stress, the vast majority of cases are reported when stress is definitely not a prevailing factor. Indeed, the converse is true. People are often in a deeply relaxed state when the OBE occurs, making many researchers believe that peace and calm are predicates for an OBE. Moreover, many who claim to be able to consciously exit from the physical body hold the view that stress functions as an inhibiting factor for inducing an OBE successfully.

The major consideration that dismisses the fantasy hypothesis is the obvious fact that OBEs frequently have a profound impact on the lives of those who have experienced them. The changes are perhaps not as profound, nor prevalent, as those that aftermath the NDE, but nevertheless personal character changes do take place.

In the late 1970s Dr Karlis Osis and researcher Donna McCormick surveyed 304 Americans who believed they had experienced one or more OBEs and asked them how their experiences had changed their philosophies and everyday lives. A massive 88 per cent believed that significant beneficial change directly resulted from their OBEs. These changes included discovering a new meaning of life and death; a capacity to view situations and people in a more holistic way; and becoming more aware of spiritual values and new levels of consciousness. Also, like those who had an NDE, a fear of death was greatly diminished if not totally overcome. For instance, in the Osis and McCormich sample, 23 per cent believed their fear of death was less intense as compared to before their OBEs, while 43 per cent believed they were completely freed of their thanatophobia as a result of their experience.[6] Clearly, mere fantasies are not known to precipitate such profound changes in people's lives.

Some psychologists believe the OBE is nothing more than a mental image or archetype. But a British study conducted by Dr Robert Crookall effectively ruled this out as a plausible explanation. Dr Crookall investigated over 700 cases of spontaneous OBEs. After his exhaustive study, he concluded that separation and re-entry of the non-physical, or astral body, into the physical body usually occurs in two distinct stages. He proposed that in the first stage a composite double of the physical body separates from it. This composite double is believed to consist of what he called a 'soul body' and a second entity, which he termed the 'vehicle of vitality'. Dr Crookall was convinced that in the second stage, the composite double sheds the 'vehicle of vitality' leaving only the 'soul body'. Therefore, he subsequently concluded that within '...the entire history of psychology no one has described either mental images or 'archetypes' that appear, and disappear, in two stages!'[7]

Furthermore, in considering the fact that many OBE accounts include visitations to specifically desired places, where witnesses sometimes reported seeing the projected person, Dr Crookall noted somewhat sarcastically that '...these [OBEs] seem to be the only 'mental images' which (a) move to a desired place or person and (b) are, on some occasions, actually seen there by other persons.'[8]

In questioning whether OBEs are merely dreams, we need to turn to the work done by American researcher Dr Charles Tart. Dr Tart was the first person to study the psycho-physiological make-up of people who reported OBEs. He worked with the late Robert Monroe (who was able to investigate the phenomenon from his own remarkable experiences, which will be discussed in more detail later in this chapter) in a sleep laboratory at the University of Virginia, and then later with a female college student in her early twenties. For the purposes of his study, Dr Tart referred to the female student as Miss Z.

In the case of Monroe, Dr Tart found that when he reported having an OBE there was an absence of rapid eye movements (REMs), which normally occur briefly during a deep sleep phase. However, alpha brain-wave activity, which normally occurs when one is in a relaxed state with eyes closed, was detected. In the case of Miss Z, an alpha brain-wave pattern was also detected during her OBEs, as well as a decrease in her REMs. Therefore, since medical sleep researchers have learnt that dreams are usually most vivid during the REM phase of sleep, the absence of the REMs, or at least a decrease, seems to strongly suggest that an OBE is not a dream.

This conclusion was supported by the findings of a study done by the American Society for Psychical Research in 1978. A computerized frequency analysis of 304 respondents to a questionnaire found that the vast majority reported a significant difference in OBE vision compared to dream imagery or ESP. Indeed, only 4 per cent believed that their dream imagery was similar to their OBE vision.[9]

Nevertheless, it is apparent that OBEs and dreams share many common characteristics, although it is equally apparent that there is a difference between the quality of the two phenomena. Monroe believed that at least some dreams, in particular those in which one feels oneself falling or flying, are in fact OBEs with an insufficient level of awareness to realize the true nature of the experience.[10]

Therefore, everyone who dreams while asleep—and researchers believe we all dream although not all of us remember them when we awaken—may well be having an OBE but simply do not realize it because of a lack of awareness.

The Mysterious Vibrations

Almost 20 years of research by Dr Dianne Morrissey has led her to the conclusion that dreams can be a launching pad for a conscious OBE. She even goes further and identifies what she terms 'Seven Keys', including mysterious vibrations, that she believes can create the opportunity for a conscious OBE while asleep. It seems apparent that these vibrations that she cites are a manifestation of the Audible Life Stream, although it appears that Dr Morrissey is unaware of this.

Dr Morrissey has discovered that the vibrations usually precede an OBE. Her findings concur with that of Monroe, whose personal experiences were almost always preceded by him experiencing the Audible Life Stream (although he too seemed unaware of the phenomena) vibrating throughout his entire body.

It's true that not all subjects who become aware of the vibrations reported hearing any sound. Also, the converse is true. When sound or music was reported, there was not necessarily any perception of vibrations. Whether sound and/or the vibrations are perceived, much depends, say the mystics, upon one's karma, spiritual sensitivity and ability to tune into the Audible Life Stream.

One of Dr Morrissey's many students who reported the vibrations did, in fact, also hear a 'humming' sound at the same time. The student, named Fiona, recalled, 'I had been sleeping and suddenly felt as if my body were [sic] vibrating and 'humming'. Yet I knew that my physical body was not moving, and neither was the bed.'[11]

This case, once again, highlights the spiritual nature of the vibrations, because as the subject reports, her body wasn't moving at all and neither was anything else in the room. Another important point is that the 'humming' sound was correctly perceived by the subject to emanate from within her, not from any external source.

Dr Morrissey herself has also experienced the vibrations, and, at least on one occasion when she did, she had a profound experience of being enveloped by spiritual light and a feeling of absolute love—noticeably similar to her NDE. In a 1994 survey she conducted, 24 per cent of subjects reported experiencing the vibrations.[12]

The Sound of Thundering Hooves

Here are two cases reported by a couple of her students in which the Audible Life Stream was perceived as quite different tones. The first comes from a female medical assistant named Nicole, who described the sound like that of a blaring radio. In perceiving electrical currents passing through her body, it is apparent that she was unknowingly also referring to the Audible Life Stream, which, say the mystics, can even be as subtle as this. Nicole reported:

> I was in bed asleep when I suddenly woke up for the first time. I felt as if electrical currents were passing through my body... The next thing I experienced was total blackness, followed by a bright Light that appeared at my left and continued to expand until my whole range of vision was filled with beautiful golden Light.[13]

She then saw a being dressed in a luminous garment appear, before the scene changed to that of a ballroom filled with color-fully and elegantly dressed men and women who were dancing. She explains that the scene then faded and she '...heard what seemed to be a radio with the volume turned up high. The noise sounded like a western movie, with lots of thundering hooves beating the ground.'[14]

Dr Morrissey noted that such a sound is usually heard when the person experiencing the OBE is pulled back into their physical body.

Sound and Visions

Lynn, a university student, reported a ringing in her ears with nothing to suggest that she was suffering from tinnitus, which certainly is not associated with life reviews and futuristic visions, which she believes she experienced, as she explains:

143

I was sitting on a sofa in the home of a friend when I heard a ringing in my ears. My vision began to blur and a mist appeared in front of me. Pictures of my whole life began to flash before my eyes. Everything was in black and white, the good and the bad. Then a peace came. I felt a Presence with me, comforting me, enveloping me in pure love, in brilliant white Light.[15]

Before, once again, becoming aware that she was sitting on her friend's sofa, Lynn visited a beautiful field and then had horrific futuristic visions of battles, famines and 'unspeakable agonies'.

Some may disregard these two preceding cases, saying that in the context of the OBE course that Dr Morrissey offers, suggestions as part of her lectures could well be a major factor in her students' experiences. There is also the question of some students willing themselves to have an OBE simply to be seen to have achieved something by doing the course. There is some merit in these arguments, but the cases cited are so similar in nature and content (specifically referring to the Audible Life Stream aspect) to other cases that will soon follow that such arguments can be seen to be a little too critical and somewhat cynical.

The following cases, unrelated to Dr Morrissey's course, date back to almost the turn of the twentieth century and occurred spontaneously, without any desire on the part of the persons involved to have an OBE. Indeed, since the subject of OBEs was given little public attention at that time, there is good reason to expect that in all the cases cited next, percipients were most likely ignorant of the phenomenon altogether.

The testimonies were collected by American Psychical researcher Sylvan Muldoon, who used the term astral projection, instead of the now more commonly used acronym OBE, for the phenomenon, but he was undoubtedly dealing with the same type of experience.

Flashing Lights and Ringing

Dr I. K. Funk was a reputable theologian, writer and publisher. He was so affected by his OBE he related his experience in one of his books entitled, *Psychic Riddle*. He described a ringing in his ears and a flashing of lights immediately prior to his experience. The experience itself he described as death, having observed his apparently lifeless physical body as a separate entity. The incident happened one morning while Dr Funk was lying in bed, as he recalls:

...there came a flashing of lights in my eyes and a ringing in my ears and it seemed for an instant as though I had become unconscious. When I came out of this state I seemed to be walking on air. No words can describe the exhilaration and freedom that I experienced. No words can describe the clearness of mental vision. At no time in my life had my vision been so clear and so free... I became conscious of being in a room and looking down on a body propt-up [sic] in bed, which I recognized as my own... This body, to all intents and purposes, looked to be dead. There was no indication of life about it, and yet here I was, apart from the body, with my mind thoroughly clear and alert, and the consciousness of another body to which matter of any kind offered no resistance...[16]

Reverberations in the Brain

This next case is from another writer named William Gerhardi, who testified to having had five OBEs. One of his novels, *Resurrection*, was in fact based upon one of his experiences. In his testimony that comes from a letter dated June 15 1936, Gerhardi hears what seems to have been the Audible Life Stream immediately prior to returning to his physical body. His description of the sound, which he describes as having a distinct mechanical tone, was obviously disconcerting for him. This reaction is understandable for one who would not expect to perceive any sounds beyond the realm of our normal hearing faculty.

He recalls that the incident took place in his flat at some time during the night and began as a dream to which he was able to bring conscious awareness:

> But I awoke with a start. For I had stretched out my hand to press the switch of the lamp on the bookshelf over my bed, and instead, found myself grasping the void, and myself suspended precariously in mid-air... The room, except for the light of the electric stove, was in darkness, but all around me was a milky pellucid light, like steam. I was that moment fully awake, and so fully conscious that I could not doubt my senses, astonished as I have never been before, amazed to the point of proud exhilaration...[17]

He then moved about his flat and realized that he didn't need to open any doors because he could pass directly through them! Venturing outside, he considered travelling to New York but decided against this, fearful of severing the link with his physical body. He described the link as a luminous garden hose— commonly known as the silver cord. It was at this point that he became aware of what to him was just a mysterious sound:

> ...it seemed to me as if a dozen coolies, among much screeching and throbbing, were lowering me with the utmost precaution under expert direction from a noisy crane, which seemed to reverberate in my brain, some precious burden which was myself, into some vessel which presently became myself...and then with a jerk which shook me as though the machinery dropped into my bowels weighed a ton, I opened my eyes.[18]

Precious Minutes in Eternity

In April 1928, another writer of the time, William Dudley Pelley recorded his OBE (should all writers, therefore, consider OBEs to be an occupational hazard?). The full account was published in *American Magazine* in March 1929 before being reproduced in a booklet entitled, *Seven Minutes in Eternity—With Their Aftermath.* Apparently, Pelley was a case-hardened materialist and so his experience certainly shattered his worldview.

On the night of the incident, Pelley had retired for bed feeling quite normal in every respect at his home in the Sierra Madre Mountains near Pasadena, California. His experience began with what he describes as a shriek, which is quite a dramatic way to describe what mystics say is sometimes a high pitched tone of the Audible Life Stream. Again, the percipient is convinced that the sound came from within himself and not from any external source. Pelley later recorded that '...between three and four in the morning a ghastly inner shriek seemed to tear through my somnolent consciousness...'[19]

He then told of how he felt himself plunge down through blue space and heard singing that corresponds precisely to some NDE reports cited previously. Next, he perceived himself to be whirling chaotically downwards, likening the sensation to being in a plane in a downward tailspin, something which he actually had once experienced. Then two benevolent spirits came to his assistance and comforted him. He testified to having been shown wonderful things and having met people who he knew had already died.

Resentful of having to return to his physical body, Pelley then described how his OBE ended. Like William Gerhardi, Pelley also says he perceived a mechanistic metallic sound:

> ...I was caught in a swirl or bluish vapor that seemed to roll in from nowhere in particular. Instead of plunging prone I was lifted and levitated. Up, up, up I seemed to tumble, feet first...

And then something clicked. Something in my body. The best analogy is the sound my repeating deer-rifle makes when I work the ejector mechanism—a flat, metallic, automatic sensation...[20]

Vibrating at High Speeds

Being a writer, we can't be in any way surprised to learn that Sylvan Muldoon himself also experienced an interesting OBE. It occurred some 21 years prior to his account being published; however, he points out that he recorded the experience soon after it occurred. Therefore, it cannot be argued that he fabricated elements to compensate for a vague memory. It was this experience that inspired him to devote his life to psychical research.

Muldoon testifies that immediately before exiting and returning to the physical body he felt, what were to him, bizarre vibrations. The experience happened at night after he awoke from a natural sleep that lasted several hours. Having awakened he found he could not get back to sleep and, indeed, discovered that he was unable to move. In describing what eventuated he wrote:

...I tried to move, to determine my whereabouts, only to find I was powerless—as if adhered to that on which I rested. Eventually the feeling of adhesion relaxed but was replaced by another sensation, equally as unpleasant—that of floating. At the same time my entire body (I thought it was my physical but it was not) commenced vibrating at a high rate of speed in an up-and-down direction. Simultaneously I could feel a tremendous pulling pressure in the back of my head... This pressure was very impressive and came in regular spurts, the force of which seemed to pulsate my whole being... I knew not what was taking place. Amid this pandemonium of bizarre sensations—floating, vibrating, zigzagging and head-pulling,

I began to hear somewhat familiar and seeming far-distant sounds...[21]

Muldoon gives no details about these sounds, but since it's obvious that by this time he had clearly transcended the physical body, any auditory sensations he would have perceived would almost certainly have been spiritual in nature.

In an excited state, he moved through the house and tried unsuccessfully to wake up the other occupants, but all attempts to touch anything were fruitless. After what he perceived to be a lapse of some 15 minutes, he again felt the awesome power of what was almost certainly the Audible Life Stream, and his astral form was drawn back to his physical body. About returning to his physical body he wrote:

Again I was in the grip of the powerful unseen directing power... It was the reverse procedure of that which I had experienced when rising from the bed. Slowly the phantom lowered, vibrating again as it did so. Then it dropped suddenly, coinciding with the physical counterpart once more. At this moment of coincidence, every muscle in the physical organism jerked, and a penetrating pain—as if I had been split open head to foot—shot through me... I was physically alive again, filled with awe, as amazed as fearful, and I had been conscious throughout the entire occurrence...[22]

The pain that Muldoon mentions is most unusual and could be the result of some psychological resistance on his part and the fact that at the time of his OBE, at least, he probably had no idea how to tune into the Audible Life Stream correctly. Regardless of this, from these preceding cases it's obvious that the OBE is often not as deep as the NDE. This accounts for the fewer cases reporting hearing the heavenly music that many NDE percipients reported, for the music is believed to be apprehended only at the higher levels of consciousness, which the factor of physical death makes more easily attainable. But this fact doesn't preclude these types of OBE reports altogether.

Music and Tinkling Water

An extraordinarily descriptive case of this type was originally published in 1918 by J. Arthur Hill, one of the early members of the American Society for Psychical Research, in his book entitled, *Man is a Spirit*. In the testimony, Hill intuitively described the spiritual music as the voice of God:

> About five years ago I awoke from sleep to find 'myself' out of the body... I was not conscious of leaving the body, but woke up out of it. It was not a dream, for the consciousness was an enhanced one, as superior to the ordinary waking state as that is to the dream state. After lying in this healing light I became conscious of what, for want of the better term, I must call music; gentle and sweet it was as the tinkling of snapping water in a rocky pool and it seemed to be all about me. I saw no figure, nor wished to, the contentment was supreme. The effect of these sounds was unutterably sweet, and I said to myself, 'This must be the voice of God'. I could not endure the happiness, but lost consciousness there and returned unconscious to the body and woke next morning as though nothing had happened.[23]

Close to Heaven

Mrs Emma Powell gave the following testimony to researcher D. Scott Rogo in the late 1960s after her son had met him following a lecture he gave at UCLA. In Mrs Powell's description, it's clear that she easily distinguished between the unearthly music she heard and mundane sound which, in this instance, was her baby crying. She told Rogo:

I had an out-of-the-body experience in 1926 in November. My daughter was a baby, I had been ill but was out of bed and doing pretty well. But this night, I lay down to go to sleep and I left my body and went straight up, very slowly, but all the time I could hear music and the higher I got the louder the music became. It was the most beautiful music I have ever heard. But I could hear my baby crying and it seemed like she was a way, way off, and I asked the Lord to let me come back, she needed me. And instantly I was back in my body... I knew I had been close to heaven or another world.[24]

Robert Monroe also perceived what must have been the Audible Life Stream as music and did so more than once. Indeed, it's impossible to discuss OBEs and not mention Monroe, who was regarded as a pioneer in OBE research. Monroe's research was different from many others because it was based almost entirely on his personal experiences, which began quite unexpectedly in 1958. At the time he was an accomplished writer and successful businessman having established his own radio company.

What makes Monroe's experiences and subsequent research so poignant is the fact that almost all his experiences were preceded with the vibrations. Unlike the other researchers, however, Monroe soon learnt that the vibrations are the most important factor in exiting the body. Therefore, by developing the ability to induce the vibrations virtually at will, he was able to exit the physical body consciously on countless occasions over many years.

A Mysterious Beam of Light

Monroe's first encounter with the vibrations occurred on a Sunday afternoon after he was struck by a mysterious beam of light while lying down in his living room. Naturally, like anyone who unexpectedly begins to feel their body shaking uncontrollably, he was very fearful initially. In his book, *Journeys Out of the*

Body, he described what happened:

> I thought it *was* sunlight at first, although this was impossible
> on the north side of the house. The effect when the beam
> struck my entire body was to cause it to shake violently or
> 'vibrate'. I was utterly powerless to move. It was as if I were
> being held in a vise. Shocked and frightened, I forced myself
> to move. It was like pushing against invisible bonds. As I
> slowly sat upright on the couch, the shaking and vibration
> slowly faded away and I was able to move freely.[25]

For the next six weeks, Monroe experienced the vibrations on nine
separate occasions whenever he lay down to rest or sleep. At first
he thought he was suffering from epilepsy but soon ruled this out
because he knew that epileptics usually have no memory of their
seizures. Also, he knew that there was no history of epilepsy in his
family, which apparently is an affirming factor in the diagnosis of
this condition. Yet, feeling highly uneasy about what he was
experiencing, he decided to consult his family doctor. Unable to
find any physiological or psychological discrepancy, his doctor
was able to reassure him that nothing was wrong.

Monroe returned home relieved, but nevertheless determined
to observe the experience as objectively as possible should it
happen again. That very evening the experience returned, and
this time the vibrations were accompanied by a roaring sound in
his head—precisely how some NDE subjects described the
Audible Life Stream. He wrote:

> As I lay there, the 'feeling' surged into my head and swept
> over my entire body. It was not a shaking, but more of a
> 'vibration,' steady and unvarying in frequency. It felt much
> like an electric shock running through the entire body without
> the pain involved. Also, the frequency seemed somewhat
> below the sixty-cycle pulsation, perhaps half that rate.

Frightened, I stayed with it, trying to remain calm. I could still see the room around me, but could hear little above the roaring sound caused by the vibrations.[26]

Monroe's numerous OBEs enabled him to delineate three quite different spiritual regions where he would find himself while in the 'Second Body' state, as he termed it. He labeled these regions with scientific candor: Locale I, Locale II and Locale III.

The Music of God

In venturing to Locale II, Monroe periodically experienced what he describes as a most unusual event, one which obviously had a profound impact upon him. For Monroe the experience went straight to the heart of the question: What or who is God? More than once while in this region, he would be awestruck by the unearthly melodic strains of music resonating all around. He intuitively believed this to be a manifestation of God.

While the scene in which Monroe found himself on one of these occasions is wholly different to the ones reported previously, and certainly the behavior of the characters encountered is most unusual (relative to social customs with which most of us are familiar), the spiritual nature of the extraordinary episode is intrinsically the same as that reported by others. Quite possibly, such differences constitute a subjective element of all spiritual experiences since these are filtered by a mind conditioned to vary degrees. However, these variances should not deflect from the objective core experience that the music of the Audible Life Stream represents. In Monroe's case, there were no beings of light or picturesque valleys, yet for him there was an unmistakable divine presence in the music, which he naturally found irresistible. He recalls his observations which began after becoming conscious of being in Locale II when he hears the trumpets, that in all likelihood are the same as those mentioned in ancient scriptures:

In the midst of normal activity, whatever it may be, there is a distant Signal, almost like heraldic trumpets... It is the Signal that He (or They) is coming through His Kingdom... At the Signal, each living thing lies down... The purpose seems to be to form a living road over which He can travel... The purpose of the abdominal exposure is an expression of faith and complete submissiveness, the abdomen being the most vulnerable part of the body or the area that can suffer damage most easily... As He passes, there is a roaring musical sound and a feeling of radiant, irresistible living force of ultimate power that peaks overhead and fades in the distance... Is this God? Or God's son? Or His representative? [27]

Monroe claimed to have experienced this unusual event, characterized by irresistible music, on three occasions. He was convinced that that the experience was the state of heavenly bliss that is referred to by various religions, and the nirvana or samadhi to which mystics throughout the ages have intimated.

Although the experience clearly impressed Monroe profoundly, it is unlikely that mystics of the highest order will agree that this is the supreme experience because they say that there are even greater realms than this. Nevertheless, his intuition linking the music with a supreme force is well-founded.

In further comments about the magnificent music that he found in the astral world, Monroe, like Betty Eadie, makes a clear distinction between it and the worldly music with which most of us are familiar. Also, he is unambiguous about the music being very much a part of each individual. Monroe observed:

It [the spiritual music] is not something of which you become aware. It is there all the time, and you vibrate in harmony with the Music. Again, this is more than the music you knew back there [in the physical world]... The mundane is missing. Choirs of human-sounding voices echo in wordless song.

Infinite patterns of strings in all shades of subtle harmony interweave in cyclical yet developing themes, and you resonate with them. There is no source from which the Music comes. It is there, all around you, in you, you are a part of it, and it is you.[28]

Years later, Monroe revisited this 'Home' as he referred to it, and was once again overwhelmed by the sweet music reverberating all around him. His poetic comments begin describing what took place after having already transcended the physical body and he entered the Astral realm. Interestingly, he also mentioned hearing the sound of the wind just as one NDE percipient did, and how Jesus, on at least one occasion, seems to have referred to the Audible Life Stream. Monroe described a '...sensation of movement...a sound like the wind flowing around me. Before me...around me...and there is the music...a thousand instruments, thousands of voices...melody weaving upon melody...perfect counterpoint, the harmonic patterns I know so well...'[29]

To facilitate research into the OBE phenomenon, Monroe established the Monroe Institute in Faber, Virginia, in 1971. Today it continues to research the effects of sound patterns on human consciousness. Based on the tried and tested theory that particular sound patterns induce higher states of consciousness, the research team has developed what they believe to be a sound pattern that enables both left and right hemispheres of the brain to function in synchronization. The institute's findings show that a highly productive and positive state of mind is achieved when both hemispheres of the brain function together. The research findings have been successfully applied to enhance physical and mental health, learning and memory capabilities, creativity and problem solving. It's also believed that the institute has successfully developed sound patterns that facilitate the separation of consciousness from the physical body.

Although the research is all based on the effects of worldly sound, as opposed to the primordial Audible Life Stream, the Monroe Institute's work, like the work of other similar organizations, has proved to be beneficial for many, many people, not only on a mental and physical level but also spiritually. Such work must be considered one of many reasons for creating widespread interest in the use of specific vibrational frequencies as a therapeutic tool. This being so, there is merit in outlining the importance of this increasingly popular and remarkably successful form of therapy in the next chapter because it adds further credence to the belief that underling all matter, including ourselves, is a vibratory life force that permeates the entire universe.

8

Sound Healing

...And Joy hath welled up in me and the Unstruck Melody Ringeth in
my mind
And all my Maladies, Sins and inner Afflictions are dispelled...
Adi Granth

Although NDE and OBE percipients made clear distinctions
between the profound spiritual music they heard during their
amazing experiences and the music of this world, everyone
knows that worldly music can also be extremely powerful. No
doubt, this is one reason why music plays a significant role in
virtually all aspects of our lives, including religious ceremony.
The inherent power of music prompted the German poet,
Heinrich Heine (1797–1856), to describe it as a miracle because
'...it stands halfway between thought and phenomenon, between
spirit and matter, a sort of nebulous mediator, like and unlike
each of the things it mediates—spirit that requires manifestation
in time and matter that can do without space.'[1]

Heine's observations are given much credence when considering the important relationship that music has with the illusory
concept of time. Music not only takes place within the construct
of time but it also has the extraordinary capacity of breaking this
illusion too.

Joachim-Ernst Berendt remarked that through music not only
does the past and present somehow merge but that the future
does too, into the NOW:

> The future is also involved to the extent that within the
> harmonious progression of music the note sounding 'now'

anticipates the future note in which it will be resolved. The note to come is, as it were, contained in the present note, which could not otherwise 'summon' it. Anyone musical knows that it is hardly possible to break off certain cadences before the final note. The final note is 'there' whether it is played or not. It may sound out later—or not at all—but, viewed in a higher sense, it was to be heard much earlier. Time only completes what became necessary outside of time. It merely makes manifest what would otherwise have remained hidden.[2]

Few, if any of us, can honestly say we have never been touched by a strange feeling of timelessness when listening to a beautiful piece of music. Fine music can be so moving that we can be magically transported to a non-place and non-time that is impossible to articulate with sufficient detail or accuracy. We somehow literally lose ourselves, or at least to a degree, our sense of 'I-ness' while enjoying the music because it can temporarily liberate us from the prison of our own creation—time.

Healing through Music

This ineffable power of music has been recognized by music therapists who appreciate the transcendental unity that music inculcates, and view it as a significant factor in the healing process. Commenting on this particular aspect, music therapist, Barbara Crowe, believes '...that the potential for music to heal comes not just from music's ability to break through normal consciousness and open us to transcendent awareness, but from the fact that music is the ultimate manifestation of this wholeness.'[3]

As a powerfully therapeutic manifestation of wholeness, albeit of this world only, it's easy to understand why music of quality has the capacity, at least in a limited way, to serve as a vehicle for the transcendence of the normal ego-based consciousness. Such a view is supported by music therapists like Grant Rudolph, who in expressing this notion writes:

> The precise language of music directly communicates what cannot be said with words. The experience at the moment of crossing a threshold with music is one of surrender. Our controlling nature gives up to a creative presence... Our ego opens for that moment and a more complete awareness enters; attention focuses on a musical event too fast or complicated for the thinking mind to encompass.[4]

Logically, if worldly music can temporarily break the illusion of time and 'I-ness' then it's not too difficult to accept that the music of the Audible Life Stream can shatter the illusion of death. This, of course, is the essence of ancient spiritual teachings. And since mystics say that all sound, indeed all phenomena, emanates from this vibratory life force, it's easy to understand why music is proving to be so effective as a therapeutic tool, even for the dying.

Music for the Dying

Music-thanatology is how Therese Schroeder-Sheker describes the work she and her teams of musicians perform in American hospitals. Over three decades ago, she established the Chalice of Repose Project, a palliative hospice program in which live music is played for the dying. It's an idea that was first pursued by the eleventh century Cluniac monastics in France who calmed dying patients with gentle music, believing their subsequent death would be a blessed one.

In her first death-bed experience using music, Schroeder-Sheker attended to a terrified man in his 80s who was beyond medication for his chronic emphysema. The man was unable to even swallow and could barely breathe. When she entered his room, the ill-tempered man was so terrified of dying that he was thrashing about erratically. Schroeder-Sheker calmed him by climbing into his bed and sitting in a midwifery position behind him with her legs folded around his waist so that her head and heart were aligned with his. She first prayed then gently sang a Gregorian chant softly into his left ear. She recalls that the man '...rested in my arms and began to breathe much more regularly and we, as a team, breathed together. It was as if the way in which sound anointed him now made up for the ways in which he had never been touched or returned touch while living...'[5]

When the man died he did so peacefully. The stopping of his heart filled the room with a sacred silence that regularly follows the death of one who is calm and accepting of the inevitable process of spiritual transition.

Human Vibratory Transformers

Why musical vibrations should have such profound calming/healing potentialities even in the final moments before the physical body dies can, to a large degree, be explained by the all-pervasive Audible Life Stream. Regarded as the primal force of the universe, mystics say it is the seed from which all things manifest, including all material sound and music, and, of course, ourselves. In other words, the spiritual vibratory essence of the universe is believed to manifest in the physical world in such a way that results in all material objects displaying an essential vibratory nature. The experiments conducted by Swiss scientist, Hans Jenny and others, which were cited in Chapter 3, certainly support this argument. This then would also provide plausible explanation as to the efficacy of all forms of vibratory therapy, but in particular music therapy.

Music therapists acknowledge that our physical bodies are resonating systems of vibratory energy. Therapist Cathie Guzzetta confirms this fact, observing:

The human body vibrates, from its large structures, such as the aorta and arterial system, down to the genetically preprogrammed vibrations coded into our molecular cells. Our atoms and molecules, cells, glands, and organs all have a characteristic vibratory frequency that absorbs and emits sound. Thus, the human body is a system of vibrating atomic particles, acting as a vibratory transformer that gives off and takes in sound.[6]

The fact that we absorb vibrations, just like any other object, means, therefore, that we can be affected by the vibrations to which we are exposed. That effect can be positive if, for instance, the vibrations that we receive resonate with our own vibratory capacity for higher levels of consciousness. On the other hand, the effect can also be negative if the vibrations we absorb pull our own vibratory pattern down by creating disharmony within us.

When an object is exposed to an external vibration that reinforces its own vibration because it is at a similar rate, a phenomenon known as sympathetic resonance takes place. If you were to place two identical tuning forks next to each other then strike one, the sound produced would spontaneously affect the second tuning fork by causing it to vibrate as if it had been struck in exactly the same way. This is due to the fact that the forks contain similar vibratory characteristics, allowing energy transfer from one to the other. When two objects share a similar vibratory pattern that allows them to resonate at the same frequency, they form a resonant system.

Sonic Entrainment

While sympathetic resonance is essentially passive in nature, whereby one object is meeting the natural vibrations of another object with its own vibrations, a closely related phenomenon, known as entrainment, is more active. With entrainment the natural vibrations of one object are replaced with a different vibratory pattern of another.

The phenomenon of entrainment was first noticed in 1665 by the Dutch scientist, Christian Huygens, when he observed two wall-mounted pendulums alongside each other were swinging together in precise rhythm. Huygens realized that the synchronization between the two pendulums could not be explained in mechanical terms, because it was as if the pendulums 'wanted' to swing together. After closer observation, he discovered that the pendulums were synchronized by the faint vibration that was travelling through the wall on which they were mounted.

Scientists have since determined that entrainment, or 'mutual phase-locking', is a universal phenomenon. Whenever two or more oscillators are in close proximity and beating in nearly the same rhythm there will be a tendency for them to 'lock in' and vibrate with the same rhythmic pattern. Author and lecturer George Leonard explains that the reason for this '...is that nature seeks the most efficient energy state, and it takes less energy to pulse in cooperation than in opposition. Entrainment is so ubiquitous, in fact, that, as with the air we breathe, we hardly notice it.'[7]

Tuning in to others

Oscillators in television sets, radios and other similar equipment are also subject to entrainment. When you adjust the tuning dial on your radio to find your preferred station, you are altering the frequency of the oscillators in the radio. When the frequency of the radio's oscillators gets close to the frequency of the radio station's oscillators, the sudden locking together that occurs is as a result of entrainment.

Like radios, human beings are subject to the phenomenon of entrainment too, because our vibrating organs are like in-built oscillators. Moreover, entrainment takes place not just through the sounds that we can detect through our ears. We also detect sounds through our skin and even bone conduction, as Dr Alfred Tomatis discovered.[8] Also, our other senses, like sight, smell and touch, enable us to perceive an even wider range of vibrations that our ears simply cannot detect.[9] The implications of this is quite profound because it means that our environment and the people we encounter have the potential to alter our own vibratory pattern. For instance, someone with a very powerful vibratory pattern can, therefore, affect many others. This has been shown through scientific research done some years ago at Boston University's School of Medicine by Dr William S. Condon.

Using a technique known as microanalysis, Dr Condon was able to observe the remarkable 'dance' that takes place between a speaker and the listener. After filming two people in conversation (at 48 frames per second) then breaking down the film to reveal every micro-movement of both the speaker and listener, Condon matched these with the tiny units of syllables of the speaker's voice. After meticulously reviewing the film, together with the tiny units of speech, he learnt that the listener responds to the words and actions of the speaker in an often very subtle but nonetheless discernible way. In one case, Condon reviewed film of a four and a half second conversation for a year and a half (and in the process wore out 130 copies of the film!) that confirmed his findings.[10]

However, Dr Condon's research shows more than a listener simply reacting to the subtle sounds and movements of a speaker. At the fundamental vibratory level the ubiquitous phenomenon of entrainment automatically takes place. This means, of course, that the listener is not merely reacting to a speaker in a outwardly way only but also that, in a very real sense, the listener and the speaker become *one* resonant system as individual vibratory patterns synchronize. For Leonard, this is unambiguously clear '...when there is silence in one of the conversations filmed by Dr Condon. *At the precise 1/48 second the speaker resumes talking, the listener begins his or her series of synchronized movements.* Exactly how this is possible cannot be explained in terms of conventional psychology or physical theory.'[11]

Entrainment, therefore, not just at a physical level but also at the deeper spiritual level of consciousness itself, provides a scientific explanation for the efficacy of all vibratory therapy. The rhythm of the voice, the rhythm of the breath, the rhythm of the heart-beat, the rhythm of various bodily functions, as well as the more subtle rhythms of cells and molecules, and ultimately the rhythm of consciousness are all subject to the phenomenon of entrainment.

Thus, we can see how music, as well as people who we are in close contact with, can exercise such a powerful influence on the rhythms of our bodies, minds and souls. As stated earlier, the influence can either be positive or negative, depending upon the type of vibration to which we are exposed. Music, for instance, can stimulate or calm us, or even create discord by disrupting our natural spiritual vibratory pattern. Illness, therefore, can be seen to be a phenomenon of disharmony in our own vibratory pattern, and which the vibratory pattern of music is capable of addressing. Put another way, it's disharmony and dis-ease that result in disease. This is a view reinforced by the German poet, Novalis (1772–1801), who was a brilliant man educated in law, science and philosophy. He asserted that any sort of '...sickness is a musical [vibratory] problem. The healing, therefore, is a musical resolution. The shorter the resolution, the greater the musical talent of the doctor.'[12]

Musical Medicine

Classical music, which to a degree is said to mirror the musical tones of the Audible Life Stream, has been proved to have remarkable therapeutic qualities for a wide variety of physical and emotional conditions. In fact, since ancient times music has been linked with gods and with healing. The ancient Greek god

Apollo was not only considered the Sun god but also the god of music. His son, Asclepius, was deemed the god of medicine and healing. Hence, the ancient Greeks believed music had the power to heal not only the body but also the soul. According to Greek mythology, Apollo gave Orpheus a lyre and was instructed by the muses, the nine celestial sisters who presided over song, as to how to play it.

Plato apparently attached a great deal of importance to the beneficial effects of music, particularly in psychotherapy and education. He wrote:

Music is a moral law. It gives a soul to the universe, wings to the mind, flights to the imagination, a charm to sadness, gaiety and life to everything. It is the essence of order, and leads to all that is good, just, and beautiful, of which it is the invisible, but nevertheless dazzling, passionate, and eternal form.[13]

Plato's sagacious pupil, Aristotle, believed there are also various positive functions of music, including as a mechanism for emotional catharsis. Even in earlier times, Pythagoras believed certain melodies and harmony could have purifying and healing influences on human behavior and are the means to facilitate the harmonizing of body, mind and soul. It's believed he calmed his students at the end of each tiring day with soothing music. And each morning he purportedly sang special songs and played exquisite melodies to remove any sleepiness from them. It's also said that on one occasion, when Pythagoras was at first unable to reason with a drunk man who was intent on setting fire to a house as an act of revenge, he succeeded in pacifying him by means of melodious music. Pythagoras aptly called his method musical medicine.

Scriptures also contain references to the healing power of music. In the Old Testament there is a reference to David expelling an evil spirit from Saul with music:

> And whenever the evil spirit from God was upon Saul, David took the lyre and played it with his hand; so Saul was refreshed, and was well, and the evil spirit departed from him.[14]

The Medicine of Mozart

In our modern era, one of the most famous exponents of music therapy is American Don Campbell, who discovered that the compositions by Mozart, in particular, are most efficacious in bringing the body into harmony and recharging the brain. He outlined the healing potential of Mozart's music in his book, *The Mozart Effect*. Why the music of Mozart is specifically able to achieve this is difficult to pin down. But Campbell observes that the simplicity and purity of Mozart's rhythms and melodies, together with the optimum high frequencies, all combine to establish the ideal atmosphere in which healing can take place— more so, according to Campbell, than the beautiful but largely more complex compositions of other great classical composers.

Innovative research into the effects of Mozart's music has been carried out at the University of California's Center for Neurobiology of Learning and Memory. Researchers found that 36 undergraduates from the psychology department scored eight to nine points higher on the spatial IQ test after listening to 10 minutes of Mozart's *Sonata for Two Pianos in D Major*. Although the effects of the limited exposure to the music only lasted some 15 minutes, the research team concluded that there was a strong relationship between listening to music and spatial reasoning. Follow-up studies have substantiated the original findings. The logical conclusions were that listening to Mozart's compositions helps 'organize' brain functioning, especially creative right-brain processes associated with spatial-temporal reasoning. This means that one's ability to focus and concentrate on a particular task is improved. And no matter what field of endeavor one may be engaged in, concentration is the number one key factor to achieving success. This is an important point to which we shall return in Chapter 11.

Findings at the University of California correlate with those of the late Dr Tomatis, who saw the magic of Mozart's music calm his patients with learning and/or communication difficulties, allowing them to express themselves more clearly. While Dr Tomatis knew that the music of other classical composers had a similar effect, he found that Mozart's compositions achieve the best results.

A Sonic Tonic

Dr Tomatis' lifetime of research into the function of the ear and sound also enabled him to identify that a particular range of sounds recharge the brain and, therefore, act as a sonic tonic for the whole body. He learnt that high frequency sounds, generally between 3,000 and 8,000 hertz, are the most effective in energizing the brain because sounds within this range affect memory, spatial perception and thinking. Moreover, he believed that the ear translates all the energy impulses that come from all parts of the body, directly to the brain. Consequently, he proved that for someone to remain wide awake the brain requires at least three billion (that's 1 followed by 9 zeros) stimuli per second for at least four and a half hours per day.[15]

Gregorian chanting, as practiced by Benedictine monks, is another form of vibratory therapy that Dr Tomatis utilized because not only does it contain all the frequencies within the spectrum of the human voice (approximately 70 to 9,000 cycles per second) but also because it comprises frequencies within the upper range for normal talking. It's this range which gives a voice its timbre, and it's the timbre of a voice—its rich overtones—that imbibe the charging stimuli. Dr Tomatis saw for himself the disastrous effect on Benedictine monks when they were disconnected from this charging stimuli through their chanting.

Normally, Benedictine monks chant for between six and eight hours a day. However, in the late 1960s a new abbot at one of the French monasteries believed there was no necessity for such monastic indulgences, which is how he regarded the chanting tradition. The residing abbot believed that by rendering the chanting ritual obsolete there would be more time available for what he perceived to be more important duties. However, soon after discarding the daily chanting practice, the monks began to feel increasingly fatigued. So concerned about this were they that they met to discuss the matter and decided the reason was that they were getting insufficient sleep. Consequently, they changed their daily schedule by retiring to bed earlier. But as most people know, excessive sleep only makes one feel more tired the next day. This is exactly what the monks discovered.

They then consulted physicians. One concluded that the monks were under-nourished because they were vegetarians. But what the good doctor didn't realize, or chose to ignore, was that the Benedictine Order has been vegetarian since at least the twelfth century. Notwithstanding this, the desperate monks added meat to their diet. Understandably, this only made them feel worse, and the reason for this will be shown in Chapter 10.

When Dr Tomatis was eventually consulted, he discovered 70 out of the 90 monks 'slumping in their cells like wet dishrags.'[16] He assessed their listening skills and reintroduced their legendary chanting schedule. Within six months, almost all the monks felt they were back to their normal levels of energy.

Not only did the chanting energize the monks, but the slow rhythm and lack of tempo that is characteristic of Gregorian chant tranquillized them too, and anyone who is familiar with this form of chanting will know that listeners are calmed also. The chanters' slow rhythm of breathing actually induces those listening into the same breathing pattern as Dr Tomatis explained:

...if you take an *Alleluia* for example, you have the impression that the subject never breathes. This slowest possible breathing is a sort of respiratory yoga, which means that the subject must be in a state of absolute tranquility in order to be able to do it. And by inducing the listener to enter into the same deep breathing, you lead him little by little to something of the same tranquility.[17]

While therapists like Dr Tomatis and Campbell have used vibratory therapy to treat people all over the world who have been afflicted with a variety of psychological, physiological and neurological disorders, including: hearing loss, speech impediments, acute pain, stress and a range of other serious physical and psychological conditions, they, like other therapists haven't failed to appreciate the spiritual significance of sound/music. Dr Tomatis, for example, considers listening (as distinct to hearing) to be the 'royal route' to the divine. And Don Campbell's amazing experience on the brink of death seems to poignantly illustrate the healing power of the Audible Life Stream, which he refers to as a mysterious 'inner sound' thereby intimating of its spiritual nature.[18]

Healed by the Audible Life Stream

Campbell's moving story begins when he was diagnosed with a large, precariously positioned blood clot under his skull that developed after an accidental knock to his head. For weeks he had suffered increasingly intense headaches, flashing lights and acute visual impairment. His right eye-lid became swollen and he could barely continue working. A specialist later confirmed that the blood clot was the cause of Campbell suffering from Horner's Syndrome, a condition whereby the fifth cranial nerve associated with the nerves in the eye and eyelid, is inflamed.

When Campbell first consulted a specialist he underwent a brain scan in a Magnetic Resonance Imager (MRI) at the Kaiser

Permanente Center in Denver. He spent two hours in the tube that he describes as something between a giant tin can and a space capsule. It was during this time in the MRI that he unexpectedly first perceived what could only have been the Audible Life Stream as an array of tones, rhythms and vibrations. He also experienced travelling through tunnels of spiritual light and sound, as well as having visions, notably like countless NDE and OBE percipients. Significantly, as Campbell explains, he heard the sounds with some perceptual faculty other than his ears because he realized the sounds emanated from within himself:

> I began to hear sounds, loud hammers that turned into loud drums...the drumbeats that shot through me were among the most compelling manifestations of sound, vibration, and magnetism I had ever experienced... But it wasn't my ears that were hearing all this. It seemed as if my entire body were [sic] being tuned into one spiritual FM station after another and now played back some vital truth that was already encoded inside me.[19]

The MRI scan confirmed that a blood clot was a major threat to Campbell's life. He and his specialist were concerned that the clot would dislodge and travel via the blood-stream to the brain, causing a massive stroke. Consequently, he was given three options: (1) undergo major surgery as soon as possible, which would mean removing a third of his skull on the right side of his head, but no guarantees of success could be given; (2) be admitted into hospital for a six to eight week period and be monitored on an hourly basis; or (3) wait a few days to see if his condition would improve. Having faith in the body's ability to heal itself and being unprepared for major surgery, Campbell chose the third option.

Understandably, the possibility of a stroke and even death

made him acutely reflective by the time he returned home. He knew that if he was going to be healed he would need to rely on every ounce of his more than a decade of experience as a sound therapist, and much more.

The next day he cautiously did some humming and toning exercises which helped calm him. Seeking further assistance to facilitate his own healing, the following day he phoned Jeanne Achterberg, the mind/body researcher who has authored a number of books on imagery and healing. Achterberg assisted Campbell for almost two hours to create imagery in his mind to ignite his own healing potential. At the start of the conversation he wanted to use the imagery of flowing water but Achterberg warned against this, believing it might incite a stroke. She urged him to create another image.

After concentrating deeper, Campbell again seemed to have unexpectedly contacted the Audible Life Stream, as an image of him sitting on a wooden chair in a wooden-floored room near an open window filled his mind. In the image, a lace curtain gently waved in a cool breeze brushing against the right side of his head where the clot was dangerously located. Campbell knew instantly that the image was appropriate and, interestingly, it was preceded by what must have again been the Audible Life Stream because he realized that the mysterious sound was not a physical sound. He, in fact, remarks that the sound he perceived was inaudible, clearly alluding to the fact that the Audible Life Stream is not perceived by the physical ears.[20]

Several days later, Campbell was feeling a little better so he fulfilled an engagement to give a series of lectures at the New York Open Center, an organization dedicated to holistic learning. Campbell's audience was so large he was forced to rent a larger room in a nearby building. During the morning session, he was suddenly overwhelmed by an unexpected burst of energy that forced him to sit down in a chair near a window. At that instant he realized that he '...was actually sitting in a wooden chair, next to an open window, in a wooden-floored room where a lace curtain was ever so gradually moving near the right side of my face...the overpowering sense of that image and the inner sound came over me.'[21]

Three weeks later, the headaches that had plagued him had subsided and he was feeling a good deal better. But he still needed to undergo a second series of exhaustive medical tests, including another session in the MRI tube. Inside the tube, he once again unexpectedly heard the mysterious songs, chants and drumming. Checking the results, the radiologist was amazed to find that the life-threatening blood clot had reduced in size significantly. Campbell's life was no longer in danger from the clot and he intuitively believes that it was the 'music of the spheres' that actually healed him.[22]

Regarded by mystics as the most powerful force in the universe, the Audible Life Stream is believed to purify gross levels of mind of all karmic dross. In using the Arabic word *sawt-e-sarmad* to refer to the Audible Life Stream, the Sufi teacher, Inayat Khan, affirmed:

> Those who are able to hear the *sawt-e-sarmad* and meditate on it are relieved from all worries, anxieties, sorrows, fears and disease, and the soul is freed from captivity in the senses and in the physical body. The soul of the listener becomes the all-pervading consciousness, and his spirit becomes the battery which keeps the whole universe in motion.[23]

Nevertheless, mystics caution about seeing the Audible Life Stream solely as a substitute for medicine prescribed by doctors. Certainly, by tuning into it, our physical bodies can be healed as Don Campbell's experience shows, but there are so many karmic factors involved that it's futile trying to consciously heal oneself in this way. It should also be noted that mystics are concerned only with our spiritual condition. And with good reason, considering that every man, woman and child that is born will at some time be struck down with the always fatal disease we know of as death. Every year countless millions contract the condition. Sometimes there may be no symptoms, with death striking swiftly without warning. At other times it may linger for weeks, months and even years. The greatest medical doctors cannot help us resist the Lord of Death because, in truth, they are unable to help themselves. Inevitably, they too will one day succumb to the same deadly illusion.

Yet, say the mystics, there has always been an antidote— abundantly available—and within each and every one of us. But while the magic serum is within our keeping, we still require expert help for it to be administered correctly. As with the taking of any form of potent medication, we need to consult trusted and suitably qualified people. Concerning the disease of death, the same wisdom applies. Thus, those who have the deepest spiritual understanding of death and dying are, in a very real sense, doctors of the soul. It's believed that these doctors of the soul have penetrated the mystery of mysteries, having mastered the art of dying while living. So their role in the process of dying while living will be the theme of the next chapter.

9

Sound Physicians of the Soul

No man can reveal to you aught but that which already lies half asleep
in the dawning of your knowledge... If he is indeed wise he does not
bid you enter the house of his wisdom, but rather leads you to the
threshold of your own mind.
Kahlil Gibran (1883–1931) from *The Prophet*

The terms 'master' and 'guru' will likely create an immediate aversion in the minds of those who value their independence. For others, desperate for spiritual guidance, being able to identify someone as their master and guide will engender in them some pride and confidence. Although many believe a master or guru is essential for spiritual development, a word of caution must be given about the choice of master because of the psychological forces that inevitably influence a relationship between a so-called master and their student.

Psychological Research into Obedience and Authority

Social psychologists have conducted some revealing experiments into conformity, compliance and obedience, which highlight some of the influences individuals will likely be faced with when dealing with others in positions of power and authority. Of particular interest are the experiments conducted by American Dr Stanley Milgram in the 1960s into obedience and authority.[1] Although highly controversial because of the serious ethical issues raised by the way the experiments were conducted, Dr Milgram's research is regarded by some as being a key contributor to the field of social psychology. Clearly, his studies have increased our understanding of the forces of destructive obedience to authority figures.

Dr Milgram set-up his study by falsely telling participants he was investigating the effects of punishment on learning. He used two confederates—one as an 'experimenter' who acted as an authority figure, and a second who played the role of a 'learner'. As confederates, both these people knew the true intent of the research. Unaware participants took on the role of a teacher and were told by the authority figure they were to test the learner's memory. However, in testing the learner's memory, participants were then told they had to administer electric shocks of increasing intensity whenever the learner failed to recall something they were expected to have memorized. Fortunately, the learners weren't actually shocked at all, but to convince participants that they were inflicting an electric shock, participants were put in control of an electrical generator with several voltage switches labeled from 15 volts to 450 volts. Electrodes were also pasted to the learners' arms to further strengthen the deception.

Following a script, the confederate learner deliberately made errors of recall which meant participants (as teachers) had to administer 'electric shocks' as instructed. What Dr Milgram did was follow the classic 'foot-in-the-door' sales technique by having the teacher initially give small 'electric shocks' before progressively increasing the voltage.[2] Despite learners screaming hysterically in some instances, as if they were really being shocked, the overwhelming results of the initial study showed that a startling 65 per cent of a group of 40 male participants were prepared to obey the authority figure and inflict what they believed to be high voltage electric shocks to innocent strangers.[3] While it should be said that most participants tried to resist giving the shocks; nevertheless, in the final analysis the results show a high degree of cruel obedience to an authority figure.

Forty women were used in a follow-up study and 65 per cent

displayed the same level of cruel obedience. To the surprise of many, Dr Milgram's experiments were conducted in several countries, sometimes using children, university students and older adults, and the basic findings have always been the same.[4]

Together with the proximity of the experimenter to the participant (or 'teacher') and the experimental procedures followed, the authority figure was also considered a key factor in the level of obedience displayed by participants. This is significant in the context of why many consider a master is necessary for spiritual development because the role that a master plays is essentially one of authority.

Beware of Cult Figures

Consequently, the dangers of accepting an authority figure into one's life in matters spiritual are clearly evident when one considers the harm inflicted on themselves and others by leaders like Marshall Applewhite of the infamous Heaven's Gate cult. In 1997, Applewhite and 38 of his followers committed suicide in California after the leader convinced them they would be taken to the Kingdom of Heaven in a spacecraft trailing the comet Hale-Bopp. Similarly, in 1978 Jim Jones, the leader of the People's Temple cult, and over 900 of his followers committed suicide in Jonestown, Guyana. And more recently, in March 1995 followers of Shoko Asahara, leader of the Aum Supreme Truth sect in Japan, obeyed their master and released deadly sarin gas into the Tokyo underground network. The result was that 12 people were killed and thousands of others were injured.

Cleary, the human mind's propensity to obey authority figures under certain situations, its willingness to conform and comply with irrational and murderous orders, make taking on a guru a decision requiring very careful consideration, particularly in light of the fact that many so-called gurus have charismatic personalities. But let's begin our discussion proper about the importance of a guru with some definitions.

The Sanskrit term guru comes from the root word *gri*, which means to speak or utter a sound. Although this probably relates to the fact that in ancient times spiritual teachings were handed down from the master to the student through the spoken word; in a very real sense, only those who actually teach others how to tune into the Audible Life Stream are apt to be called a guru. As Tulsi Sahib, the eighteenth century poet-mystic of India wrote, it's only the true guru who is familiar with the Word, or the Audible Life Stream:

> He who knows the different divine Sounds
> He is indeed a great Saint [Guru].
> He knows the Unknowable,
> He knows the Word.[5]

There are many levels of spiritual teachers and, since one can only reach a level no higher than that of the teacher, it is essential to be guided by a teacher whose level of consciousness is unsurpassed. Mystics emphasize that genuine gurus, having merged their individual consciousness into the Audible Life Stream, are the best qualified for assisting others to penetrate the illusion of death. They are believed to be the only ones who can properly advise others about how to avoid those spiritual sounds which can, in fact, be detrimental. Recall that it was Betty Eadie who, during her NDE, learnt that not all spiritual sound is necessarily beneficial, but that some can do damage.

Jagat Singh (1884–1951), who many regarded as a mystic, offered this advice about the importance of a proper spiritual teacher by using a house as a metaphor for the physical body:

> Try to find someone who knows the secret of the 'house', who has himself been inside it and can take you 'within'. What do we do when we do not know the way to a place? We inquire of someone who knows the way. Likewise, before starting on

our Spiritual Journey within, we have to seek the help of a Perfect Guide. Call him Guru, Master, Friend, Teacher, Guide or Brother; the name makes no difference.[6]

This important tenet is found in many scriptures and mystical literature because, say the mystics, it is an essential element of learning how to die while living. Scholar of religion, Daniel Gold, observes that a teacher or '...guru...can serve as an esoteric master for serious disciples and can, according to his specific tradition, lead them to apparently different kinds of realizations... Both the esoteric and the more popular traditions of holy men [gurus] are found in Hinduism, Buddhism, and Indian Islam.'[7]

We may also consider that Hafiz, the fourteenth century Persian mystic, emphasized the necessity of a spiritual teacher when he wrote:

Do not tread this path without a guide:
There is utter darkness;
Beware of going astray.[8]

In the *Bhagavad-Gita*, Krishna tells Arjuna that only self-realized souls can impart real spiritual knowledge, thereby overcoming the web of illusion:

Just try to learn the truth by approaching a spiritual master... The self-realized souls can impart knowledge unto you because they have seen the truth. Having obtained real knowledge from a self-realized soul, you will never fall again into such illusion...[9]

Also, in the *Adi Granth* it's written:

Let no one be deceived. None will cross the Ocean of the universe without a True Master, a Perfect Guide.[10]

In the same text, it's explained that only one who has found a perfect Audible Life Stream master can firstly connect with the Word and thus shatter the illusion of death:

> And, through the Perfect Guru...his Consciousness is awake to the Word, and he feeds himself upon the Lord's Nectar with abandon.
> He Dies not: yea, he Lives ever,
> And becomes Immortal and Deathless...[11]

Also in the Katha Upanishad we find:

> This sacred knowledge [of death] is not attained by reasoning; but it can be given by a true Teacher.[12]

The Need for a Living Mystic

Clearly, the great mystics of the past, having left the physical realm, are unable to be contacted by most of us. Therefore, their message is open to varied interpretation as history shows. Genuine living mystics, on the other hand, can be seen and heard, they can directly answer questions put to them about death, spirituality, and the essential mystical teachings upon which all religion is based can be revealed. By being in our midst, living mystics are examples of the fact that what they have achieved can also be achieved by others.

Moreover, and of immense importance, is recognizing that someone else is wiser than oneself in matters spiritual, and then being prepared to be advised by that person. This is the first crucial step in stripping the ego of its entrapping power and overcoming the Lord of Death's deceptive spell.

The Hidden Meaning of the Holy Trinity

As noted previously, Jesus was a mystic in Palestine some 2000 years ago. There were mystics before him and there have undoubtedly been mystics after him. His title, 'Christ', means the anointed one. All living mystics are believed to be anointed ones of the universal power—the Audible Life Stream. The title, 'Christ', like 'Messiah', which is central to Jewish belief, are both simply other terms for a living spiritual teacher. As such, it's hardly surprising, there being ample evidence of Jesus making this point throughout Christian scriptures. However, like most of the essential teachings of the great sages, it seems this message has failed to reach the masses.

It can be argued that the concept of the Holy Trinity points to the fact that Jesus emphasized the need for a living spiritual teacher. The Holy Trinity is a fundamental tenet of Christianity that has been debated over for centuries, even causing serious schisms amongst the faithful. This alone highlights the need for a living teacher that no amount of intellectualism could ever replace. Quite simply, it is likely that the lost meaning of the Holy Trinity—being the Father, the Son and the Holy Ghost—is that only a living teacher (the Son) can put one in touch with the God-power (the Father) through the Audible Life Stream (the Holy Ghost). This is possible because all three elements of the trinity are essentially the same if one accepts that living teachers are God-realized souls who have merged their consciousness with the Audible Life Stream. Living mystics are, therefore, considered the necessary intermediaries between the unknown spiritual regions and our physical world.

Many of us wisely engage tour guides to travel in foreign countries because the guides have local knowledge and can consequently ensure the journey is smooth and unhindered. The role of the genuine mystic can be seen in exactly the same way, except their area of expertise is the vast undiscovered country we will all journey to at the time of death.

Being considered to be the personification of the Audible Life Stream, we can see why Jesus' disciples referred to him as the 'Word made flesh' in the Gospel According to John:

And the Word became flesh and dwelt among us, full of grace and truth...[13]

In the same gospel, the author also makes the point that only the Son of God can make God, the Father, known to others because no one has seen God. This is just another way of saying that a living teacher is necessary for making the God-principle known to others:

No one has ever seen God; the only Son, who is in the bosom of the Father, he has made him known.[14]

Recently discovered scriptures also make it evident that Jesus made it quite clear that a living teacher is of paramount importance for unveiling the mystery of death. This contentious claim is substantiated in the Gospel of Thomas, which is part of the revealing *Nag Hammadi* codices discovered in Egypt only in 1945 by two brothers collecting rich soil for their fields. These 12 manuscripts that the farmers found were buried in an earthenware pot that was sealed with bitumen, indicating that someone went to great lengths to conceal them. The reason for this is apparent when we consider that the documents present the teachings of Jesus in an undeniable mystical light, clearly contradicting the official views ratified by the religious authority of the time.

The Gospel of Thomas is essentially a collection of Jesus' sayings. In it we find Jesus giving his disciples stern advice about the importance of seeking a living teacher, which he calls the 'Living One', before they die:

Take heed of the Living One while you are alive,
lest you die and seek to see him
and be unable to do so.[15]

Even in the New Testament gospels, Jesus makes it very clear that he can only help other physical beings while in the physical world. He tells his disciples:

> As long as I am in the world, I am the light [the living mystic] of the world.[16]

The *Dhammapada*, a Hinayana scripture that's believed to consist of the important sayings of the Buddha, contains the same advice. In the following aphorism, the Buddha tells us to associate with one who is spiritually wise, which, of course, can only be done if the sage is actually alive:

> If an intelligent man be associated for one minute only with a wise man, he will soon perceive the truth, as the tongue perceives the taste of soup.[17]

And again in the same document, the Buddha enjoins us to follow a sage whose life is a good example of a saint. Such an example can surely only be validated if the mystic is alive:

> Therefore one should follow the wise, the intelligent, the learned, the much enduring, the dutiful, the noble, one should follow a good and wise man, as the moon follows the paths of the stars.[18]

The fact that Krishna, Buddha and Jesus, like all the other past mystics, are no longer in the world means that others embodying the same universal power are the current 'lights' of the world. And when these lights are extinguished we can expect others to lead the way along the spiritual path. Thankfully, living Audible Life Stream teachers don't only appear once every 2000 years. If this was the case it would seem those born in the intervening years would have a strong case of discrimination to argue.

Instead, living teachers themselves say that there are always mystics in the world, often leading very simple quiet lives away from public attention.

Even the most hardened skeptic can surely accept that without a living Audible Life Stream teacher all we have are scriptures that are often questionably translated and edited. No matter how eloquently written, or how saintly the author, these cannot provide guidance on the inner spiritual planes. Books can give us knowledge but cannot impart wisdom and first-hand experience.

Summing up the pivotal role of the living teacher on the path of spirituality, Daniel Gold concludes:

> The redemptive power of *sants* [gurus] of the past is thus made available through the living guru. His words convey their instructions, explain the meaning of scripture, and make known the will of the highest divine. And as a direct manifestation of the divine guru within everyone, each of the master's actions is weighted with significance.[19]

The Living Teachers Prepare the Way

Therefore, with the guidance of a living Audible Life Stream teacher, it seems both logical and prudent to gain experience of the inner spiritual worlds while alive before we are thrust into this domain at the time of death. Preparation in all things is most wise. In the context of an inevitable death, it's advice that is most apt because, say the mystics, the spiritual journey is fraught with danger and deception. Jesus alluded to these dangers when, in the Gospel According to Matthew, he is quoted as saying:

> For the gate is narrow and the way is hard, that leads to life [beyond death], and those who find it are few.[20]

Rumi reiterated this same point when he wrote:

Seek a Master for this journey;
Without a Master it is full of risks and dangers.[21]

Some of these dangers pertain to the fact that the spiritual journey necessitates an expansion of consciousness that chips away at the wall of 'I-ness'. An Audible Life Stream teacher, both outwardly and inwardly prepares the neophyte for this evolutionary transformation. Even though the sense of 'I' is illusory, hastily shattering this illusion is quite likely to result in delusion and serious mental illness. Without the adequate mental and spiritual preparation that Audible Life Stream teachers offer, messianic hallucinations and/or psychosis are very real possibilities.

Drug-taking is one example where rapid fluctuations of consciousness affecting the sense of 'I-ness' take place. Depending on a number of factors, including the mental disposition of the person and the type and quantity of the drug taken, the experience can be described as something between being highly ecstatic and raw stark terror. Sometimes drug users on a trip believe they have met and communicated with God. Perhaps some have, but the experience definitely cannot be sustained and the risks they take are certainly enormous. More often than not, the consequences are frightening short-term trips that may have disastrous long-term effects on their lives and the lives of their families and friends.

It's not uncommon for drug-users, even first-timers, to develop schizophrenia and other mental disorders. Some may be drawn to suicide, as a direct result of a rapid and completely unprepared expansion in awareness about which they know nothing. In advising about the need to be psychologically prepared for a natural mystical experience, Joseph Campbell sees a mechanical drug-induced experience as something quite different in that '...the one who cracks up is drowning in the water in which the mystic swims. You have to be prepared for this experience.'[22]

Venturing into matters spiritual, which is the greatest journey that we can ever take, should never be embarked upon lightly or approached with selfish motives, because the end result could be disaster. On the other hand, those who are under the wing of a genuine teacher can be secure in the knowledge that the journey will be accomplished without insurmountable turmoil.

Karmic Managers

As a predicate to preventing disturbing scenarios unfolding and providing guidance on the inner planes, it's believed the living mystic mitigates, to varying degrees, the enormous karmic burden that we all bear primarily as a result of countless previous lives. The mystics are said to be able to do this because their level of consciousness is believed to be beyond the levels within which the law of karma functions. Although they have a physical appearance like any ordinary person, the Audible Life Stream teachers' level of consciousness is thought to be beyond that of the average mind. Thus, it's argued that they have shattered the illusions that the ordinary mind perpetuates. So while they respect the law of karma and work within its limitations, mystics are said to be in control of their karma and are believed to not act from an 'I-centered' sense of awareness.

In a letter to a spiritual seeker who, among other things, queried how the law of karma affects an Audible Life Stream, teacher, Charan Singh, replied:

No one can live in this world without karmas. It is our karmas which give us the body in which we live. But the difference between the karmas of the Master and those of an ordinary person is that...Karmas are the masters of ordinary men, whereas the...Masters have complete control over their karmas.[23]

Being in complete control of their own karmic account, it seems that mystics can also manage their students' karmic debts. They do so, it seems, with the utmost wisdom and compassion. Fully realizing that their neophytes must learn important lessons so that past negative deeds will not be repeated, they also know that too severe karmic repercussions can result in an even heavier karmic load for the unprepared. So, in managing their students' karma, the law of causation is still abided by but instead of the debt being paid entirely by the one who originally incurred it, the mystic may deem it appropriate to pay the debt, to varying degrees, on their students' behalf.

One example of this relates to a painful accident suffered by Sawan Singh, while still a student of his teacher, Jaimal Singh (1839–1903). After breaking his leg while trying to mount his horse, Sawan Singh desperately arranged for a telegram to be sent to his master because doctors feared for his life since he could neither defecate nor urinate properly.

After receiving the telegram, it's said that Jaimal Singh went into deep meditation that lasted the entire night. Coming out of his meditative equipoise in the early hours of the following morning, he had a telegram sent to reassure his student that even though the karma was very heavy, he would not die as a result of the accident. The telegram in reply implied that Jaimal Singh had helped mitigate some of Sawan Singh's karma because he would suffer for five months rather than five years as karmic law apparently dictated.[24] The moment the telegram was received, Sawan Singh is said to have been able to defecate and urinate as normal.

However, generally speaking, Audible Life Stream teachers do not interfere with their students' current-life karma for to do so would alter what has already been destined at the time of birth. Yet, the ways of Audible Life Stream teachers and the largely unknowable complexities of karmic law means there can be no hard and fast rule applied in this matter, as the aforementioned incident illustrates.

The Mystics and the Sound are One

Audible Life Stream masters are also believed to fulfill another important role, which is to accompany their students' souls at the time of death when they pass through the spiritual gateway alone. It should be mentioned, however, that those who have learnt how to contact the Audible Life Stream and have earnestly practiced dying while living would probably have already been assured of this, having quite possibly encountered their teacher on the inner planes before actually dying. But for those without this experience, Sawan Singh explained:

> A Master alone knows everything about death. At the time of death, when family and children, our wealth possessions and body, all leave us, it is the Perfect Master alone who accompanies the disciple. For this reason he is our true and genuine friend.[25]

Ultimately, this true friend is the Audible Life Stream. Substantiating this, Charan Singh, using some of the other terms to denote this force, once wrote:

> Our real Master is the Word, the *Logos*, *Shabd*, *Nam*, the Audible Life Stream, or whatever name one may choose to give it. The Master is that Power manifested in human form.[26]

Naturally then, it's acknowledged that the Audible Life Stream masters' physical vibratory energy is extremely powerful and magnetic, easily capable of entraining the physical and spiritual vibratory pattern of anyone coming into their physical presence to a higher frequency. Some report being soothed and emotionally uplifted in their teacher's presence. Needless to say, the past mystics, having no physical presence, cannot readily provide this type of spiritual and emotional security.

The Masters Find You

So how does one then recognize a genuine living mystic among so many false ones—the infamous so-called 'wolves in sheep clothing' that we have all heard about? Well, in fact, it's perfectly true to say that just as you may be eagerly searching for the Audible Life Stream teacher, the teacher is just as keenly 'searching' for you—after all this is why they are here. The ancient edict: 'When the student is ready, the master will appear' is as true today as it has always been. But this doesn't mean that someone wishing to be taught how to die while living can sit at home waiting patiently for a knock at the door. Certainly the mystics are searching for those who seek liberation from the clutches of the Lord of Death but not in the sense that they will do letter-box drops or go door-knocking. Moreover, it would be expecting too much to find an advertisement in the telephone directory under the heading 'Living Audible Life Stream Teachers'. Rather, genuine masters don't need to do such things because their search is not a physical one but instead a spiritual one—far superior to the best mass marketing techniques that are employed in the corporate world today. And for those seeking a genuine mystic, the search will normally preclude dangerous solo treks though remote mosquito-infested jungles or oxygen depleted snow-capped mountains. But somehow, no doubt through an infinitely complex spiritual network, when the seeker is ready the teacher will assuredly be found. Just as bees can instinctively hone in on the sweet nectar of a flower that other insects are ignorant of, the sweet scent of the nectar of truth is always intuitively detected by sincere spiritual seekers.

Yet, finding an Audible Life Stream teacher may not necessarily mean in the physical sense of a meeting, although there's no reason why this isn't possible. But since mystics have only one physical body, it's more likely one will at least become aware of them through their timeless message. Sometimes we may be aware of a mystic but will not be drawn to them, or else doubt their spiritual acumen because of one's unpreparedness for the spiritual path. Others may spend a whole lifetime searching for a teacher and will recognize one immediately. But even if the search takes a whole lifetime and does not result in evident success, mystics themselves say, that time spent earnestly seeking for a teacher is not wasted because the exercised sincerity will definitely produce fruit in a future birth.

Recognizing a True Mystic

Since there are so many so-called spiritual teachers in the world today, mention can be made of some very general characteristics of a true mystic. Dr Julian Johnson presents his views of such characteristics in his book, *The Path of the Masters*. These characteristics should in no way be seen as a rigid set of criteria in determining a true mystic from a false one because even Audible Life Stream teachers have varying personalities despite apparently rising above the illusion of 'I-ness'. Let's remember that all who attain the highest level of consciousness become perfect instruments of a divine will, whose sense of diversity is apparent in the world around us. Thus, mystics shouldn't be expected to be akin to robotic clones.

So, notwithstanding relatively minor personality differences and acknowledging that intellect alone cannot judge someone to be a mystic or not, all genuine mystics will earn their own living and will, therefore, not ask for any money in return for revealing the secret of life and death. This, apparently, is a universal law. In a world where the worth of something is measured only by its dollar value this will seem most unusual. Many believe that if something is free then it must be worthless. Yet, when it comes to rediscovering the soul one should ask: what value can be placed on something that is priceless? Moreover, the true mystics say that they don't give others anything that we don't already have. Realization of the immortality of spirit is not a commercial commodity that can be bought and sold like a car or a piece of jewelry. Instead, it is our inherent nature. Mystics merely reveal to their students how to rediscover their innate spiritual nature so that they too can become mystics in their own right.

A second characteristic of genuine mystics is that they will never speak boastfully about any personal spiritual attainments. Oneness with the Audible Life Stream equates to perfect unity with the entire cosmos, so to consider oneself better than others belies this realization. A more subtle aspect of this is that mystics won't advertise their apparent humility for public attention. Genuine humility can be judged against a so-called mystic's behavior in trying circumstances, or conversely when among devoted followers full of praise. To determine if behavior is genuinely humble, carefully considered observation of the person will be required. Also, true sages should never be violent or spiteful for this would be counter to the tenet of compassion.

While many regard someone who performs 'miracles' (which may, in fact, simply be undetected magic) as being highly spiritually evolved, a true mystic should never display their spiritual powers publicly as a means to attract followers. Such displays are a contradiction to any sense of genuine humility. Mystics are not entertainers who perform like stage-show magicians.

Finally, the true mystic will instruct their students in the art of dying while living by teaching them how to tune into the Audible Life Stream. Anyone in a position of being a so-called spiritual leader but who does not teach this process, may well be highly evolved but they can't be said to be a master of the highest order. There is no logical reason to seek the assistance of a pharmacist (or drug-dispenser) rather than a fully qualified medical physician when disease threatens one's life. It's surely sensible to engage an expert in the field if one wants the best diagnosis and treatment. The same reasoning applies for treading the path of spirituality and learning how to die fully conscious.

Yet, it must be added that not all those who purportedly teach others how to contact the Audible Life Stream and how to die while living are necessarily genuine mystics. Just as there are always genuine teachers in the world, there are also those who have only reached a limited level of spiritual attainment but who, for various reasons, believe they can guide others. This doesn't imply that such people are deliberately out to deceive others as to their spiritual acumen. Unfortunately, some perhaps are, but often these less than perfect teachers are sincere people who may truly believe that they are fully qualified masters of the Audible Life Stream, however, who are sadly really just deluded. This, of course, highlights the countless hidden traps in which the ego can be ensnared anywhere along the inner journey.

In addition, researchers of cults also give the following advice: avoid becoming involved with groups lead by charismatic leaders who make outlandish promises and are erratic in their behavior; avoid attributing to the so-called guru or their senior followers an infallibility that negates rational questioning of what they say and do; and be watchful of those who endeavor to use guilt, shame and fear to de-individuate others.[27]

Taking these points into consideration, it may also be prudent when trying to decide if someone is a genuine mystic, to look at their background. Unimportant details like what country they come from, their gender, or whether or not they are physically appealing can be ignored. However, the sort of lifestyle that they lead and have led prior to taking on the mantle of mastership is worth considering, as is whether they had a genuine master who instructed them on their spiritual journey.

Yet caution should be exercised in expecting a genuine mystic to have an unbroken lineage of teachers that can be traced all the way back to Jesus or Buddha, for example. Obviously, the lack of properly documented evidence makes such an expectation impossible to fulfill. Also, one needs to bear in mind that mystics can apparently appear at any time and in any region of the world depending on the demand of sincere seekers and the conjunction of favorable karmic circumstances.

In the case of Jesus, he too would have had a teacher. As author and scholar of mysticism, John Davidson, asserts, 'Jesus...like all other Masters, would most certainly have had a Master and the individual most likely to have been his teacher was one who flits mysteriously in and out of the pages of the gospels—John the Baptist.'[28]

If one accepts that John the Baptist was a master of the Audible Life Stream, he would have performed an important job that all mystics perform, which is to baptize (as his name suggests) spiritual seekers, although it is not always referred to as this. In the modern era it is more commonly referred to as initiation. Christians understandably regard baptism with great importance because, being the first religious rite in a person's life, it establishes and theoretically shapes one's spiritual destiny after death. Other religions have similar rites to which they attach equal importance. Mystics, on the other hand, regard the modern-day ritualistic interpretation of baptism that's perpetuated by most religious traditions as being inaccurate and without any spiritual substance. Consequently, baptism, as performed today, is regarded by mystics as having no spiritual benefit for preparing for the after-life. This is yet another highly contentious issue requiring a more detailed argument. Genuine mystics believe that baptism, or initiation, is a very necessary step in learning how to die while living. So in the following chapter the true mystical meaning of baptism, its correct spiritual significance, and what should really take place at such an important event will be outlined.

10

The Journey of Death

The father came back from the funeral rites. His boy of seven stood at
the window, with eyes wide open and a golden amulet hanging from
his neck, full of thoughts too difficult for his age. His father took him
in his arms and the boy asked him, 'Where is mother?'
'In heaven,' answered his father, pointing to the sky.
...The boy raised his eyes to the sky and long gazed in silence. His
bewildered mind sent abroad into the night the question, 'Where is
heaven?'
No answer came: and the stars seemed like the burning tears of that
ignorant darkness.

Rabindranath Tagore (1861–1941) from *The Fugitive*

Some religious traditions enact a form of baptism that was originally a deeply spiritual initiation into the mysteries of death.
Today, however, it's true to say that the process is merely a ritual,
full of sincerity and often deep emotion, but empty of real
spiritual significance. For example, people ceremonially 'take
refuge in the three jewels' (the Buddha, the *dharma* or teachings,
and the *sangha* or community of Buddhists) to become
Buddhists. Interestingly, the use of water is central to Christian
baptism. Millions of Christians around the world regard the rite
of baptism as taking a 'new birth', which many believe makes for
a type of down-payment for a reservation into the so-called
kingdom of heaven. Based on the belief that John the Baptist
immersed people into the flowing waters of the river Jordan,
today would-be Christians queue up to be plunged into
swimming pools, lakes, rivers and even oceans, believing that
they will be spiritually 'born again' by doing so. But does it seem

logical that something as profound as spiritual communion can be foreshadowed by an outward and highly ceremonial dunking? It seems most unlikely if one fully appreciates the mystical tenets of spirituality. As is often the case, the correct spiritual meaning of the words of the past mystics understandably eludes those who are uninitiated into the mysteries of life and death by a genuine Audible Life Stream teacher. Of genuine spiritual initiation, the ancient Greek philosopher, Plutarch (c.46–120) wrote that when one dies '...the soul experiences the same impressions and passes through the same process as is experienced by those who are initiated into the Great Mysteries.'[1]

The Water of the Audible Life Stream

In contrast to this, it seems most apparent that the ritualistic religious baptisms that are performed today around the world stem from a misunderstanding of genuine spiritual initiation. Accordingly, proper spiritual initiation precludes all outward ceremony and ritual. Moreover—aqua-phobics can be securely assured—with proper spiritual initiation one stays firmly on *terra firma* because there is no need for any physical substance like water within a process that is purely spiritual in nature. As Jesus himself is quoted as saying:

> That which is born of the flesh [physical matter] is flesh; and that which is born of the Spirit is spirit.[2]

Recall that in Chapter 6 the New Testament was also cited with a quote attributable to Jesus in which he says that to be born anew one needs to hear the spirit, comparing it to the sound of the wind—precisely how people who reported NDEs and OBEs in earlier chapters described their respective experiences of the Audible Life Stream:

> The wind blows where it wills, and you hear the sound of it,

but you do not know whence it comes or whither it goes; so it is with everyone who is born of the Spirit.[3]

Furthermore, the sacred writings of an extant Gnostic sect called the Mandaeans, that regards John the Baptist as a savior, also reveal that the word 'water', mentioned therein, has a deeper spiritual meaning than just ordinary water. This particular sect, like the others of the time and region, used the term 'jordan' to refer to any river or stream, and in this case it's almost certain that it's the Audible Life Stream to which their scriptures refer.[4] So, in all likelihood, being baptized in the 'Jordan' really meant a spiritual immersion not a physical one. But like other religious adherents it seems the Mandaeans, who today are found in border regions between Iraq and Iran, are unaware of the deeper spiritual meaning imbedded in their scriptures.

Mystics throughout history have associated the audible essence of the universe with water because when apprehended, it can sound very much like a moving body of water—and this is perhaps one reason why it is referred to as a 'stream'. Sometimes it can be perceived like a rushing river, sometimes like a gentle stream, or even the rolling waves of an ocean. And, of course, the best way to explain a mystical concept to someone is to put it in symbolic terms to which the person can readily relate. The fact that water is essential for sustaining physical life also makes it an apt symbol for the Audible Life Stream that is the underlying sustenance of spiritual life.

Die to be Born Again

It's accepted by students of mysticism that proper spiritual initiation, when mystics reveal the way to tune into the Audible Life Stream, is the first step in actively becoming aware of our innate spiritual lives. It has been traditionally regarded as a 'new birth' because initiates are given the means by which to reveal their spiritual lives. One is effectively born anew to the spirit. So to be truly born again spiritually, the key is to be in touch with the spiritual water of the Audible Life Stream and not, as it's believed by many today, submersed into the material water of this world.

Being purely of spiritual significance, void of ritual, at the time of Audible Life Stream initiation, mystics say an eternal spiritual link is established between themselves and their initiates. It's through this link, which mystics advise is maintained even beyond the death of their physical bodies and that of the initiates, that the teacher guides their students on the inner planes as well as manages their karmic accounts.

Reducing the Burden of Karma

Mystics emphasize that whether this link is a strong one or not is primarily dependant upon the initiate's ethical disposition. Hence, sages will usually request potential initiates to carefully consider a simple set of moral guidelines that ensure the spiritual link is firmly established and maintained. In this respect, never will a genuine mystic rush a potential initiate into making a decision about whether to be initiated or not. Rather, they will advise the spiritual seeker to be absolutely convinced that they are ready to accept the moral guidelines and the mystic, regardless of how long such convictions take to be engendered. The guidelines basically constitute an important foundation of adequate preparation for the spiritual journey.

One can be assured, however, that learning to die while living will not require the abandonment of our secular existence. Nor should anyone expect to swap their suburban plot for an unserviced cave in the hills, shave one's head and acquire a begging bowl, or even take a vow of celibacy. Nevertheless, ethical codes of conduct, although being perfectly rational and reasonable, will be seen by some to be outside of the norm of most Western societies where the gratification of the senses is actively promoted and the sense of 'I' is overtly encouraged. But it's clearly senseless for anyone wishing to reach the pinnacle of wisdom and realize the secrets of life and death to continue feeding the ego by engaging in negative behavior like deceit, theft, drug abuse, or any form of violence (directly or indirectly). To this end, genuine mystics will outline the two most important prerequisites for receiving initiation which are:

1. A vegetarian diet (lacto-vegetarian or vegan).
2. Avoidance of mind-altering substances, including recreational drugs like alcohol.

Despite its widespread social acceptability, it important to consider that alcohol is a toxic substance that has been shown to kill brain cells, and thus severely affects brain function in the short and long term. It is also highly addictive and impairs one's ability to focus the attention and concentrate—the significance of this will be made clear in Chapter 11.

Vegetarianism and Spirituality

As to the vegetarian diet: consider that the word vegetarianism, that was first coined in 1847 by the founding members of the Vegetarian Society of Great Britain, was done so not because it depicts the fact that people practicing the ethos eat mainly vegetables, but because it comes from the Latin word *vegetus* meaning to feel lively.[5] Following a plant-based diet, lively is exactly how the founders of the society felt, as should anyone who follows a balanced vegetarian diet. Ideally, the vegetarian diet should be based on organic products because, if for no other reason, the science shows that conventional food is simply unsafe. The US Food and Drug Authority has acknowledged that at least 53 carcinogenic pesticides are used liberally on conventional crops.[6] In other countries, like Australia, conventional farmers are known to also use unsafe pesticides, in addition to antibiotics and growth hormones, on their produce. The same would be true in many other countries.

Also, the ecological and health benefits of being vegetarian have been well documented. The worldwide network of vegetarian societies can provide detailed information about this. But briefly, it's worth mentioning that the increasingly limited resources required to sustain animals for slaughter, like land (usually precious rain forests) and water, is many times greater than is necessary to support plant-based farming industries. Author, Keith Ackers, makes some sobering comments about this:

> Land, energy, and water requirements for livestock agriculture range anywhere from 10 to 1000 times greater than those necessary to produce an equivalent amount of plant foods. And livestock agriculture does not merely *use* these resources, it *depletes* them... Most of the world's soil erosion, groundwater depletion, and deforestation—factors now threatening the very basis of our food system—are the result of this particularly destructive form of food production.[7]

Quantifying this gross inefficiency, research has found that to produce one kilogram (2.2 pounds) of beef that can feed at most four people, feed-lot cattle need to consume 16 kilograms (35.2 pounds) of beans or grain. The same quantity beans or grain could adequately feed 80 people directly as wholesome vegetarian fare! This lamentable situation means that about 70 per cent of crops grown in USA need to be fed to animals rather than humans. Meanwhile, starvation claims a life somewhere in the world about every four seconds.[8] And in light of the potential devastating effects of climate change as a result of global warming, consider that the United Nations Food and Agricultural body reported in 2006 that the livestock industry contributes 18 per cent of all greenhouse emissions—more than all forms of transportation, which contributes 13.5 per cent.[9] The livestock industry is a significant contributor to greenhouse gases because of emissions of carbon dioxide (from the burning of fossil fuels), nitrous oxide (from the use of inorganic fertilizers), and methane, which is produced from cattle digestion and manure.[10]

Furthermore, ponder over the fact that a meat-based diet, which is loaded with fat, excessive protein and contains little or no fiber, is linked with many degenerative diseases like heart disease, cancer, osteoporosis and obesity.[11] Needless to say, that the sicker a society is, the greater the financial burden on industry, through losses in productivity and worker absence, as well as society at large. A higher social medical bill forces health service-providing governments to set higher tax rates and, of course, hospital patients themselves have to pay more and more for treatment. In contrast, researchers have learnt that the best illness-preventative medicine available is a well-balanced vegetarian diet because it provides all the nutrients that a human body needs through all stages of its development—millions of people on the Indian sub-continent who are vegetarian from birth are a testament to this.

Naturally though, the mystics are more concerned with the spiritual implications of someone being a link (albeit an indirect one) in the chain of unnecessary violence, in this case, in the form of animal slaughter. In the *Dhammapada*, the Buddha is quoted as saying:

He who, seeking his own happiness, does not injure or kill beings who also long for happiness, will find happiness after death.[12]

Sages contend that even only purchasing the slaughtered animal flesh will incur a negative karmic debt because if there was no demand for the meat there would be no reason to kill the animal for food in the first instance. So the measured karmic justice associated with eating animal flesh will assuredly be meted out at some stage—if in this life then, more often than not, in the form of illness and disease, as over-burdened hospital systems in most Western societies will testify.

Mystics argue that it's quite foolish trying to reduce our karmic burden and raise our level of consciousness without taking the necessary steps to minimize creating new karma. Since it's impossible to avoid creating some new karma during our physical lives—because even the innocuous act of breathing results in millions of microscopic beings being exterminated—mystics say we need to choose the path of *minimum* debt. So while they recognize that even following a vegetarian diet will incur karma, they point out that it is of a much lesser burden than would be incurred in eating the flesh of animals. And, after all, we all need to eat something to maintain healthy bodies. The lesser karmic burden from following a vegetarian diet can be more easily eliminated by contact with the Audible Life Stream, whereas a much heavier burden will make it more difficult to even tune into it in the first place. As Sawan Singh once confirmed:

> There is karma even in vegetable eating, but not so heavy as in animal food. The holy Sound alone is potent enough to wash away karma of all kinds. The lighter the karma, the greater is the attraction of the soul towards the Sound.[13]

Not only does our karmic burden determine how far we can evolve spiritually, but few can reasonably disagree with the mystics' claim that the food we eat also conditions our way of thinking. As Sawan Singh once intimated, non-vegetarian foods perpetuate animalistic tendencies, ensuring the higher spiritual dimensions will likely remain unattainable:

> Meat, eggs (fertile or infertile), and...intoxicants do not suit those who wish to subdue [the] animal nature in them and

who wish to still their mind and gain access to subtle planes.[14]

The Indian mystics like Krishna, Buddha, Guru Nanak and so on, were all strict vegetarians, which is why many Indians are vegetarians today. Many Buddhists would dispute the assertion that the Buddha was vegetarian. However, aside from the extract from the *Dhammapada* (which is a Hinayana Buddhist text) cited earlier in the chapter, Mahayana texts also suggest that the Buddha was vegetarian. For example, in the *Lankavataea Sutra* that dates back to at least AD 443 there is an entire chapter on avoiding meat-eating. During a long discourse with a *bodhisattva* (someone motivated by great compassion to achieve enlightenment), the Buddha purportedly says:

So with Bodhisattvas whose nature is compassion, [the eating of] meat is to be avoided by him.[15]

Further, if one accepts that the Buddha mastered the art of dying while living through the Audible Life Stream (as has been evidenced in Chapter 4) then assuredly he must have been vegetarian.

Jesus the Vegetarian
In the Christian world, the commandment 'Thou shall not kill' is interpreted by most to mean only the prohibition of murder. In fact, recent modern translations of the Bible (for example *The Good News Bible: Catholic Study Edition*, Catholic Bible Press, 1979) have substituted the world 'kill' with 'murder'—proof that changing and editing of the scriptures is continuing and is a good example highlighting how easily the intended original meanings can be altered.

Most in the Christian world would be quite astounded to learn that there is substantial evidence pointing to Jesus having been a vegetarian. If true, he would have undoubtedly taught his followers to abstain from eating meat. In the *Essene Gospel of Peace*, found and translated by Dr Szekely, Jesus is depicted enjoining a sickly group of people to strictly abstain from eating animal flesh if death is to be conquered. Jesus implores the group:

For I tell you truly, he who kills, kills himself, and whoso eats the flesh of slain beasts, eats of the body of death.[16]

In the same document, Jesus later offers advice that corresponds almost word for word to a passage in the Old Testament book, Genesis:

Obey, therefore, the words of God: 'Behold, I have given you every herb bearing seed, which is upon the face of all the earth, and every tree, in which is the fruit of a tree yielding seed; to you it shall be for meat'.[17]

But what of the stories of Jesus eating fish and turning water into wine, may you well ask? Once again it's important to recognize the symbolism used to convey the mystical meaning of such stories, as well as appreciate the fact that there have been many things included and omitted from the scriptures as we see them today. For example, biblical scholar, Reverend V. A. Holmes-Gore, discovered that the use of the word 'meat' in the New Testament gospels doesn't accurately reflect the original Greek words used. The Greek words used include: *broma* (food); *brosis* (the act of eating); *phago* (to eat); *trophe* (nourishment); and others were all translated erroneously to English as 'meat'.[18]

Similarly, wine, like water and even bread are believed to be mystical metaphors for the Audible Life Stream because of its life sustaining qualities and the wine-like sweet 'intoxication' one is said to experience when in communion with it.

The use of the word 'fish' is also believed to have been mistranslated from the original Greek (*ichthus*) because its intended mystical meaning (the Christ) has been totally lost. It's believed that the word *ichthus* was used as a conversational password by the original Christians because it is an acronym for the Greek phrase *Iesous Christos Theou Uios Soter*, which means 'Jesus Christ, Son of God, Savior'.[19]

Other researchers have discovered much evidence supporting the belief that Jesus, as well as John the Baptist, the apostles, Judaic Christians, the Gnostics, and some desert fathers of the time, were all teetotalling vegetarians. Summing up his research into this matter, author and scholar, John Davidson writes in his impressive tome, *The Gospel of Jesus*:

> We have seen, then, that there is considerable evidence that Jesus taught and practiced vegetarianism and abstention from alcohol... And if he really did teach the path of the Creative Word [the Audible Life Stream], then—like all the other mystics of the world who have taught this path—it is certain that he would have been.[20]

Therefore, we can be quite certain that if any so-called spiritual teacher does not follow a vegetarian diet and abstains from alcohol, nor advises their students to do so, while they may have attained a higher spiritual level than most ordinary people, it's highly unlikely that they can be considered Audible Life Stream masters of the highest order.

So, having outlined briefly the broad moral guidelines necessary to walk the spiritual path successfully, what of the initiation itself?

Death's Journey

At the initiation, apart from being taught the ancient technique through which one can practice the process of dying while living by tuning into the Audible Life Stream, an overview of the soul's journey at death is also given. This overview is characterized by the different sounds and lights that the Audible Life Stream manifests as at the various levels of consciousness. These spiritual lights and sounds constitute validating 'sign posts' along the journey of death that are determined by various levels of consciousness. Being levels of consciousness, they are not structured one on top of the other like the ascending storeys of a building. Instead, their dimensions are structured purely on the basis of vibratory frequencies. Mystics speak of five levels of consciousness—the physical realm being the one with the lowest vibratory frequency.

Providing a 'map' of the journey is an important aspect of the initiation because without knowing the complete journey of death many travelers of the inner spheres can be easily deceived into thinking that the end has been reached when, in fact, only the lower levels of consciousness have probably been traversed. This is even true in the physical realm where the vast majority of us consider this world to be all there is to existence. But spiritual travelers guided by the melodious Audible Life Stream know that this world is only the bottom rung in the ladder of consciousness.

The Five Trees of Paradise

Naturally, trying to describe in any detail what is essentially ineffable is really an exercise in futility, which is why the five levels of sound and light make this task somewhat easier. In ancient times, these five levels were described as the Five Trees of Heaven—recall that the term 'tree' is believed to be another mystical metaphor for the Audible Life Stream. Consistent with this notion, in the Gospel of Thomas, reference is made to the Five Trees of Paradise, which is also considered a mystical reference to the five levels of consciousness. In this gospel, Jesus is quoted as saying:

For there are Five Trees for you in Paradise which remain undisturbed summer and winter and whose leaves do not fall. Whoever becomes acquainted with them will not experience death.[21]

Similarly, a third century Iranian mystic known as Mani, who asserted that his teachings were the same as those of Jesus, also referred to the five levels of Creation as the Five Greatnesses.

Today some spiritual leaders speak of more than five levels but this doesn't necessarily mean that they have penetrated deeper into ultimate reality. Ultimate reality is just that— ultimate reality, and nothing more can be added to or taken from its totality. The variances in the number of levels of consciousness just depend upon how the different spiritual regions are 'classified'. For instance, a cake can be cut into halves, or quarters or eighths and so on. But having more pieces doesn't make the cake any larger. Since, historically, great mystics have taught that there are five levels of consciousness it's hardly surprising that most present-day mystics teach the same thing.

As mentioned previously, connecting each of the five levels of consciousness is the Audible Life Stream. Therefore, it is the only means to traverse through the different spiritual regions and from one level to the next.

At the physical level, dense matter interacting with our physical senses establishes the greatest veil of illusion that, for the most part, obscures the Audible Life Stream from being experienced. The mind and the senses are the rulers here and the spirit waits patiently in the tomb of the body for death when it will be freed like a bird once its cage-like prison is destroyed. Here, the mind vibrates at such a low rate that some mystics describe the physical realm as being 'frozen' in comparison to the vastly higher-vibrating spiritual dimensions. Here, attachments to sense gratification are the fuel for the illusion of only a physical world. And the more we relate to the physical world the less we are aware of the spiritual realm. The death of the physical body shuts down the channels for physical sensory input thereby allowing the realm of spirit to be revealed. This is why central to any spiritual path worthy of being pursued should be the practice of dying while living so that acquaintance with the spiritual dimensions can be made before we are forced to travel through death's door totally unprepared.

The Astral Realm

Mystics say that when the physical body finally dies, all souls will encounter the first spiritual realm known as the Astral realm. Where in the Astral realm one finds oneself will be determined by the law of karma, which is why some have described beautiful scenes while others may speak of a foreboding environment. According to the mystics, there are over 100 sub-regions within the Astral realm alone—some very pleasant and heaven-like yet some terribly menacing. Each sub-region is believed to have its own characteristic tone of sound, explaining the different tones that NDE and OBE percipients reported because almost certainly it was to lower levels of the Astral realm where all these people found themselves. As the testimonies showed, without knowledge of how to tune into the Audible Life Stream it is most unlikely one will ascend further.

However, once here, having discarded the physical body, mystics tell us that one's Astral or Light body becomes one's primary vehicle. They say that the Astral body has sense faculties that directly correspond with our physical senses, but which, of course, are sensitive to much higher and finer vibrations. The Astral body is with us even in the physical realm. The colors that some people have the ability to see around others, which are sometimes referred to as an aura, are believed to be the Astral body of the person. The colors and shape of the Astral body accurately reflects the character and emotional state of an individual. Therefore, it's believed that in the Astral world no deception is possible because everyone's true nature is apparent to all others there.

For those practicing dying while living, rising up into the Astral realm consciously on the waves of vibration of the Audible Life Stream, mystics advise that one can expect to see flashes of lights very much like the stars on a clear night sky, or perhaps even like a night-time fireworks display. Suns and moons, like the physical galactic bodies, will also appear. These scenes are the dividing curtain between the physical and Astral realm. The advice from mystics is that when the largest and brightest of these lights becomes centered and bursts open, the luminous or radiant form of the Audible Life Stream teacher who bestowed the initiation will appear and will then guide their student through the spiritual region.

It's believed that, initially, the teacher's radiant form will be identical to the physical form, but as the spirit ascends higher and consciousness becomes more subtle the radiant form will be perceived simply as light and sound. Meeting with one's teacher on the Astral plane is regarded as the proper starting point on the spiritual ascent.

Mystics say that those who die and who were not initiated into the mysteries of death will, in all probability, remain in the Astral realm until the law of karma determines that another physical rebirth is necessary. This may be a very short time or perhaps aeons. On the other hand, those who have been initiated and who have either died finally or temporarily, having contacted the Audible Life Stream as instructed, will have the opportunity to ascend further if the teacher, as manager of all karmic accounts, deems it beneficial for the student's spiritual evolution. Initiation, however, doesn't necessarily preclude future rebirths because the sense of 'I-ness', although more subtle than at the physical level, still prevails within the Astral realm. So, only once all the karma pertaining to the physical and

Astral realms have been eliminated can the spiritual journey continue into higher spiritual spheres.

The Causal Realm

Beyond the Astral realm, say the mystics, is the Causal realm where the Audible Life Stream is of a finer vibration once again. In this region, the soul is said to function within a luminous Causal body, so named because it is in this body where the seeds of karma take root and the illusion of time and 'I' are born. As Sawan Singh explained to his students, within the Causal body '...a perfect record is left of every experience of the individual, running through all the countless ages of his existence. Out of all these experiences character is formed, and from that character all actions flow.'[22]

At the Causal level, mystics say that one is able to fully understand the complex intricacies of the law of karma as it applies to any individual, including oneself, because the fruit of all karmic seeds can be known instantly. Being still within the domain of illusion, although of a much more subtle kind than what we are accustomed to at the physical level (and consequently at the Astral level), the Causal realm is also referred to as the region of universal mind. Consciousness is said to be so powerful in the Causal realm that anything that is imagined manifests immediately. Naturally, with such power it is very easy to get entrapped here fulfilling every kind of desire imaginable. Mystics insist that if not for the help of a genuine Audible Life Stream teacher, whose only objective is for the soul to return to the highest level of consciousness, further ascension would most likely be curtailed by the inevitable pangs of ego-centered desire. Thus, even in this highly elevated region, the soul is still believed to be within the transmigration cycle of birth and death.

So despite being able to enjoy immense pleasures instantly, the fact that the law of karma still applies in the Causal realm means that eventually one would be forced to take a rebirth in the

Astral, and most likely the physical, realms again. It is only beyond the Causal realm, say the mystics, by penetrating the last remaining veil of illusion with the aid of the sound and light of the Audible Life Stream, that the region of pure spirit can be reached.

Bathing in the Pool of Immortality

About the region of pure spirit, the fourth realm of consciousness, the mystics tell us that the soul is immersed into what is termed the Pool of Immortality. At this ineffable level, all ties with the three lower levels of consciousness are said to be severed. The illusions of 'I-ness', time, karma, birth and death have been finally exposed and the soul has achieved liberation— well in a sense. For despite the soul having reached this stage of pure consciousness, unfettered by the dross of ego, the mystics caution that it is still not in perfect vibratory union with the source from which level the Audible Life Stream emanates. Even though, strictly speaking, the law of karma does not apply here, this realm is still said to be subject to a phenomenon known as dissolution.

According to mystics, there are two types of dissolution. The first is believed to occur after several millions of years and includes all the levels of consciousness up to and including the Causal realm. This is somewhat euphemistically known as simple dissolution. The second type of dissolution, known as a grand dissolution, is said to occur after even longer intervals and includes all the realms up to and including even this first region of pure spirit. This concept of dissolution resonates beautifully with new physics theories that predict that the universe will contract and die at some time in the far distant future—the big crunch as noted in Chapter 3. Thus, the collapse, or death, of the physical universe could correspond to either a simple or grand dissolution that would also include other higher levels of consciousness.

Dividing this realm of pure spirit and the next higher and 'final' realm is, according to the mystics, a region of intense darkness. Although it is said that here the light of the soul is so bright that it can be compared to the luminosity of several suns, the darkness is so deep that even this light cannot dispel it. It's believed that only genuine mystics know the way to successfully traverse through this intense blanket of darkness, having been guided through by their respective Audible Life Stream teachers, to the highest level of consciousness.

The Infinite Ocean of Consciousness

Crossing this region of darkness with the aid of the Audible Life Stream, finally the droplet of pure soul is said to completely merge with the infinite ocean of consciousness—the source of the Audible Life Stream. Yet, because it's only at this vibratory level that perfect unity is achieved, at this level of consciousness there is no possibility of an Audible Life Stream concept, or any concept for that matter. Concepts predicate separateness, and this is a misnomer when perfect unity is established. This is made clear by the nineteenth century Indian spiritual teacher, Seth Shiv Dayal Singh (1818–1878), who was regarded by many as a mystic, when he wrote:

> Be it known that in the final region...there is no form, color, or delineation, as we know them here; even the *Shabd* [Audible Life Stream] is not manifested there. No description of the region can be given by word of mouth or by writing. This is the final resting place...[23]

Hence, only at this point can it be said that all is one because one is all. The seeker's soul, the Audible Life Stream, the ocean of consciousness are seamlessly interwoven and lost to each other by an unsurpassed unity often associated with love and bliss generated by infinite inexhaustible levels of pure energy. This must surely be the ineffable of the ineffable.

Not even subject to a grand dissolution, the highest realm of consciousness, the realm of deathlessness, is regarded as unchanging and eternal. As Sawan Singh once related to his students:

> It is the only perfectly pure region. It is the realm of absolutely pure spirit and is the region of Truth, of Ultimate Reality. It knows neither death, nor dissolution, nor change, nor any imperfection. It is the great center about which all other worlds revolve. It is the grand capital of all creation... No sort of understanding of it can be conveyed to human intelligence. From the center of Light, Life and Power, the Great Creative Current...flows to create, govern and sustain all other regions.[24]

At the time of initiation more details of the different levels of consciousness are given. Specifically, this information pertains to the various types of lights and sounds that one can expect to perceive along the complete journey of death. But, of course, this doesn't imply that once one is initiated into the path of the Audible Life Stream that when the physical body finally dies one will be guided all the way to the highest level of consciousness. This is certainly possible but will depend on how well rehearsed one is in the art of dying while living. Obviously, the better prepared one is, the higher the level of consciousness that can be reached. But Audible Life Stream teachers assure their students that whatever level of consciousness one reaches at the time of death, and no matter how many future rebirths may be required in the lower levels of consciousness, one's spiritual journey will continue with their help until the highest level of pure spirit is attained.

The only other element of the spiritual initiation still to be discussed is the scientific methodology by which one can have a foretaste of death while still very much alive. Therefore, in the final chapter we shall examine the scientific basis of the methodology and its two primary principles.

Dying to Truly Live

Meditation and action—he who knows these together,
Through action leaves death behind and through meditation gains
immortality.
The Upanishads

Mystics believe that for discovering the secret of life and death, the mind is the best investigative tool. The simple reason for this is that the mind is the source of the illusion of 'I-ness'. Equally important from the mystics' point of view, is that the mind is also the seat of consciousness, and that consciousness is the most fundamental element of ultimate reality. Regarding the all-pervasive consciousness we temporarily house in our physical bodies as being a microcosm of the infinite universe, the sages' ancient message is that each and every one of us has access to the macrocosm and the ultimate nature of reality.

In its purest form, consciousness is really energy. Energy, scientists know, is an inherent aspect of all physical matter. Einstein's famous formula, $E=mc^2$ (where E=energy, m=mass and c=the speed of light), proves that all physical matter is really bound-up energy.

Mystical Scientists

Although, generally speaking, scientists tend not to equate energy with consciousness as the mystics do, some modern-day physicists do accept that the universe does appear to be like an enormous thought. For example, professor of physics, Freeman Dyson, holds the view that '...it is reasonable to believe in the existence of a...mental component of the universe. If we believe in this mental component of the universe and call it God, then we can say that we are small pieces of God's mental apparatus.'[1]

Also, in the last century, the English astronomer-physicist, Sir James Jeans (1887–1946), wrote that those '...concepts which now prove to be fundamental to our understanding of nature...seem to my mind to be structures of pure thought...the universe begins to look more like a great thought than like a great machine.'[2]

Interestingly, these opinions resonate perfectly with the words of the mystic, Rumi, who hundreds of years ago penned the following:

This world is a single thought of the Universal Intellect; the Intellect is like the king and forms are its messengers.[3]

Professors Dyson and Jeans are certainly not alone among scientists whose open-mindedness has enabled them to see the immense wisdom that imbues the ancient spiritual teachings of the East. In fact, some of the greatest scientists of the twentieth century, like the physicists Einstein (who incidentally was vegetarian in his later life), Prof. Erwin Schrodinger (1887–1961), mathematician Dr Kurt Godel (1906–1978) and others, were well-known for their views concerning the unified non-physical nature of the universe. Like the great mystics, these eminent scientists all believed in a universal consciousness that somehow encapsulates all the individual droplets of consciousness, which is how we ordinarily perceive ourselves.

Prof. Schrodinger, who is regarded as one of the prominent architects of the new physics, saw much wisdom in the ancient Vedas and refused to accept that consciousness would cease when the physical body dies. His views were largely based on the quantum physics investigation into the nature of time that was touched on briefly in Chapter 2. As was noted, physicists regard time as 'elastic' and without any definitive phases that we normally refer to as the past, the present and the future. Thus,

Prof. Schrodinger could not accept that consciousness would ever be extinguished because time is dependent upon consciousness—not the other way around. Prof. Schrodinger described time as '...a figment of my thinking. That as such it might some day put an end to my thinking, as some believe, is beyond my comprehension.'[4]

Prof. Schrodinger's opinion paralleled those of Dr Kurt Godel. Godel's Theorem, for which he is best remembered, proves that complete knowledge of any system cannot be derived from within the given system. Applying Dr Godel's reasoning to, for example, a house, it would be impossible to know everything about the house if we only had access to the living room. From within the living room only we could not know the layout of the remainder of the house, anything about the exterior or perhaps the gardens. Complete knowledge of the house is only possible if we have unhindered access to all rooms and all the surrounds. If one accepts that there is nowhere in the universe where consciousness does not prevail, then Godel's Theorem substantiates the mystics' belief about each of us having the potential to realize ultimate reality through consciousness.

Understandably, Godel's Theorem is so conclusive that many regard him not only as one of the greatest logicians of the twentieth century but also one of the greatest philosophers. In a telephone conversation with mathematician, Dr Rudy Rucker, Dr Godel responded affirmatively to the question of whether he believed in a universal consciousness as opposed to only billions of individual entities of consciousness residing separately in people's brains and added emphatically that such a view is '...the basic mystic teaching.'[5]

Einstein also had a strong leaning to the ageless wisdom of mysticism. An often quoted remark of his, about a human being's place in the universe that fully supports the spiritual tenet of a universal unity of reality, is:

A human being is part of the whole, called by us 'universe,' a part limited in time and space. He experiences his thoughts and feelings as something separate from the rest—a kind of optical delusion of his consciousness. This delusion is a kind of prison for us... Our task must be to free ourselves from this prison by widening our circle of compassion to embrace all living creatures and the whole of nature in its beauty.[6]

Of particular interest is the fact that Einstein seemed unafraid of death, and as such regarded the demise of the physical body philosophically. When during a serious illness he was asked if he was afraid to die, he reportedly answered, 'I feel such a sense of solidarity with all living things that it does not matter to me where the individual begins or ends.'[7]

Mystics certainly concur with this, saying that the individual does not begin nor end, but instead that such a concept is merely an illusion. Let's remember that the crux of their simple message is to awake from these dreamy illusions of time and space, the sense of 'I-ness', life (as we normally see it) and death.

Material Science Cannot Reveal Ultimate Reality

But let's not get entrapped in the beguiling web of intellectual back-slapping. Although much perfectly logical modern-day scientific thought and opinion is aligned with ancient spiritual tenets, in that both recognize the illusory nature of the physical world and the fundamental reality of the all-pervasiveness of consciousness, we need to do more than just accept this on an intellectual level. Like any scientific theory it must be subjected to proper validation. It's seems that the timeless path of the mystics does provide a mechanism for validation, and this is essentially why mystics regard their teachings as a science. This is in contrast to the material sciences, which, it seems equally apparent, cannot offer such proof of the spiritual nature of ultimate reality—a view shared by Dr Godel and Prof.

Schrodinger. As Prof. Schrodinger put it bluntly, '...we shall not expect the natural sciences to give us direct insight into the nature of spirit.'[8]

Thus, even to some scientists themselves, it's evident that the material sciences with their traditional physical tools and methods of observation are certainly fully equipped to answer many of the 'how' questions pertaining to worldly phenomena. However, it appears that the material sciences are quite incapable of addressing the questions as to why things are a particular way. So unless the material sciences acknowledge consciousness alone as a valid tool of investigation, it's likely that there will always be questions about even the material universe that will go unanswered. For mystics would contend that all physical laws are a reflection of underlying spiritual laws. This, it could be argued is the essential meaning of the ancient Hermetic maxim: 'As above, so below'.

Meditation—the Path to Ultimate Reality

So how can consciousness, unsupported by immensely sophisticated and usually highly expensive machines, assist us in learning how to die while living and in understanding the nature of ultimate reality? Well, in some ways it's not too surprising that some eminent scientists have themselves intimated of the answer. Prof. Paul Davies makes the point that some well-respected '...scientists, most notably the physicists Brian Josephson [who shared the Nobel Prize for Physics in 1973] and David Bohm, believe that regular mystical insights achieved by quiet meditative practices can be a useful guide in the formulation of scientific theories.'[9]

Mystic sages, once again would whole-heartedly agree. Perhaps they can be regarded as scientists of the soul since through the practice and perfection of deep meditation they have achieved insights into the very nature of ultimate reality. They have done this by no other means than dying to the illusory physical world while living. The fact that they have achieved this by a methodology no less scientific in its approach and application than that used by material scientists is perhaps one reason why some of the finest physicists and mathematicians of the modern era have intuitively recognized the merit in the path of mysticism.

Therefore, meditation, mystics advise us (with measured support from at least two forward-thinking scientists of the physical world), makes for the logical starting point to understand the true nature of ultimate reality. Mystics say that meditation, if done sincerely and with correct guidance, can reveal the doorway leading to ultimate reality. This hidden door is believed to normally only open fully at the time of death. Consequently, while we are alive to the physical world we are dead to the ultimate realm of spirit and vice-versa. But these two states of consciousness are not permanently mutually exclusive, which is the popular belief apparently rooted in a complete misunderstanding of the process of death and also of meditation.

Contemplative Meditation is an Objective Experience

Many regard meditation as a purely subjective experience, believing it to be solely dependant upon the mind. In one sense this is true because, as we all know, subjectivity is an obvious and often displayed trait of all mindful beings. However, proper meditation delves deeper than just the gross level of mind that, as we've previously established, acts merely as a 'filter' of consciousness. As such, subjectivity cannot be regarded as the sum total of consciousness, which is what Brian Hines, author of the book, *God's Whisper, Creation's Thunder*, contends.

Hines classifies four different aspects of consciousness: feeling, thinking, observing and contemplating. He posits that feeling and thinking are both subjective and so cannot be relied upon for objective information. In considering the aspect of observing, he notes that it relies on the five senses, which creates obvious problems. As was outlined in Chapter 1, the physical senses together with the conniving brain give us only a limited view of reality. This leaves one remaining aspect of consciousness—contemplation. Consequently, it is the contemplative aspect of consciousness that is central to the process of correct meditation.

Mystical Insights are a Shared Vision

Furthermore, transpersonal psychologist, Ken Wilber, argues that insights derived in contemplative meditation constitute an objective experience. He answers criticism of contemplative meditation being purely a subjective and private pursuit by explaining that the knowledge and wisdom acquired through the experience is as verifiable as any scientific experiment for those who are actually prepared to practice it. Wilber contends:

> ...a *trained* eye is a *public* eye or it could not be trained in the first place; and a public eye is a communal or *consensual* eye. Mathematical knowledge is public knowledge to trained mathematicians (but not to nonmathematicians); contemplative knowledge is public knowledge to all sages. Even though contemplative knowledge is ineffable, it is *not* private: it is a shared vision... And a trained contemplative eye can *prove* the existence of God with exactly the same certainty and the same public nature as the eye of flesh can prove the existence of rocks.[10]

Similarly, physicist Dr Fritjof Capra, author of *The Tao of Physics* (and other thought-provoking books), draws a notable parallel between scientific experimentation and mystical experience: He posits that:

> A mystical experience...is not any more unique than a modern experiment in physics. On the other hand, it is not less sophis-

ticated either, although its sophistication is of a very different kind. The complexity and efficiency of the physicist's technical apparatus is matched, if not surpassed, by that of the mystic's consciousness—both physical and spiritual—in deep meditation.[11]

Therefore, this indicates that anyone willing to practice contemplative meditation can expect the same objective results as anyone else willing to follow the same methodology. In the same way, two scientists who separately perform an identical experiment, and with all things being equal, they will both arrive at the same results. Contemplative meditation is, therefore, no different. Although it begins in an individual consciousness (which is an illusion anyway) the end result can be an objective perfectly unified reality.

Audible Life Stream Yoga

Yet, today there are many forms of meditation that one can practice, and not all are strictly forms of contemplative meditation. The one and only method taught by true mystics is one where the Audible Life Stream is apprehended. In apparently referring to the Audible Life Stream as 'The Voice of The Silence', Helena P. Blavatsky (1831–91), who was the principle founder of the Theosophical Society, made this significant point when she wrote:

> There is but one road to the Path; at its very end alone the 'Voice of the Silence' can be heard.[12]

Throughout the ages, this 'one road' has no doubt been given many different names in various languages. Indian mystics have traditionally used the Sanskrit expression *Surat Shabd yoga* to refer to the practice. *Surat* means soul, *Shabd*, as we already know, is another name for the Audible Life Stream, and *yoga* means union. So, as the name suggests, the objective of *Surat Shabd yoga* is to unite the soul with the Audible Life Stream.

In the West, the word *yoga* is used almost exclusively to refer to only one popular form of *yoga* called *Hatha yoga* (and sometimes to another increasingly popular form called *Ashtanga yoga*), where participants position themselves in a variety of sometimes mind-boggling postures. Undoubtedly, with a well-qualified teacher, there is also a deeper mental aspect to the practice beyond just contorting the body as if it were a rubber band. And although the obvious health benefits of such a practice are noteworthy, in contrast, *Surat Shabd yoga* is strictly a path based on stillness of body and mind. So although *Hatha yoga*, like all forms of *yoga* for that matter, has the same objective, which is to unite the individual soul with the universal soul, the methods believed to achieve this vary. However, it's significant to note that regardless of the different approaches for complete spiritual union, included in all forms of *yoga* is a meditative aspect. In terms of *Surat Shabd yoga*, meditation is the entire practice.

Surat Shabd yoga, contend the mystics, is the only practice whereby death's doorway can be found and passed through temporarily before the physical body actually perishes. This was summed up by Charan Singh, who, when asked about the real purpose of spiritual practice and specifically meditation, replied:

Actually, this meditation [on the Audible Life Stream] is a process of dying daily. Meditation is nothing but a preparation to leave the body. That is the real purpose of meditation. Before you play your part on a stage, you rehearse the part so many times, just to be perfect. Similarly, this meditation is a daily rehearsal to die, so that we become perfect at how to die...[13]

Thus, mystics have always regarded Audible Life Steam

meditation as the highest form of spiritual practice because it enables the process of death to be rehearsed—safely and without any danger of a premature death. Bodily functions like breathing and heart-rate continue at a subtle and barely perceptible level. But nevertheless one is said to undergo the same spiritual experience that is precipitated by the eventual demise of the physical body, invoking many of the elements reported in the classic NDE. In effect, therefore, tuning into the Audible Life Stream is a way to safely induce an NDE.

Confirming this, Sawan Singh, explained what an adept of Audible Life Stream meditation can expect to experience while dying temporarily with full consciousness:

...the limbs will become senseless first, as the attention is withdrawn from them. Later on, as the process of withdrawal proceeds, the trunk of the body becomes senseless. Ultimately the entire body below the eyes will become senseless. Breathing will continue normally, as in sleep. Only the attention, instead of being out, will be within. It will not be below the eyes as in sleep, but above the eyes. There will be full consciousness within, but unconsciousness as far as the outward world is concerned. This is death, of which the world is so much afraid. Those who go on this path die daily, and for them death has no terror; for them it is a beaten path.[14]

Accordingly, there seems to be essentially no difference between the death experience during Audible Life Stream meditation and actually dying, other than, of course, while meditating one is fully conscious and the physical body remains alive. As Sawan Singh pointed out, the fear of death can be naturally overcome because by perfecting the meditation one becomes intimately familiar with the whole process of death. No longer can the fear of the great unknown be perpetuated because the unknown becomes known.

Meditation is Concentration

Since details of the ancient technique should only be revealed by a genuine living Audible Life Stream teacher, but even then never publicly and only to those who understand and accept the moral guidelines of the path, the specifics of the simple method should never be detailed in any book. However, what can be outlined are the two fundamental principles that make the meditative practice a unique method of dying while living. The first of these principles is one of concentration. Inayat Khan emphasized this crucial aspect of concentration when once asked what is meditation. His reply was:

> Concentration is the beginning of meditation, meditation is the end of concentration; it is an advanced form of concentration. The subtle working of the mind is called meditation. It is more profound than concentration, but once concentration is accomplished fully it becomes easy for a person to meditate.[15]

Consciousness, we've already established, is essentially energy. So Audible Life Stream meditation is effectively a way of concentrating energy. And, at this point it's worthwhile recalling the fact that it's the inability of physicists to devise a way to concentrate energy to sufficiently high levels that makes for the biggest obstacle they face in trying to test the so-called Theory of Everything discussed in Chapter 3. In contrast, it seems that Audible Life Stream meditation can achieve this. In fact, it's perhaps perfectly reasonable to say that it is the only means by which to achieve this. And given the astronomical costs of building particle accelerators, it is also the most economical means—being totally free of charge.

Professor of physics, Steven Weinberg, in conceding that the most powerful particle accelerators imagined could never sufficiently concentrate energy to the required levels, writes there is a greater likelihood that '...breakthroughs in theory or in other sorts of experiments will some day remove the necessity of building accelerators of higher and higher energies.'[16]

Perhaps the breakthrough that Prof. Weinberg speaks of is dependant upon the scientific community first acknowledging the spiritual nature of reality and then specifically the Audible Life Stream, which some already have to a degree through acceptance of superstring theory.

Death's Doorway

An ancient Zen koan that is attributed to a ninth century monk named Tozan advises:

> Let your eye catch the sound.
> Then you will finally understand...[17]

It is no coincidence that in Audible Life Stream meditation the point of concentration is commonly called the wisdom eye, or third eye, or even the eye center, to which the Zen master Tozan was almost certainly referring. The eye center is 'located' in the center of the brain behind the forehead, a little above the eyebrow line (but it shouldn't be regarded as a physical organ with a physical location). It's only at this point, say mystics, that the Audible Life Stream of pure energy can be contacted because it's only here where it's continually resounding. As Jagat Singh once explained:

> You can have a full and clear view of the Macrocosm and all that it contains by gaining access into the human body, at the eye center. Christ says 'The Kingdom of God is within you.' It is nowhere to be found in the outside world. By studying oneself, one can study the universe. The whole 'Secret' will be found in the portion of the human body which is above the eyes [at the wisdom eye].[18]

Closely connected with the crown *chakra* at the top of the head, the eye center is regarded by mystics as the doorway to ultimate reality that, as mentioned earlier, automatically opens when we die. *Chakra* is a Sanskrit word which literally means vortex or whirlpool. Mystics contend that there are six main *chakras* in the human body, and that the value of meditating on the highest wisdom-eye *chakra* is that, once activated, all the lower *chakras* are automatically opened and balanced. However, traversing through this wisdom-eye doorway at the time of death, most of us don't get very far because once we have entered we don't know what to expect nor what to do. Since the physical world through our senses normally keeps this door hidden, we are advised to die to this world while still alive to be able to find it and become accustomed to passing through it—and, of course, returning. Consequently, one is able to prepare for the eventual demise of the physical body.

According to mystics, normally our consciousness diffuses out to all parts of the body from the wisdom eye, specifically to our sense receptacles that are essentially the nine apertures of the body (that is the two eyes, two nostrils, two ears, mouth and the two lower bodily orifices). And recall that it is through our senses that our ego is continually bolstered.

So, when consciousness is concentrated at the wisdom eye, the effect is to reverse its normal outward and downward flow and disentangle it from the senses. This is precisely what will take place automatically at the time of physical death, as Charan Singh explained:

When the soul [consciousness] withdraws from the nine apertures and comes to the eye center, it leaves the body. To die daily means to practice the withdrawal of the consciousness to the eye center every day.[19]

Thus, for meditation, Audible Life Stream teachers emphatically caution against focusing the attention at any point lower than the wisdom eye. Regarded as being the seat of the soul—the true 'heart' of our being—and the point where the soul departs from the body at the time of death, makes the wisdom eye the proper launching pad for the spiritual journey.

When Jesus spoke about the single eye being the lamp of the body, it's almost certain he was referring to the eye center and was probably again referring to the Audible Life Stream when he said that this eye can be sound:

The eye [center] is the lamp of the body. So, if your eye [center] is sound, your whole body will be full of light...[20]

This explains why many people who practice methods of meditation other than the technique taught by Audible Life Stream teachers, but which are also based on concentrating at the wisdom eye, will possibly perceive spiritual light and even sometimes hear the Audible Life Stream. In fact, if one is engaged in any sedentary activity like, for instance, reading, where the attention is strongly focused at or near the wisdom eye, there's the possibility that one will unwittingly contact the Audible Life Stream very briefly. These experiences are certainly better than no experience at all (and should, at least, personally confirm the existence of the Audible Life Stream). However, these happenstance experiences are of no great spiritual benefit because the Audible Life Stream will rarely have the affect of drawing the soul upwards without knowledge of how to tune into it.

In such instances, being uninformed about the spiritual sound, some may think they have contracted tinnitus, which remains a little understood medical condition. Perhaps some have if, for example, in the recent past they were exposed to extremely loud noise, but quite often no plausible explanation can be found to explain the sudden and unexpected occurrence of these mysterious sounds. Also, it's fascinating to note that many of the same sounds that these people report hearing like running water, crickets, swarming bees, whistling, and so on, correspond to the same sounds that one can expect to perceive in the early stages of Audible Life Stream meditation. Writes long-time student of mysticism and professor of philosophy, Lekh Raj Puri, about what those starting on the spiritual path can expect to encounter:

> First we hear confused sounds like those of a flowing river, a running train or of showers of rainfall. Gradually the sounds change into those of the insect cicada...and of small tinkling bells (metallic ringing)... Finally when our concentration has reached a high pitch, we hear the clear sound of a big bell, resounding and reverberating. That is the first real sound of the Word... It has a great power of attraction; it draws the soul up...[21]

The Magnetic Attraction of the Audible Life Stream

The Audible Life Stream's attractiveness is another reason why tuning into it is so important. Its entraining magnetism far exceeds any kind of experience in this physical world that normally entices the restive mind. Mystics counsel that while in contact with the Audible Life Stream the mind is so satiated that it doesn't have the desire to chase ephemeral sense pleasures. Rather, it becomes totally absorbed in the sound. Consequently, mystics say consciousness is slowly entrained to higher and higher frequencies and, therefore, higher and higher levels of reality beyond time and space where the energy is infinite and eternal.

Mystics advise that at an advanced stage of the practice, where the skill of concentration is well-honed, the enfeebled waves of habit and attachments recede in the lake of the mind as it evolves beyond the realm of ego. The mind's metaphorical lake surface becomes automatically stilled. Such an experience is very much what professor of psychology, Mihaly Csikszentmihalyi described as 'flow'.

The concept of flow is essentially a theory of happiness that Prof. Csikszentmihalyi developed based on years of systematic research. He describes flow as a rare state of unified consciousness in which one is totally absorbed in a challenging task requiring intense concentration.[22] According to Prof. Csikszentmihalyi, this focusing of attention results in a loss of one's sense of self because we become so involved in the challenge at hand.[23] He writes that in these flow experiences we usually, '...feel a sense of transcendence, as if the boundaries of the self had been expanded.'[24]

Interestingly, there are eight elements of the flow experience, including (but not limited to): concentration, a loss of self-consciousness, transcendence of the ego, a feeling of being connected to a greater whole, a sense of personal growth, and an altered sense of time.[25] Prof. Csikszentmihalyi makes the point that self-discipline and self-mastery are the conduits through which the flow experience is possible. He also notes that the loss of self-consciousness does not mean that one's mind is dulled. Rather, the opposite is true. A greater mental clarity emerges because more mental energy is devoted to the task at hand instead of being diverted to how one looks or feels.

An experience of flow can occur whenever one is fully engrossed in any challenging mental or physical activity, so it is no surprise that the elements that Prof. Csikszentmihalyi identifies to describe the concept are also present in Audible Life Stream meditation, as any well-disciplined practitioner would attest.

A Unified Circle of Consciousness

Consistent with the concept of flow, mystics say that only when the mind is stilled and attention is concentrated firmly at the wisdom eye does the Audible Life Stream have the magnetic effect. As the point where mind and soul are believed to interlock, the wisdom eye center can be imagined to be like the droplet of ink in water that was mentioned in Chapter 2 to illustrate the second law of thermodynamics. Consciousness constantly dispersing from the wisdom eye center throughout the body is analogous to the droplet of ink diffusing in the glass of water. In the same way that when the ink is completely diffused in the water we cannot differentiate between the water and the ink, the constant diffusion of consciousness throughout the body makes it normally impossible to differentiate between consciousness and the physical body, even though originally the two (like the ink and water) were quite separate. Hence, we can see why we normally believe the physical body and the material world are all there is to existence.

So, by collecting our consciousness successfully at the eye center what we are in fact doing is reversing this entropic outward flow of consciousness, which is effectively like reversing the flow of ink from countless outward directions that lead to total diffusion, to one inward direction resulting in complete symmetry and order. Therefore, reigning in consciousness to the eye center in this way and separating it from the remainder of the body can be imagined to be like the ink droplet returning to its perfect spherical shape as it was before diffusing in the water. We can now see that we have returned to that ubiquitous religious symbol—the circle; the reconstituted spherical shape of the ink droplet being ideal to denote perfect consciousness, unity, deathlessness.

This is really what the mystics mean when they say to go within and 'know thy self'. They are, in fact, telling us to reverse the flow of consciousness from an outward direction orientated to a physical world, to an inward direction and a state of pure deathless consciousness. This, say the mystics, is only possible if we focus our consciousness at the eye center. Sawan Singh once remarked:

This 'going inside' means gathering the attention at the headquarters of the soul in the body. In other words, the attention which is diffused in the outside world and is pervading and agitating every cell of the body should be gathered at the headquarters, the eye center, to the extent that it becomes oblivious of the body.[26]

Breaking the Illusory Flow of Time

This reversal of the flow of consciousness is theoretically, but also practically, like reversing the flow of time; indeed, it's actually a process of breaking the illusion of time. Time, you will remember, is the cornerstone of the second law of thermodynamics. Yet, the notion of breaking the illusion of time obviously opposes this fundamental law of physics. But consider two points. Firstly, consciousness being energy, can, just like the energy of quantum waves, function in a 'forward' or 'backward' direction. Secondly, the all-pervading force of gravity functions in direct opposition to the ubiquitous law of disorder, and to which even energy (that is consciousness) is subject. Professor Weinberg explains that '...according to general relativity, gravitation is produced by and acts on energy as well as mass. This is why photons [particles of light] that have energy but no mass are deflected by the gravitational field of the sun.'[27]

We also know that black hole theory has proved that when the force of gravity is rampant, time and space are distorted. Indeed, physicists know that intense gravity can actually stop time. For this to occur, gravity essentially becomes the only prevailing force because it would be equal with all other forces. As Prof. Weinberg remarks, at a sufficiently high energy level '...the force of gravitation between two typical elementary particles becomes so strong as any other force between them.'[28]

The energy required for this to happen is known as Planck energy, which was mentioned in Chapter 3 in relation to superstring theory. Recall that superstring theory is hoped to be the

Theory of Everything where the four forces of nature are unified. However, physicists accept that the Planck energy level is only possible at an event like the big bang when everything was unified—matter and even time didn't exist.

And this brings us to another important point that we've previously established. In Chapter 2 we determined that time (as a forward flowing phenomenon) is an illusion intrinsically linked to our illusory concept of 'I'. Also, remember that the mystics regard the law of karma as the motor that drives the endless cycle of birth and death. This law can only be enacted within the illusion of time—an effect can only happen *after* a cause. So breaking the illusion of time and establishing an eternal, but nonetheless timeless NOW would logically undermine the illusory sense of ego and make the law of karma impotent. Of course then, when an eternal NOW prevails, void of any notion of 'I' and karma, there simply can be no concept of death. For, at this point, there is nothing left that can die, nor any cause even if there was.

The Big Crunch of Consciousness

So, since it is consciousness via the brain that determines the illusory linear forward flow of time, if consciousness is 'gravitationally' reversed away from the physical world and collected at the wisdom eye, then we can logically see that as a result this consciousness-brain-material-world link is broken, and time and space are turned upside-down. A timeless NOW would theoretically be established. Only pure consciousness, unalloyed by any illusory sense of 'I', would prevail: Pure energy—without beginning, without end—birthless and deathless.

Bear in mind that this is what precisely happens when a star dies. The force of gravity becomes so rampant that a black hole is created. On a universal scale, the same processes are expected to take place some time in the far distant future when physicists expect the big crunch to occur—the 'death' of the universe. This is truly a long way off because the universe is still expanding, in other words, the entropic outward flow of the universe is stronger than the currently weaker force of gravity. However, when the force of gravity becomes stronger, the universe will begin to collapse in on itself at a faster and faster rate.

Now, since the second law of thermodynamics denotes increasing disorder and decreasing gravity with time, an increasing of gravity naturally results in greater order and, as we also know, a concentration of energy too. When sufficiently concentrated, physicists know that all forces of nature unify. This was the case at the big bang, is the case in black holes, and is expected to be the case at the big crunch.

Thus, the parallel being drawn between our individual, normally entropic outward flow of consciousness, and how the physical universe is expanding (remembering that even some physicists regard the universe as a vast thought) should be very clear. At the individual level, this reversal of the flow of consciousness is believed to take place in Audible Life Stream meditation when the concentration of consciousness is drawn to a single point at the eye center, which perhaps can be conceived as a one-dimensional circular superstring. At the universal level, this reversal of expansion is a concentration of energy too. At the time of the big bang, energy was so concentrated that gravity was the overriding force. The same scenario is expected to prevail at the big crunch when the physical universe will die. As we know, when there is so much concentration of energy, time and space become irrelevant concepts because gravity shrinks space to an unimaginable 'point'. Naturally, without space, matter cannot be present either. Physicists acknowledge that in such a scenario, time stretches to an all-embracing NOW without a past, present or future, just timelessness. This is a state of perfect unity because gravity would be the dominant and primary force.

If we draw an analogy between the unifying force of gravity and the force of attraction we know of as spiritual love, we can perhaps see why mystics always describe the notion of an Absolute (or God, Allah or whatever name you wish to choose) as pure love. For when only gravity—pure attraction—exists then there is perfect unity. This is the crux of the physicists Theory of Everything, which will inevitably and naturally unfold when the universe will eventually collapse in on itself and die. But let's be mindful of the fact that physicists also predict that, at some fantastic concentrated energy level, the universe will begin expanding again. Importantly, the same can be said of the process of dying while living in the perfection of Audible Life Stream meditation because mystics advise that in practicing the technique, while death in a sense is fully experienced it is not irreversibly enacted.

'As Above, So Below'

Thus, one should be able to see that in the process of Audible Life Stream meditation, by collecting consciousness to a single point (the wisdom eye), it seems likely that the very same processes take place as when stars die and eventually when the universe will die. In each case, energy is concentrated at a single point. Perhaps we can now look at the ancient maxim, 'As above, so below', and see it with a new deeper meaning. For, it seems that just as stars and the physical universe are expected to die, so too does the physical body when the ego perishes and the potentiality of a state of pure unified energy prevails. The microcosm is indeed the macrocosm. The result is a concentration of energy to a point where only the force of attraction exists—gravity for the scientists and love for the mystics—absent of any matter or time. For the scientific community, this is the Theory of Everything but for those who meditate on the Audible Life Stream and practice dying while living this is spiritual unity and ultimate reality. One attains a realization of pure consciousness. Oneness. Deathlessness.

Naturally, reaching this stage in the meditation, where one

succumbs to the unity of consciousness, is dependant on the level of concentration. But, advise the mystics, the desired level of concentration is attainable, like all things, only with the necessary practice. With practice, just as in the physical world where the force of gravity becomes stronger and stronger when matter and energy approach a black hole; in Audible Life Stream meditation the force of unifying consciousness increasingly becomes the dominant force too as it is withdrawn from the body and collected at the wisdom eye. Precisely in the same way that if caught in the gravitational field of a black hole it would become impossible to resist the pull to its center, in the meditation practice one can expect to reach a stage when the spiritual law of unification at the eye center becomes so compelling it is irresistible. On one level, this is the manifestation of the irresistible nature of love that mystics speak of. So those scientists who fantasize about dying by plunging into a black hole somewhere in deep space, or who speculate on the death of the universe, or dream of a final theory of everything, can actually experience the same processes in those events while remaining in the safety and comfort of their own homes by practicing Audible Life Stream meditation. This then is perhaps the ultimate scientific experiment.

Spiritual Listening is an Act of Selflessness
Apart from concentration, a second and equally important principle of Audible Life Stream meditation is the act of listening. Once concentration at the wisdom eye is achieved then, say the mystics, we can truly listen to the enchanting tones of the Audible Life Stream.

Just like concentration has been shown to undermine the illusions of time and ego, and therefore death, so too does the act of listening. This is even true, to a limited degree, for listening with our physical ears, as was mentioned in Chapter 3. To listen is arguably the most often used advice in all scriptures across the world. For instance, the word 'hearing', in the context of listening, is referred to at least 91 times in the first five books of the Old Testament.[29] Also, it's no accident that the phrases 'to listen' and 'to obey' have common etymological roots, because to listen to the Audible Life Stream in meditation is really an exercise in obedience and selflessness. An act of genuine selflessness is, of course, the antithesis of egotism.

To listen effectively we obviously need silence. So to meditate on the Audible Life Stream a sacred silence needs to be engendered. This necessarily precludes the practice of chanting aloud or the playing of musical instruments, for all mundane sound is, in the spiritual sense, noise because it is a barrier between the Audible Life Stream and consciousness.

Mystics throughout the ages have reminded us of the importance of absolute silence. Alluding to the spiritual significance of absolute silence, an eleventh century Zen master posed the following koan to his students:

If you blot out sense and sound—what do you hear?[30]

And the German mystic and Christian theologian, Meister Eckhart (c.1260–1328), wrote:

Nothing in the universe is so like God as silence.[31]

Also, presumably cryptically referring to the Audible Life Stream, Helena P. Blavatsky told us that complete silence must first be established before it can be apprehended:

Before the Soul can hear the image (man) has to become as deaf to roarings as to whispers, to cries of bellowing elephants as to the silvery buzzing of the golden fire-fly... For then the soul will hear, and will remember. And then to the inner ear will speak—THE VOICE OF THE SILENCE...[32]

More recently, Joseph Campbell eloquently said of the universal spirituality of silence:

> All final spiritual reference is to the silence beyond sound... Beyond that sound is the transcendent unknown, the unknowable. It can be spoken of as the great silence, or as the void, or as the transcendent absolute.[33]

Thus, Audible Life Stream teachers instruct people how to enter the great silence through concentration and spiritual listening to begin dying to the world of illusion and become enlivened to the realization of immortality. Although other forms of meditation may include these two important aspects, none seem to encompass both in the same way to allow the mind to firmly attune to the Audible Life Stream. Once attuned to the Audible Life Stream, then say the mystics the 'transcendent unknown' can become known.

Even brief periods of meditative communion with the Audible Life Stream are said to have transformative effects on the mind. Believed to be the purest of energy, any contact with it is a step towards the ego becoming starved of power and eventually dying a natural death. As a result, consciousness is said to become purified and holistically expansive. The benefits of achieving this level of consciousness while still living in our imperfect ego-dominated world with all its problems should be plainly apparent.

Therefore, by properly attuning to the Audible Life Stream, not only is the journey of death well prepared for, but equally important is that the journey we call life is also given the paramount importance that it deserves. Potentially, one's life can be transformed for the better, as is evidenced by some of the testimonials from people who have undergone an NDE.

History records that throughout the ages Audible Life Stream teachers have emerged to offer those who search for meaning and purpose in life the ancient secret of dying while living. Clearly, learning the ancient secret of dying while living is an important lesson to learn because one day we will die. As the eighteenth century Indian mystic, Paltu, advised, those who learn how to die while still alive will conquer the illusion of total extinction that most normally associate with the demise of the physical body:

All have to die,
But they conquer death
Who die before their death.[34]

Epilogue

Let us deprive death of its strangeness, let us frequent it, let us get used to it; let us have nothing more often in mind than death...We do not know where death awaits us: so let us wait for it everywhere. To practice death is to practice freedom.'

Michel Eyquem de Montaigne (1533–92)

The day after completing the draft manuscript for this book, news was received that my 83 year-old maternal grandmother had died in her sleep the previous night. My parents say that she had spent many long hours and sleepless nights caring for their three bothersome infants.

In a reverential tone, the eulogy at my grandmother's funeral reminded those gathered of the priceless gift of death she had bestowed upon us. For the death of a loved-one not only reminds us of our true spiritual inheritance, but also of our own tenuous physical mortality. The Lord of Death can come for us at any time—not only when we are retired and old with a family swollen with grandchildren to spoil. Conceivably, he could arrive this very day. As such it makes perfect sense to be spiritually prepared.

Mystics emphasize that controlled conscious experience of death itself, under the guidance of a genuine teacher, is the best form of preparation. It will also enable us to overcome the secret fear of death that most of us unconsciously harbor. Joseph Campbell acknowledged that conquering our thanatophobia is a revelation of the joy of life when he wrote:

The conquest of the fear of death is the recovery of life's joy. One can experience an unconditional affirmation of life only when one has accepted death, not as contrary to life but as an aspect of life. Life in its becoming is always shedding death, and on the point of death. The conquest of fear yields the courage of life. That is the cardinal initiation of every heroic adventure — fearlessness and achievement.[1]

Overwhelming anecdotal and even scientific evidence strongly suggests that such an important heroic adventure can only begin by learning how to tune into the vibratory frequencies of the Audible Life Stream. By doing so, we can begin to realize that we are inherently spiritual beings and that death is only the discarding of the ephemeral physical body. Furthermore, and of equal importance, we naturally develop an appreciation of the sanctity and significance of our physical lives too.

Genuine mystics always teach that life in the physical realm is just as much a spiritual journey as that which will inevitably transpire at the moment of death. For first and foremost we are spiritual beings who happen to be in the midst of a physical experience. And although social conditioning and our beguiling minds of illusion tell us differently, this physical experience is not separate from the total evolutionary experience that we are all continually undergoing.

Certainly, we are here as physical beings for a specific purpose. Preparing spiritually for the inevitable journey of death is the key to discovering that purpose. For life and death are really two sides of the coin of existence. To know only one side is to really devalue life because only half of our conscious awareness will be active, or in other words, we will be effectively only half awake (and equally half asleep). Until both sides of our total being are realized, we can never appreciate the full value of life or what it really means to be whole, complete and fully conscious.

So, we can remain in blissful (or perhaps not so blissful) slumber or choose to finally fully awaken and potentially realize what it means to truly live. Although much less travelled, mystics throughout the ages have advised that the latter path inevitably leads us to the mysterious doorway of death. And, they say, that the one safe and tried way to enter unhindered, and penetrate all the secrets of the universe, is with proper guidance from the sonorous Audible Life Stream—the ancient secret of dying while remaining alive to the illusory physical world.

...Two roads diverged in a wood, and I—
I took the one less travelled by,
And that has made all the difference.
Robert Frost (1874–1963) from *The Road Not Taken*

Chapter Endnotes

Introduction

1 R. Monroe, *Journeys Out of the Body*, Souvenir Press, 1972, pp. 122–123.

2 D. Campbell, *The Mozart Effect*, Hodder and Stoughton, 1997, p. 8.

3 R. Moody, *Life After Life*, Bantam Books, 1975, p. 29.

4 S. Nuland, *How We Die*, Alfred A. Knopf, Inc., 1993, p. xv.

Chapter 1

1 J. Barker, *Scared to Death: An Examination of Fear, its Causes and Effects*, Frederick Muller Ltd., 1968, pp. 2–3.

2 Barker, p. 12.

3 E. Becker, *The Denial of Death*, The Free Press, 1973, p. ix.

4 Metropolitan Anthony of Sourozh quoted in D. Cohn-Sherbok & C. Lewis (ed.), *Beyond Death*, Macmillan Press Ltd., 1995, p. 28.

5 R. Kavanaugh, *Facing Death*, Penguin Books, 1974, p. 24.

6 D. Reanney, *The Death of Forever*, Longman Cheshire, 1991, p. 129.

7 Barker, p. 15.

8 J. Davidson, *The Gospel of Jesus*, Element Books, 1995, p. 3.

9 E. Underhill, *Mysticism*, Oneworld Publications, 1993, p. 72.

10 Underhill, p. 81.

11 D. S. Rogo, *Beyond Reality*, The Aquarian Press, 1990, p. 86.

12 Freud quoted in Reanney, p. 123.

13 R. Descartes, *Meditations On First Philosophy*, J. Cottingham (trans.), Cambridge University Press, 1986, pp. 9–10.

14 J. Campbell, *The Power of Myth*, Anchor Books, 1988, p. 18.

15 D. Darling, *After Life*, Fourth Estate Limited, 1995, p. 172.

16 M. Csikszentmihalyi, *The Evolving Self: A Psychology for the New third Millennium*, HarperCollins, 1993, p. 80.

17   Csikszentmihalyi, pp. 81–82.

18   J. Johnson, *The Path of the Masters*, Radha Soami Satsang Beas, 1993, p. 299.

19   *Holy Bible*, Revised Standard Edition, The British and Foreign Bible Society, 1952, Matthew 18:4.

20   G. Singh, (trans.), *Sri Guru Granth Sahib*, World Book Center, 1989, Vol. 4, p. 1045.

21   Singh, Vol. 4, p. 1043.

Chapter 2

1   A.C.B. Swami Prabhupada, *Bhagavad-Gita as it is*, Bhaktivedanta Book Trust, 1984, p. 399.

2   Hume quoted in P. Davies, *God and the New Physics*, Penguin Books, 1983, p. 89.

3   D. Myers, *Psychology*, 6th edition, Worth Publishers, 2001, p. 329.

4   Myers, p. 321.

5   D. Darling, *After Life*, Fourth Estate Limited, 1995, p. 116.

6   Davies, p. 101.

7   N. Herbert, *Quantum Reality*, Rider, 1985, p. 194.

8   Rumi quoted in B. Hines, *God's Whisper, Creation's Thunder*, Threshold Books, 1996, p. 174.

9   Davies, p. 100.

10   Davies, p. 107.

11   Davies, p. 120.

12   Einstein quoted in D. Morrissey, *Anyone Can See the Light*, Stillpoint Publishing, 1996, p. 158.

13   Davies, p. 121.

14   F. A. Wolf, *Parallel Universes*, Simon & Schuster, 1988, pp. 223–224.

15   Davies, p. 121.

16   C. Pickover, *Black Holes*, John Wiley & Sons, Inc., 1996, p. xi.

17   Reanney, *Music of the Mind*, Hill of Content Publishing Co., 1994, p. 90.

[18] Reanney, p. 90.

[19] Reanney, p. 40.

[20] Reanney, pp. 38–39.

[21] T. Cleary (trans.), *The Essential Tao*, HarperSanFrancisco, 1991, p. 43

[22] Reanney, *The Death of Forever*, Longman, 1991, p. 35.

[23] Davies, p. 204.

[24] J. Berendt, *The World is Sound: Nada Brahma*, Destiny Books, 1983, p. 192.

[25] Berendt, p. 191.

[26] Berendt, p. 192.

[27] J. Johnson, *The Path of the Masters*, Radha Soami Satsang Beas, 1993, p. 304.

[28] S. Singh, *Philosophy of the Masters (Abridged)*, Radha Soami Satsang Beas, 1973, p. 17.

[29] S. Singh, p. 17.

[30] *Holy Bible*, Revised Standard Edition, The British and Foreign Bible Society, 1952, Galatians 6:7.

[31] *Holy Bible*, Matthew 5:38–40.

[32] *Holy Bible*, 2 Corinthians 4:18.

[33] S. Singh, p. 71.

[34] C. Singh, *Quest for Light*, Radha Soami Satsang Beas, 1993, pp. 183–184.

[35] Einstein quoted in L. Dossey, *Recovering the Soul*, Bantam Books, 1989, pp. 147–148.

[36] Rumi quoted in Hines, p. 228.

[37] Johnson, p. 395.

[38] S. Singh, p. 204.

[39] *Holy Bible*, Genesis 1:3.

[40] S. Singh, *Spiritual Gems*, Radha Soami Satsang Beas, 1996, p. 64.

Chapter 3

[1] P. Tompkins & C. Bird, *The Secret Life of Plants*, Harper &

Row, 1973, pp. 146–147.

2 Tompkins & Bird, p. 147.

3 Tompkins & Bird, p. 155.

4 J. Berendt, *The World is Sound: Nada Brahma*, Destiny Books, 1983, p. 59.

5 Berendt, p. 66.

6 D. Campbell (ed.), *Music: Physician for Times to Come*, Quest Books, 1991, p. 234.

7 S. Weinberg, *Dreams of a Final Theory*, Pantheon Books, 1992, p. 203.

8 Weinberg, pp. 213–214.

9 C. Singh, *Quest for Light*, Radha Soami Satsang Beas, 1993, pp. 92–93.

10 Weinberg, pp. 234–235.

11 P. Davies & J. Gribbin, *The Matter Myth*, Viking, 1991, p. 249.

12 M. Hayes, *The Infinite Harmony: Musical Structures in Science and Theology*, Weidenfeld and Nicolson, 1994, pp.1–3.

13 Hayes, pp. 3–4.

14 Hayes, pp. 6–7.

15 D. Reanney, *The Death of Forever*, Longman Cheshire, 1991, p. 189.

16 Marius Schneider quoted in J. Berendt, *The Third Ear*, Henry Holt and Company, 1988, p. 9.

17 D. Myers, *Psychology*, 6th ed., Worth Publishers, 2001, p. 213.

18 Berendt, *The Third Ear*, p. 19.

19 Berendt, *The World is Sound*, pp. 140–141.

20 Aristole quoted in Berendt, *The Third Ear*, p. 12.

21 Berendt, *The Third Ear*, p. 16.

22 Berendt, *The Third Ear*, p. 28.

23 Elsie von Cyon quoted in Berendt, *The Third Ear*, p. 36.

24 I. Khan, *The Mysticism of Sound and Music*, Shambhala, 1991, p. 27.

Chapter 4

1   J. Berendt, *The World is Sound*, Destiny Books, 1983, p. 18.

2   J. Miller, *The Vedas*, Rider & Co., 1974, p. 64.

3   Miller, p. 153.

4   A.C. B. S. Prabhupada, *The Bhagavad-Gita as it is*, I. S. K. C., 1984, p. 378.

5   M. Z. Khan (trans.), *The Quran*, Olive Branch Press, 1991, Sura 14: 25–28.

6   E. B. Szekely, *From Enoch to the Dead Sea Scrolls*, International Biogenic Society, 1981, p. 23.

7   Szekely, p. 22.

8   E. B. Szekely, *The Essene Gospel of Peace: Book Four*, International Biogenic Society, 1981, p. 44.

9   *Holy Bible*, Revised Standard Version, The British and Foreign Bible Society, 1952, Genesis 2:9–16.

10 *Holy Bible*, Genesis 3:8–10.

11 Kabir quoted in C. Singh, *Die to Live*, Radha Soami Satsang Beas, 1995, p. 29

12 *Holy Bible*, John 4:13–14.

13 *Holy Bible*, John 6:50–51.

14 *Holy Bible*, Matthew 4:4.

15 *Holy Bible*, John 1:1.

16 *Holy Bible*, John 5:25.

17 *Holy Bible*, 1 Corinthians, 15:31.

18 *Holy Bible*, Matthew 10:39.

19 Bhikkhu Nanamoli (trans.), *The Middle Length Discourses of the Buddha*, Wisdom Publications, 1995, p. 263.

20 Nanamoli, p. 262.

21 C. Luk, *The Secrets of Chinese Meditation*, Rider & Company, 1964, p. 37.

22 Luk, p. 37.

23 M. Morse, *Closer To the Light*, Villard Books, 1990, pp. 81–82.

24 Budge, E. A. W., *The Book of the Dead*, Dover Publications,

1967, p. xlv.

25 W. Evans-Wentz, *The Tibetan Book of the Dead*, Oxford University Press, 1960, p. 104.

26 Evans-Wentz, p. 128.

27 David-Neel quoted in J. Berendt, *The World is Sound: Nada Brahma*, Destiny Books, 1983, pp. 178–179.

28 Khan, Sura 6:72–74.

29 Rumi quoted in C. Singh, *Die to Live*, Radha Soami Satsang Beas, 1979, p. 30.

30 Rumi quoted in Hines, *God's Whisper, Creation's Thunder*, Threshold Books, 1996, p. 285.

31 *Holy Bible*, Exodus 19:17–19.

32 *Holy Bible*, Revelation, 1:15.

33 *Holy Bible*, Revelation, 1:17–18.

34 *Holy Bible*, Revelation, 2:7.

35 G. Singh, *Sri Guru Granth Sahib*, World Sikh University Press, 1978, Vol. 3, p. 707.

36 Cleary, T. *The Essential Tao*, Harper & Row, 1991, p. 10.

37 Cleary, p. 87.

Chapter 5

1 D. Darling, *After Life*, Fourth Estate Limited, 1995, pp. 48–49.

2 US Census Bureau report 'Annual Estimates of the population by sex and selected age groups for the United States: April 1, 2000 to July 1, 2003'. Retrieved from http://www.census.gov/popest/national/asrh/NC-EST2003/NC-EST2003-02.pdf on 24 February 2005.

3 C. Sutherland, *Transformed by the Light*, Bantam Books, 1992, p. 3.

4 Australian Bureau of Statistics report '2001 Census basic community profile and snapshot'. Retrieved from http://www.abs.gov.au/ausstats/abs@census.nsf/4079a1bbd2 a04b80ca256b9d00208f92/7dd97c937216e32fca256bbe008371f

0!OpenDocument#Table1 on 24 February 2005.

5   D. Cohn-Sherbok & C. Lewis (ed.), *Beyond Death*,
    Macmillan Press Ltd., 1995, p. 164.

6   J.E. Owens, E.W. Cook & I. Stevenson. *Features of 'near-death
    experience' in relation to whether or not patients were near
    death.* The Lancet, Nov 10, 1990 vol. 336, no. 8724, pp.
    1175–1177.

7   G. Groth-Marnat & R. Summer. *Altered beliefs, attitudes, and
    behaviors following near-death experiences.* The Journal of
    Humanistic Psychology, 1998, vol. 38, no. 3, pp. 110–125.

8   Sutherland, p. 102.

9   Sutherland, p. 101.

10 Sutherland, p. 141.

11 Sutherland, pp. 158–161.

12 K. Ring, *Life at Death*, Coward, McCann & Geoghegan,
    1980, p. 175.

13 Sutherland, pp. 86–87.

14 Sutherland, p. 87.

15 Owens, Cook, and Stevenson. pp. 1175–1177.

16 M. Morse, *Closer to the Light*, Villard Books, 1990, p. 10.

17 D. S. Rogo, *Return from Silence*, The Aquarian Press, 1989, p.
    229.

18 R. Moody, *Life After Life*, Bantam Books, 1975, p. 29.

19 R. Moody, *The Light Beyond*, Macmillan London Ltd., 1988,
    p. 9.

20 Ring, p. 94.

21 Ring, p. 94.

22 Sutherland, p. ii.

23 M. Grey, *Return from Death*, Arkana, 1985, p. 31.

24 P. Fenwick & E. Fenwick, *The Truth in the Light*, Headline
    Book Publishing, 1995, p. 88.

25 E. Kelly, *NDE with reports of meeting deceased people.* Death
    Studies, 2001, vol. 25, pp. 229–249.

26 Kelly, pp. 229–249.

27 D. Barlow and V. Durand, *Abnormal Psychology: An Integrated Approach 3rd ed.*, Wadsworth, 2002, pp. 421–453.

28 Moody, *The Light Beyond*, p. 96.

29 Ring, p. 213.

30 Moody, *The Light Beyond*, p. 98.

31 Ring, p. 212.

32 Ring, p. 207.

33 E. Kubler-Ross, *Death is of Vital Importance*, Station Hill Press, 1995, pp. 87–88.

34 Ring, p. 209.

35 Kelly, pp. 229–249.

36 Moody, *The Light Beyond*, p. 140.

37 Morse, p. 8.

38 C. Sagan, *Broca's Brain*, Hodder & Stoughton, 1979, p. 304.

39 Morse, p. 188.

40 P. & E. Fenwick, pp. 183–184.

41 Morse quoted in B. Eadie, *Embraced by the Light*, Golden Leaf Press, 1992, pp. vii–viii.

Chapter 6

1 D. Reanney, *Music of the Mind*, Hill of Content Publishing Co., 1994, p. 108.

2 D. Morrissey, *You Can See the Light*, Citadel Press, 2001, p. 155.

3 C. Sutherland, *Within the Light*, Bantam Books, 1993, p. 248.

4 Sutherland, p.72.

5 M. Grey, *Return from Death*, Arkana, 1985, pp. 44–45.

6 Grey, p. 48.

7 K. Ring, *Life At Death*, Coward, McCann & Geoghegan, 1980, p. 94.

8 Ring, p. 94.

9 *Holy Bible*, Revised Standard Edition, The British and Foreign Bible Society, 1952, John 3:8.

10 P. Fenwick, & E. Fenwick, *The Truth in the Light*, Headline

Book Publishing, 1995, p. 47.

11 P. Fenwick & E. Fenwick, p. 178.

12 D. S. Rogo, *Beyond Reality,* The Aquarian Press, 1990, pp. 103–104.

13 Morse, *Closer to the Light,* Villard Books, 1990, pp. 155–156.

14 Morse, pp. 149–150.

15 Sutherland, pp. 289–291.

16 Grey, p. 33.

17 Grey, pp. 46–47.

18 Grey, p. 50.

19 Ring, pp. 36–37.

20 Ring, p. 122.

21 P. Fenwick & E. Fenwick, p. 86.

22 P. & E. Fenwick, pp. 86–87.

23 Ring, p. 63.

24 Ring, p. 63.

25 B. Eadie, *Embraced by the Light,* Golden Leaf Press, 1992, pp. 28–29.

26 Eadie, pp. 37–38.

27 Eadie, p. 80.

28 Eadie, pp. 86–87.

29 Eadie, pp. 120–121.

30 D. S. Rogo, *Return from Silence,* Aquarian Press, 1989, p. 57.

31 W. Barrett, *Death-bed Visions,* Aquarian Press, 1986, p. 99.

32 D. S. Rogo, *Beyond Reality,* p. 101.

Chapter 7

1 D. Morrissey, *You Can See the Light,* Citadel Press, 2001, p. 71.

2 C. Green, *Out-of-the-body Experiences,* Institute of Psychophysical Research, 1968, pp. 92–93.

3 J. Mitchell, *Out-of-body Experiences,* Turnstone Press, 1985, p. 40.

4 Mitchell, p. 41.

5   Mitchell, p. 41.

6   Mitchell, p. 68.

7   Crookall quoted in Mitchell, p. 44.

8   Crookall quoted in Mitchell, p. 44.

9   Mitchell, p. 54.

10   R. Monroe, *Journeys Out of the Body*, Souvenir Press, 1972, p. 187.

11   Morrissey, p. 101.

12   Morrissey, p. 179.

13   Morrissey, p. 110.

14   Morrissey, p. 110.

15   Morrissey, p. 146.

16   S. Muldoon, *The Case for Astral Projection*, The Aries Press, 1936, pp. 80–81.

17   Muldoon, pp. 102–103.

18   Muldoon, p. 105.

19   Muldoon, p. 135.

20   Muldoon, p. 137.

21   Muldoon, pp. 115–116.

22   Muldoon, p. 118.

23   Hill quoted in D. S. Rogo, *Beyond Reality*, The Aquarian Press, 1992, p. 102.

24   Rogo, p. 103.

25   Monroe, p. 22–23.

26   Monroe, p. 24.

27   Monroe, pp. 122–123.

28   Monroe, p. 124.

29   R. Monroe, *Ultimate Journey*, Doubleday, 1994, p. 25.

Chapter 8

1   E. Szekely, *Essene Communions with the Infinite*, International Biogenic Society, 1979, p. 27.

2   J. Berendt, *The Third Ear*, Henry Holt & Co., 1985, p. 44.

3   D. Campbell, (ed.), *Music: Physician for Times to Come*, Quest

Books, 1991, p. 119.
4 Rudolph quoted in Campbell, p. 116.
5 Schroeder-Sheker quoted in R. Leviton, *Rhythm, Harmony and Healing* (Sydney: Australian WellBeing, 1994 annual ed. no. 54), p. 44.
6 Campbell, pp. 149–150.
7 G. Leonard, *The Silent Pulse*, E. P. Dutton, 1978, pp. 13–14.
8 P. Madaule, *When Listening Comes Alive*, Moulin Publishing, 1994, p. 75.
9 Campbell, p. 148.
10 Leonard, pp. 15–17.
11 Leonard, p. 18.
12 Novalis quoted in Campbell, p. 34.
13 Plato quoted in Szekely, p. 34.
14 *Holy Bible*, Revised Standard Edition, The British and Foreign Bible Society, 1952, 1 Samuel 16:23.
15 Campbell, p. 13.
16 Campbell, p. 14.
17 Campbell, p. 19.
18 D. Campbell, *The Mozart Effect*, Hodder and Stoughton, 1997, p. 8.
19 Campbell, *The Mozart Effect*, p. 4.
20 Campbell, *The Mozart Effect*, p. 8.
21 Campbell, *The Mozart Effect*, p. 8.
22 Campbell, *The Mozart Effect*, p. 9.
23 I. Khan, *The Mysticism of Sound and Music*, Shambhala, 1991, p. 171.

Chapter 9
1 D. Myers, *Psychology* (6th edition), Worth Publishers, 2001, pp. 653–655.
2 Myers, p. 655.
3 S. Brehem, S. Kassin, S. Fein, *Social Psychology* (4th ed.), Houghton Mifflin Co., 1999, p. 235.

4   Brehem et al., p. 235.

5   Tulsi Sahib quoted in S. Singh, *Philosophy of the Masters (Series V)*, Radha Soami Satsang Beas, 1989, p. 69.

6   J. Singh, *The Science of The Soul*, Radha Soami Satsang Beas, 1994, p. 7.

7   D. Gold, *The Lord As Guru*, Oxford University Press, 1987, p. 174.

8   Hafiz quoted in S. Singh, p. 101.

9   Prabhupada, A.C. Bhaktivedanta Swami, *Bhagavad-Gita as it is*, International Society for Krishna Consciousness, 1984, pp. 164–165.

10   J. Singh, p. 7.

11   Gopal Singh (trans.), *Sri Guru Granth Sahib*, World Book Center, 1989, Vol. 4, p. 1025.

12   J. Mascaro (trans.), *The Upanishads*, Penguin, 1974, p. 58.

13   *Holy Bible*, Revised Standard Edition, The British and Foreign Bible Society, 1952, John 1:14.

14   *Holy Bible*, John 1:18.

15   J. Davidson, *The Gospel of Jesus*, Element Books, 1995, p. 540.

16   *Holy Bible*, John 9:5.

17   K. Ming, *Poplar Deities of Chinese Buddhism*, Kuan Yin Contemplative Order, 1985, p. 149.

18   Ming, p. 152.

19   Gold, p. 213.

20   *Holy Bible*, Matthew 7:14.

21   Rumi quoted in S. Singh, *Philosophy of The Masters (Abridged)*, Radha Soami Satsang Beas, 1990, p. 37.

22   J. Campbell, *The Power of Myth*, Anchor Books, 1988, p. 16.

23   C. Singh, *Quest for Light*, Radha Soami Satsang Beas, 1993, p. 227.

24   S. Singh, *Spiritual Gems*, Radha Soami Satsang Beas, 1996, p. 8.

25   S. Singh, *Philosophy of the Masters (Abridged)*, p. 159.

26   C. Singh, *Die to Live*, Radha Soami Satsang Beas, 1995, p. 21.

27 M. Wexler, *Expanding the Groupthink Explanation to the Study of Contemporary Cults*, Cultic Studies Journal, Vol 12, No. 1, 1995. pp. 49–71.

28 Davidson, p. 560.

Chapter 10

1 S. Singh, *The Dawn of Light*, Radha Soami Satsang Beas, 1985, p. 63.

2 *Holy Bible*, Revised Standard Edition, The British and Foreign Bible Society, 1952, John 3:6.

3 *Holy Bible*, John 3:8.

4 J. Davidson, *The Gospel of Jesus*, Element Books, 1995, p. 673.

5 S. Calvert, *We're Talking About Vegetarianism*, Wayland, 1997, p. 5.

6 Anonymous, *Killing Fields*, The Ecologist, Vol. 32, 2002, pp. 22–24.

7 K. Akers, *A Vegetarian Sourcebook*, G. P. Putnam's Sons, 1983, p. 85.

8 Information obtained from http://library.thinkquest.org/C002291/high/present/stats.htm on 18 April 2009.

9 Figures quoted from the Australian Capital Territory website at http://www.vegetariansociety.org.au/why.html/ on 16 April 2009.

10 Information obtained from the Australian Vegetarian Society website at http://www.veg-soc.org/cms/html/modules.php?name=Content&pa=showpage&pid=121 on 18 April 2009.

11 Akers, pp. 50–55.

12 K. Ming, *Popular Deities of Chinese Buddhism*, Kuan Yin Contemplative Order, 1985, p. 150.

13 S. Singh, *Spiritual Gems*, Radha Soami Satsang Beas, 1996, p. 201.

14 S. Singh, p. 86.

15 Daisetz T. Suzuki (translator) *The Lankavataka Sutra*, George Routledge and Sons, Ltd., 1932, p. 212.

16 E. Szekely, *The Essene Gospel of Peace (Book One)*, International Biogenic Society, 1981, p. 36.

17 Szekely, p. 37.

18 S. Dasa, *You Mean That's the Bible?*, ISKCON, p. 8.

19 Dasa, p. 8.

20 Davidson, p. 952.

21 Davidson, p. 360.

22 S. Singh, *Philosophy of the Masters (Abridged)*, Radha Soami Satsang Beas, 1990, p. 8.

23 S. S. D. Singh, *Sar Bachan*, Radha Soami Satsang Beas, 1991, p. 13.

24 S. Singh, *Philosophy of the Masters (Abridged)*, p. 10.

Chapter 11

1 F. Dyson, *Infinite in All Directions*, Harper & Row, 1988, p. 297.

2 Jeans quoted in L. Dossey, *Recovering the Soul*, Bantam Books, 1989, p. 201.

3 Rumi quoted in B. Hines, *God's Whisper, Creation's Thunder*, Threshold Books, 1996, p. 155.

4 Schrodinger quoted in Dossey, p. 133.

5 Godel quoted in Dossey, p. 142.

6 Einstein quoted in Dossey, p. 149.

7 Einstein quoted in Dossey, p. 147.

8 Schrodinger quoted in Dossey, p. 137.

9 P. Davies, *The Mind of God*, Simon & Schuster, 1992, p. 227.

10 K. Wilber, *Eye to Eye*, Anchor Books, 1983, pp. 34–35.

11 F. Capra, *The Tao of Physics*, Flamingo, 1991, p. 44.

12 H. P. Blavatsky, *The Voice of the Silence*, Quest Books, 1992, p. 15.

13 C. Singh, *Die to Live*, Radha Soami Satsang Beas, 1995, p. 137.

14 S. Singh, *The Dawn of Light*, Radha Soami Satsang Beas,

1985, p. 170.

15 I. Khan, *The Mysticism of Sound and Music,* Shambhala, 1991, p. 219.

16 S. Weinberg, *Dreams of a Final Theory,* Pantheon Books, 1992, p. 235.

17 J. Berendt, *The World is Sound: Nada Brahma,* Destiny Books, 1991, p. 36.

18 J. Singh, *Science of the Soul,* Radha Soami Satsang Beas, 1994, p. 162.

19 C. Singh, p. 135.

20 *Holy Bible,* Revised Standard Edition, The British and Foreign Bible Society, 1952, Matthew 6:22.

21 L. Puri, *Teachings of the Gurus,* Radha Soami Satsang Beas, 1987, p. 159.

22 M. Csikszentmihalyi, *The Evolving Self: A Psychology for the Third Millenium,* HarperCollins, 1993, p. xiii.

23 Csikszentmihalyi, p. xiv.

24 Csikszentmihalyi, p. xiv.

25 Csikszentmihalyi, pp. 179–187.

26 S. Singh, pp. 42–43.

27 Weinberg, p. 202.

28 Weinberg, pp. 202–203.

29 J. Berendt, *The Third Ear,* Henry Holt & Co., 1995, p. 24.

30 Berendt, *The World is Sound: Nada Brahma,* p. 19.

31 Berendt, *The Third Ear,* p. 72.

32 Blavatsky, pp. 2–3.

33 J. Campbell, *The Power of Myth,* Anchor Books, 1988, pp. 120–121.

34 Paltu quoted in C. Singh, p. 29.

Epilogue

1 J. Campbell, *The Power of Myth,* Anchor Books, 1988, p. 188.

B O O K S

O is a symbol of the world, of oneness and unity. In different cultures it also means the "eye," symbolizing knowledge and insight. We aim to publish books that are accessible, constructive and that challenge accepted opinion, both that of academia and the "moral majority."

Our books are available in all good English language bookstores worldwide. If you don't see the book on the shelves ask the bookstore to order it for you, quoting the ISBN number and title. Alternatively you can order online (all major online retail sites carry our titles) or contact the distributor in the relevant country, listed on the copyright page.

See our website **www.o-books.net** for a full list of over 500 titles, growing by 100 a year.

And tune in to myspiritradio.com for our book review radio show, hosted by June-Elleni Laine, where you can listen to the authors discussing their books.

MySpiritRadio